Current Directions
in
COMMUNITY
PSYCHOLOGY

aps READINGS FROM THE
ASSOCIATION FOR
PSYCHOLOGICAL SCIENCE

Current Directions
in
COMMUNITY
PSYCHOLOGY

EDITED BY

Marybeth Shinn and Emily Thaden

Vanderbilt University

Allyn & Bacon

Boston • New York • San Francisco
Mexico City • Montreal • Toronto • London • Madrid • Munich • Paris
Hong Kong • Singapore • Tokyo • Cape Town • Sydney

Acquisitions Editor: Michelle Limoges
Series Editorial Assistant: Lisa Dotson
Marketing Manager: Kate Mitchell
Production Supervisor: Patty Bergin
Editorial Production Service: TexTech International
Manufacturing Buyer: JoAnne Sweeney
Electronic Composition: TexTech International
Cover Designer: Kristina Mose-Libon

Library of Congress Cataloging-in-Publication Data

Current directions in community psychology / edited by Marybeth Shinn,
Emily Thaden.
   p. cm.
  ISBN-13: 978-0-205-68010-8
  ISBN-10: 0-205-68010-0
  1. Community psychology. I. Shinn, Marybeth. II. Thaden, Emily.
  RA790.55.C87 2010
  362.2—dc22

RA
790.55
C87
2010

2009015939

10 9 8 7 6 5 4 3 2 1   13 12 11 10 09

Allyn & Bacon
is an imprint of

ISBN-10: 0-205-68010-0
www.pearsonhighered.com ISBN-13: 978-0-205-68010-8

Contents

Introduction

Community psychology studies the mutual influence between people and their environments, including immediate environments, such as schools or neighborhoods, and broader social forces, such as poverty. Further, community psychology applies the knowledge gained to create social interventions that aim to improve the quality of life for individuals and communities. These interventions, in turn, test the underlying theories on which they are based. Community psychology links to both other aspects of psychology in the effort to understand people's behavior and well-being, and also other social science disciplines in the effort to understand larger social systems. For instance, community psychology, sociology, and anthropology all study human behavior in the context of social groups and larger society; however, community psychology typically focuses more on changing environments to foster well-being. Community psychology shares an action orientation with clinical psychology, but it emphasizes working in natural settings and promoting the health of groups and communities. Community psychology and public health both focus on preventing problems and promoting health more than treating individuals who already have problems. Because community psychology contributes to and is informed by the work of academics and practitioners in other fields, not all of the authors in this reader identify as community psychologists. However, all of these articles elucidate how individuals are embedded within micro- and macro-level social systems, which affect their development and adjustment, or report on social interventions to promote well-being. This is the crux of community psychology.

This reader is organized into five sections. The first three sections focus on *naturally occurring* effects of contextual factors on individuals, while the last two focus on *intervention* with individuals, groups, and communities to prevent negative outcomes and promote well-being. Section 1 focuses on the most immediate environments of individuals' lives, such as families or schools, and how these environments, singly or in combination, may influence individuals. The articles in Section 2 shift attention to broader social contexts, including neighborhoods and culture. Many of these authors theorize how these factors influence individual and community outcomes and identify implications for social policy or change. Section 3 explores the impacts of environmental stressors, from natural disasters to residential instability. Understanding how stressful circumstances affect people and communities and how individuals manage stressful environments is crucial to design effective interventions. Section 4 reviews prevention and promotion programs to improve individual or community outcomes. These types of programs may aim to increase the skills of individuals to manage their environments or target environmental factors to prevent negative effects on people in these settings. Lastly, Section 5 relates to the broad dissemination and practice of interventions that have been supported by researchers. This section highlights a key challenge to researchers and practitioners, which is that interventions are only as useful as the people, communities, and settings they reach. At the end of each section, questions prompt the reader to critically engage the articles and concepts across readings.

This compilation of articles captures the orientation of community psychology—that people affect and are affected by their environments and that many human problems can be prevented—but it does not capture the full breadth of the field. Some of these articles lay the foundation for empowering communities and individuals without explicit reference to the concepts of empowerment or agency. One premise of community psychology is that communities that are marginalized within society are nevertheless "experts" on the issues that affect them; hence, their expertise should drive problem identification and generation of solutions. Community members' involvement enhances their power, control, and skills and increases the likelihood that interventions will be effective. A second premise of community psychology is that social problems warrant social solutions. Several articles in this volume implicate larger social systems and invoke macro-level social issues, but they tend not to focus on changing social systems. Readers interested in this more sociological aspect of community may consult any community psychology text for more work on community development, community organizing, and social policy.

Section 1: Environmental Impact: Microsystems and Mesosystems

Community psychology invokes an ecological systems perspective to understand the relationships between individuals, communities, and larger society. One version of this perspective, based on the work of Bronfenbrenner (see Marshall article), emphasizes that people are embedded in multiple social environments, small and large. The articles in this section focus on the most immediate environments, called microsystems, such as families, peer groups, child care settings, or schools, and on mesosystems, which are comprised of the connections between microsystems, such as between a child's home and school. Ecological systems theory recognizes that person-environment interaction is complex and bidirectional. However, bidirectional relationships across multiple ecological levels pose challenges for research. Therefore, most research has been conducted on the smaller micro- and mesosystems where the impacts of environmental variables on individuals are easier to identify.

The first article by Marshall provides a more detailed introduction to ecological systems theory and addresses factors across ecological levels that may influence childcare quality and hence child development. She notes that an ecological systems perspective highlights the constraints some families face with child care options. The second article by Stephens and Franks explores the interactive impact of women's multiple roles as parent caregivers, wives, mothers and employees. It is not the number of the roles so much as their quality that matters, and experiences in one role can spill over into others. The third article by Hill and Taylor explores the mesosystem of school and family factors related to parental school involvement, which in turn is associated with children's academic achievement. They note challenges that are common to community psychology research, including difficulties in measuring multi-dimensional phenomena (e.g. school involvement), capturing reciprocal relationships among factors, and identifying potential differences in patterns across socio-economic and ethnic groups.

The fourth article by Wills and Yaeger focuses on factors within the microsystem of the family that relate to adolescent substance abuse. This article utilizes a transactional model, which identifies direct and indirect effects of risk and protective factors to predict adolescent outcomes. (Note that some community psychologists use "transactional" to refer to the roles of the person and environments within an overall system of reciprocal relationships.) In the fifth article, Graham shows not only that ethnic contexts in schools and classrooms influence peer victimization, but that the consequences of victimization for adjustment also depend on ethnic context. Thus both Graham and Wills and Yaeger show that environmental factors not only affect individual well-being but also that other processes vary depending on environmental conditions. Community psychologists have often found that findings from laboratory studies or middle class samples may not hold true in poor communities.

The final two articles in this section describe other contextual factors that may affect youth development. Patterson reviews the empirical literature to examine whether parental sexual orientation affects youth development. This article illustrates how synthesizing research with different samples and research designs may bolster the findings regarding ecologically complex phenomena. Larson describes the relationships between out-of-school activities and youth outcomes and compares how U.S. youth spend their time relative to other postindustrial populations. Time use involves patterns of exposure to different environments, and longer exposure, for example to homework and school, is associated with stronger impacts.

The Quality of Early Child Care and Children's Development

Nancy L. Marshall[1]
Wellesley College

Abstract

The past half-century saw dramatic changes in families that altered the daily experiences of many young children. As more mothers of young children entered the labor force, increasing numbers of young children spent substantial hours in various child-care settings. These changes gave rise to a large body of research on the impact of the quality of early child care on children's development. However, a full understanding of the role of the quality of early child care requires consideration of the interplay among child care, family, workplace, and society. This article places what we know about the quality of early child care and children's development in this larger ecological context, and suggests directions for future research and practice.

Keywords

child care; maternal employment; child development; child-care services

The past half-century saw dramatic changes in families that altered the daily experiences of many young children. In 1970, only 24% of mothers with a young child (birth through age 3) were in the labor force; by 2000, this figure had risen to 57%. This growth in maternal employment was accompanied by changes in children's daily experiences. By 2000, 80% of children under the age of 6 were in some form of nonparental care, spending an average of 40 hours a week in such care (National Research Council and Institute of Medicine, 2003).

Research on children's experiences saw a parallel change that was equally dramatic. Early research in the field focused primarily on the question of whether child care (or maternal employment) per se was good or bad for children; current research asks questions about the relation between children's development and variations in the quality and quantity of child care that they experience. The field also now recognizes varying types of child care, including center-based care, licensed or regulated home-based care by nonrelatives (family-child-care homes), and other home-based care, such as care by relatives or in-home sitters. There have been methodological advances as well. Early research was more likely to study small samples and examine correlations between child care and children's outcomes at a single point in time; current research is more likely to involve large samples at multiple sites, to use experimental or quasi-experimental designs, and to follow participants over time.

Perhaps the most important advance in child-care research has been theoretical. Early research tended to study the effects of child care in isolation from other significant aspects of children's lives. Current research is more likely to be grounded in ecological systems theory, which considers children's development in the context of the child-care system as well as the family system, and recognizes the links between these systems and the larger society.

In this article, I focus on one segment of current research on early child care—the links between the quality of child care and children's development—drawing on ecological systems theory to provide an overview of recent advances and to suggest directions for future research.

ECOLOGICAL SYSTEMS THEORY AND EARLY CHILD CARE

Ecological systems theory places child development in an ecological perspective, in which an individual's experience is nested within interconnected systems (Bronfenbrenner, 1989). *Microsystems,* such as families or child-care settings, are characterized by face-to-face connections among individuals. *Mesosystems* consist of two or more microsystems and the linkages or processes that combine or connect them. These mesosystems exist within the larger context of the *exosystem,* those settings in which the child does not directly participate but that influence the lives of parents and other adults in the child's world, such as a parent's workplace, educational institutions that train child-care teachers and providers, and government agencies that set regulations for child-care facilities or establish welfare-reform policies. The mesosystems and exosystems operate within the context of a *macrosystem* of societal and cultural beliefs and practices. Note that these systems are not static, but may change over time.

The Mesosystem of Family ← → Child Care

Children inhabit both families and child-care microsystems, and these systems are linked. Parents select particular types of child care, of varying quality, for children of different ages—and these decisions vary with family structure, parental characteristics, geographical location, and other factors. Singer, Fuller, Keiley, and Wolf (1998) argued that child-care researchers must consider these *selection effects* if they are to accurately model the impact of child care on children's development over time.[2]

Through their selection of particular child-care arrangements, parents have an indirect impact on their children's development (in addition to their direct impact within the family system). But this linkage between the family system and child-care system operates in both directions: The child-care system can also influence the family system. For example, Ahnert, Rickert, and Lamb (2000) described a particular mesosystem characterized by shared care; in this mesosystem, mothers adapted their interactions with their toddlers in response to the toddlers' experiences in child care.

The Exosystem

The family ← → child-care mesosystem operates within the larger context of the exosystem of parental employment—one of the primary functions of child care is to enable parents, particularly mothers, to work outside the home. Historically, the child-care system has developed in response to characteristics of parents' employment. For instance, the current child-care system includes child-care centers, which tend to have operating hours that match those of parents who are working weekdays, as well as family-child-care homes and kith-and-kin care, which are more likely to meet the needs of parents who are working evenings, weekends, or variable hours. However, in industries that operate around the clock, particularly those with highly skilled workers such as hospitals, we are more likely to see on-site child-care centers, sick-child care,[3] and other accommodations to parents' employment needs.

Another important aspect of the exosystem is government policies and regulations that affect both the demand for child care (such as welfare-reform efforts that require low-income mothers to seek employment) and the affordability of child care. Although the United States provides some child-care subsidies for families, many low- and moderate-income families do not have effective access to subsidies.[4] Given the links between the quality of care and the cost of care, it is not surprising that children in low-income families who are not in the higher-quality, government-subsidized programs tend to receive lower-quality child care than children in middle-income families (cf. Phillips, Voran, Kisker, Howes, & Whitebook, 1994). In this way, the exosystem of government policies and regulations provides an important context for the operation of the family ← → child-care mesosystem.

THE QUALITY OF EARLY CHILD CARE AND CHILDREN'S DEVELOPMENT

Using ecological systems theory as a framework, I turn now to the question of the relation between the quality of early child care and children's development. I begin with a discussion of the concept of quality, and then move on to an overview of what researchers currently know about the role of the quality of early child care in children's lives.

What Is Quality?

The underlying assumption of all definitions of quality is that a high-quality early-child-care setting is one that supports optimal learning and development. However, quality has been measured in a variety of ways across different studies. Measures of child-care quality can be categorized as either structural or process indicators. Structural characteristics include the child:staff ratio (the number of children per teacher or provider), the group size (number of children in the setting), and the education and specialized training of teachers, providers, or directors. The features of structural quality can be regulated, and most states set minimum standards for at least some aspects of structural quality, at least in center-based care. Studies that assess structural quality are most useful in evaluating the impact of features that can be regulated.

Although understanding the links between structural indicators of quality and children's development is important, we also need to understand the mechanisms by which structural quality affects children's development, which requires examining what actually happens in the early-care setting (i.e., the process).

How do adults and children interact? What materials are available for the children, and how do adults support children's use of those materials? Process quality refers to the nature of the care that children experience—the warmth, sensitivity, and responsiveness of the caregivers; the emotional tone of the setting; the activities available to children; the developmental appropriateness of activities; and the learning opportunities available to children. Unlike the features of structural quality, process quality is not subject to state or local regulations, and it is harder to measure. One of the more commonly used measures, the Early Childhood Environment Rating Scale (ECERS; Harms, Clifford, & Cryer, 1998), assesses multiple aspects of process quality. Such multidimensional process measures tell us much more about the quality of care that children receive than do structural measures alone.

Structural Indicators of Quality and Children's Development

What do we know about the links between the structural indicators of quality in early child care and children's development? The research to date has found that better ratios (fewer children per adult) and more education or training for teachers are associated with higher language, cognitive, and social skills of the children cared for (National Research Council and Institute of Medicine, 2003). However, many of the studies that have examined structural indicators have employed small samples (fewer than 100 children) or have not considered selection effects in their analyses, so studies that do not have these limitations are of particular importance. In an interesting study that assessed the links between structural quality, process quality, and children's outcomes, the NICHD Early Child Care Research Network (2002) found that the relation between caregiver training and child-staff ratio, on the one hand, and children's cognitive and social competence, on the other hand, was mediated by process quality—that is, higher levels of caregiver training and lower ratios of children to adults in child-care settings were associated with higher levels of process quality, which were, in turn, associated with children's greater cognitive and social competence.

Process Quality and Children's Development

Among studies published in the past 15 years, those that employed an ecological model[5] consistently found that higher process quality is related to greater language and cognitive competence, fewer behavior problems, and more social skills, particularly when multidimensional measures of quality, such as the ECERS, are used or quality is assessed at more than one point in time. For example, the Cost, Quality and Child Outcomes Study (Peisner-Feinberg, Burchinal, & Clifford, 2001) found that higher process quality in preschool classrooms predicted fewer behavior problems 1 year later, and predicted higher language and math scores in kindergarten and second grade, although the magnitude of these associations declined over time. This same study also found a link between the child-care and family systems, such that the association between child-care quality and children's school performance was moderated by mothers' education; specifically, the association was stronger for children whose mothers had less education.

BEYOND SELECTION EFFECTS

I began this article with a discussion of the importance of considering children's development from an ecological systems perspective, which considers the family ← → child-care mesosystem as a context for children's development. Many studies of child care now consider the role of selection effects by statistically controlling for family characteristics. However, other linkages within the mesosystem must also be considered if one is to adequately understand the role of child-care quality in children's development. For instance, aspects of the family system, such as the mother's education or depression, parenting practices, and family income, may have independent effects on children's development. In fact, in a study of 1,100 children, the NICHD Early Child Care Research Network (2001) found that although the quality of early child care consistently predicted socio-emotional and cognitive-linguistic outcomes during the first 3 years of life, family factors were more consistent predictors of children's development than quality of child care, or any other child-care factors examined.

Research on the family ← → child-care mesosystem is familiar territory for many psychologists. However, Bronfenbrenner's ecological systems theory calls attention to other influences on children's development—the exosystem of parental employment and government policy and the macrosystem of societal beliefs about the desirability of maternal employment and the desired outcomes for children. For example, there is a complex interplay between parental employment, government policy, child care, and children's development for low-income families. Government policy and the macrosystem of societal beliefs promote employment for low-income parents. However, low-income parents tend to have less education and fewer marketable skills compared with other parents, and are likely to be employed in sectors of the labor market where jobs are part-time or contingent (temporary), allow little flexibility for managing family demands, and offer few benefits. Work schedules are also likely to include hours outside of the typical Monday-through-Friday daytimes when child-care centers normally operate. Although government subsidies are available to some low-income families, most do not receive subsidies. As a result, children from low-income families are likely to be placed in lower-cost and lower-quality center care or informal care that is itself often of lower quality (cf. Henly & Lyons, 2000). Viewing this "choice" as a selection effect leads one to interpret it as parental preference—but an ecological perspective suggests a different interpretation: Regardless of their individual preferences, low-income families' choices are constrained by the operation of the exosystem of the workplace and government policy.

FUTURE DIRECTIONS

Current state-of-the-art research has provided clear evidence that the quality of early child care matters to children's development. Children who attend higher-quality child-care settings have greater language and cognitive competence and greater social competence than children who receive lower-quality child care. However, several studies have documented the prevalence of mediocre or inadequate child care in the United States (National Research Council and Institute of Medicine, 2003, pp. 53–54). In addition, the high-quality care that does exist is not equitably distributed—lower-income children are less likely than higher-income children to have access to it.

The next step is to answer the question: How can we best raise the quality of early child care for all children? Ecological systems theory draws our attention to the importance of placing this question in the context of family processes, parental employment, governmental policies, and societal beliefs and goals when developing theoretical models and models for practice. We must integrate our societal goals of supporting healthy families, economic self-sufficiency, and women's employment with our goals of supporting healthy development and school readiness for children, if we expect to advance research and practice in the area of early-child-care quality and children's development.

Recommended Reading

Lamb, M.E. (1998). Nonparental child care: Context, quality, correlates. In W. Damon, I.E. Sigel, & K.A. Renninger (Eds.), *Handbook of child psychology: Vol. 4. Child psychology in practice* (5th ed., pp. 73–134). New York: John Wiley & Sons.

National Research Council and Institute of Medicine, Committee on Integrating the Science of Early Childhood Development, Board on Children, Youth, and Families. (2000). *From neurons to neighborhoods: The science of early child development* (J.P. Shonkoff & D.A. Phillips, Eds.). Washington, DC: National Academy Press.

National Research Council and Institute of Medicine, Division of Behavioral and Social Sciences and Education, Board on Children, Youth, and Families, Committee on Family and Work Policies. (2003). (See References)

Phillips, D.A., Voran, M.N., Kisker, E., Howes, C., & Whitebook, M. (1994). (See References)

Notes

1. Address correspondence to Nancy L. Marshall, Center for Research on Women, Wellesley College, 106 Central St., Wellesley, MA 02481.

2. *Selection effects* refers to the effects of family-level and community-level factors on decisions about the selection of child care.

3. Sick-child care consists of backup child-care arrangements for children who are mildly ill and cannot go to their regular child care or school, but do not require full-time parental care.

4. Middle-income families may receive subsidies through the child-care deductions in the federal tax code and through employers' Dependent Care Assistance Plans that allow eligible families to pay for child care with pretax dollars. Low-income families may receive subsidies through federal Head Start programs or through state-administered Transitional Assistance for Needy Families (TANF) programs, as well as other state and local programs.

5. The ecological model might be explicitly specified, or implicitly indicated through statistically controlling for key selection effects, such as the effects of family income or education.

References

Ahnert, L., Rickert, H., & Lamb, M.E. (2000). Shared caregiving: Comparisons between home and child care settings. *Developmental Psychology, 36,* 339–351.

Bronfenbrenner, U. (1989). Ecological systems theory. *Annals of Child Development, 6,* 187–249.

Harms, T., Clifford, R.M., & Cryer, D. (1998). *Early Childhood Environment Rating Scale: Revised edition.* New York: Teachers College Press.

Henly, J.R., & Lyons, S. (2000). The negotiation of child care and employment demands among low-income parents. *Journal of Social Issues, 56,* 683–706.

National Research Council and Institute of Medicine, Division of Behavioral and Social Sciences and Education, Board on Children, Youth, and Families, Committee on Family and Work Policies. (2003). *Working families and growing kids: Caring for children and adolescents* (E. Smolensky & J.A. Gootman, Eds.). Washington, DC: National Academies Press. Retrieved August 14, 2003, from http://www.nap.edu/openbook/0309087031/html/R1.html

NICHD Early Child Care Research Network. (2001). Nonmaternal care and family factors in early development: An overview of the NICHD Study of Early Child Care. *Applied Developmental Psychology, 22,* 457–492.

NICHD Early Child Care Research Network. (2002). Child-care structure → process → outcome: Direct and indirect effects of child-care quality on young children's development. *Psychological Science, 13,* 199–206.

Peisner-Feinberg, E.S., Burchinal, M.R., & Clifford, R.M. (2001). The relation of preschool child-care quality to children's cognitive and social developmental trajectories through second grade. *Child Development, 72,* 1534–1553.

Phillips, D.A., Voran, M.N., Kisker, E., Howes, C., & Whitebook, M. (1994). Child care for children in poverty: Opportunity or inequity? *Child Development, 65,* 472–492.

Singer, J.D., Fuller, B., Keiley, M.K., & Wolf, A. (1998). Early child-care selection: Variation by geographic location, maternal characteristics, and family structure. *Developmental Psychology, 34,* 1129–1144.

This article has been reprinted as it originally appeared in *Current Directions in Psychological Science*. Citation information for this article as originally published appears above.

Parent Care in the Context of Women's Multiple Roles

Mary Ann Parris Stephens[1]
*Department of Psychology, Kent State University,
Kent, Ohio (M.A.P.S.)*

Melissa M. Franks
*Institute of Gerontology and Department of Psychology,
Wayne State University, Detroit, Michigan (M.M.F.)*

Abstract

This article addresses the multiple roles held by women involved in parent care and the ways in which these roles affect the women's well-being. Research on women's roles (including that of caregiver) has been guided by two opposing perspectives, the scarcity hypothesis and the expansion hypothesis. Findings from our studies of role quality, role combinations, and role spillover have provided abundant evidence that the lives of these women cannot be easily captured by either the scarcity or the expansion hypothesis alone.

Keywords

parent care; women's multiple roles; scarcity hypothesis; expansion hypothesis

Many advances in society over this century have added to the number of roles that make demands on people's resources. At the same time, such changes also have created more ways for people to experience joy in life. In the past few decades, societal change has been felt most keenly by women in their middle years. Of particular relevance has been women's provision of care to their aging parents. This article addresses the multiple roles held by women involved in parent care and the ways in which these roles affect their well-being.

Data from the Informal Caregivers Survey, based on a nationally representative sample of caregivers to older adults, indicated that more than one third (37.4%) of all caregivers were adult children of the impaired persons (Stone, Cafferata, & Sangl, 1987). Daughters were three times more likely to assume the role of primary caregiver than sons. Daughters who take on primary responsibility for parent care are often referred to as "women in the middle" (Brody, 1981). This term alludes to the multiple roles of these women, in that they frequently simultaneously occupy several major roles, including caregiver, wife, mother, and employee.

It was for this reason that the *competing-demands hypothesis* evolved to explain the negative impact that caregiving often has on caregivers' psychological and physical wellbeing. According to this perspective, multiple role responsibilities create demands on these women, and these demands compete for the women's time and energy. The competing-demands hypothesis rests on assumptions similar to those of the *scarcity hypothesis,* which assumes that individuals have limited personal resources, and that social organizations and role partners demand all of these resources (Goode, 1960). Thus, an individual's total role obligations are thought to be overly demanding, making role conflict the norm.

The scarcity hypothesis has been challenged by the *expansion hypothesis,* which emphasizes the energy gains, rather than the energy expenditures, accrued by individuals with multiple roles (Marks, 1977). This energy-expansion perspective predicts that roles have positive consequences due to the enhancement of such personal resources as mastery, self-esteem, identity, and social and material gains. Indeed, a growing literature on women's health has shown that occupying multiple roles (most often those of mother, wife, and employee) is associated with better overall well-being.

Although the scarcity and expansion perspectives make different predictions about the effects of multiple roles, both are limited in that they focus on role occupancy alone (quantity) rather than on the quality of experiences that transpire within roles. With this emphasis on quantity, each perspective predicts either a net gain or a net loss of resources, regardless of role experiences. In contrast, perspectives that emphasize the quality of role experiences assert that two similar roles could involve different cost/benefit ratios within and across these roles. Therefore, such perspectives suggest that problems and rewards in roles should be considered, so that the quality of role experiences can be determined (Barnett & Baruch, 1985).

These issues of role quality largely have been overlooked in research on family caregiving. Most research in caregiving has focused on the problems associated with parent care and, thus, has given little attention to the more positive aspects of providing care. Moreover, this work has tended to examine the caregiver role in isolation from other roles. When other roles have been considered, they often have not been given the same weight as the caregiver role.

CAREGIVING IN THE CONTEXT OF OTHER ROLES

Over the past few years, we and our colleagues have focused considerable research attention on adult daughters who provide assistance to their chronically ill and disabled parents. We have been especially interested in two opposing questions: Do the roles that these women occupy in addition to the parent-care role have deleterious effects on their well-being (as the competing-demands perspective assumes)? Alternatively, do these additional roles benefit the women's well-being (as the expansion perspective assumes)? To address these questions, we conducted a series of studies in which we conceptualized the parent-care role as an important family role that women often experience as a part of their larger family and work life.

Role Quality

First, we sought to demonstrate our most basic premise, that women not only find their parent-care responsibilities to be stressful, but also find them to be rewarding (Franks & Stephens, 1992; Stephens, Franks, & Townsend, 1994). The women in our studies did indeed report both types of experiences in their caregiving role. The most often reported stressor was the interpersonal conflict experienced when the parent criticized or complained, was unresponsive, or was uncooperative or demanding. Rewards that the women reported resulted from the satisfaction taken from knowing that one's parent is well cared for (endorsed by 100% of these women), that this role fulfills a family obligation, and that providing needed assistance increases the time spent with a parent.

Because family caregiving research had focused almost exclusively on the stress that daughters encounter in the single role of caregiver, remaining to be explored was the question of how stress in other family roles affects their wellbeing. In this research, all the women not only occupied the role of caregiver, but also simultaneously occupied the roles of wife and mother to children at home. As they did for the parent-care role, these women reported experiencing stress in both of their additional roles. Furthermore, the stress in these roles detracted from their well-being beyond the negative effects of experiences in the parent-care role.

From the perspective of role quality, a more complete understanding of the impact of multiple role experiences can be gleaned from considering the positive aspects of the women's additional roles. These women also reported experiencing many rewards in their roles as mother and wife, as they did in their parent-care role. In addition, the rewarding aspects of these additional roles were reported more often by these women than were the stressful aspects. And rewards in each of the three roles contributed to psychological well-being even after stress in all three roles had been accounted for.

Role Combinations

Drawing from the assumptions made by the competing-demands and expansion perspectives, we then explored the accumulation of stressful and rewarding roles. An "accumulation" of roles refers to having a large number of roles that are either primarily stressful or primarily rewarding. The perspective of competing demands led us to expect that stress in the mother and wife roles would further diminish well-being for those women experiencing high levels of parent-care stress. Conversely, the perspective of energy expansion led us to expect that rewards in the mother and wife roles would further enhance well-being among women experiencing high levels of rewards in parent care.

These expectations were generally supported. Women experiencing high levels of stress in only their parent-care role reported better well-being than did women experiencing high stress in the parent-care role and one other role, or women with high stress in all three roles. An opposite pattern emerged for role rewards: Women experiencing high levels of rewards in only the parent-care role evidenced poorer well-being than did women with additional rewarding roles. Taken together, our findings lent some support for both the competing-demands and the expansion perspectives.

In a subsequent study, another approach was taken to examine the effects of combining additional roles with parent-care responsibilities (Stephens & Townsend, 1997). This larger study focused on 296 women who simultaneously occupied four roles: caregiver to an impaired parent, mother, wife, and employee. The aims of this study were to investigate whether the stress experienced in the additional roles of mother, wife, and employee might exacerbate (increase) the negative effects of parent-care stress on psychological well-being and whether the rewards experienced in these additional roles might buffer (decrease) the stress effects of parent care. The evidence clearly supported the stress-exacerbation prediction in the case of the mother role and the stress-buffering prediction in the case of the employee role. Experiences in the wife role neither exacerbated nor buffered the effects of parent-care stress.

Role Spillover

Some role theories have recognized the possibility that the stressful and rewarding experiences associated with any given role may not necessarily be confined to that role. Rather, because the boundaries between roles are sometimes ambiguous, it is possible for experiences in one role to "spill over" and color the experiences in another. This spillover is thought to be bidirectional in that experiences in one role have the potential to influence experiences in a second role, and vice versa. Furthermore, the influence of one role on another may be positive as well as negative.

From this theoretical perspective, spillover between women's parent-care role and two other roles, wife and employee, has been considered (Stephens & Franks, 1995; Stephens, Franks, & Atienza, 1997). The competing-demands and expansion hypotheses once again provided the conceptual framework. Competing demands provided the perspective for conceptualizing negative spillover as demands on time and energy in one role influencing the quality of experiences in the other role; negative spillover was also conceptualized as psychological interference between the roles. Conversely, energy expansion provided the perspective for conceptualizing positive spillover as feelings of attachment, mastery, and self-esteem in one role influencing the quality of experiences in the other role.

The type of negative spillover between parent-care and wife roles that women reported most frequently was the limited time available for their husbands because of caregiving responsibilities. The spillover of self-esteem from the parent-care role to the wife role was the most frequently reported type of positive spillover. Results for spillover in the other direction indicated that very few women felt their marriage interfered with their parent-care responsibilities. In contrast, many women indicated that their marriage had helped to bolster their parent-care experiences (Stephens & Franks, 1995).

A subsequent study explored role spillover between parent care and employment (Stephens et al., 1997). Exhaustion, difficulty concentrating, and work disruptions were the most frequently reported types of negative spillover from the parent-care role. In turn, the limited time and attention that could be provided to the parent because of employment were the most frequently reported types of negative spillover from the employment role. The most frequently reported type of positive spillover in both directions was being in a good mood in one role because of positive experiences in the other role.

In both studies of role spillover, both negative and positive spillover were found to occur in both directions. Moreover, women who experienced greater negative spillover (especially negative spillover from the parent-care role to the other

15

role) tended to have poorer well-being, whereas women who experienced greater positive spillover (especially positive spillover from the parent-care role to the wife role or positive spillover from the employee role to the parent-care role) tended to have better well-being. Taken together, the results on role spillover suggest that a woman's parent-care role and her marriage or employment not only have the potential to interfere with each other (as the competing-demands hypothesis assumes), but also have the potential to enhance each other (as the expansion hypothesis assumes).

SUMMARY

Findings from our studies of role quality, role combinations, and role spillover have provided abundant evidence that the lives of women providing care to impaired parents cannot be easily captured by either the competing-demands or the expansion hypothesis alone. We have found the strongest support for competing demands when we have focused on the problems and stressors encountered in the parent-care role and in other family and work roles. Likewise, we have found the strongest support for energy expansion when we have focused on the satisfying and rewarding aspects of role experiences.

A far more complex picture emerges when one considers problematic and rewarding role experiences simultaneously. Our studies have amply demonstrated that positive experiences in one role have the potential to offset the effects of negative experiences occurring in another role. This pattern of findings is not entirely consistent with either the competing-demands or the expansion perspective.

Given the accumulated findings, we have become convinced that the two questions that guided our original work in this area are more complementary than opposing. Moreover, it is our contention that the processes governing the ways in which multiple roles affect well-being are more complicated than the ones proposed by either role theory. Thus, our research strongly suggests the need for a more comprehensive theoretical framework for understanding the lives of women who are in the middle of parent-care and other role responsibilities.

Recommended Reading

Moen, P., Robison, J., & Fields, V. (1994). Women's work and caregiving roles: A life course approach. *Journal of Gerontology, 49*, 176–186.

Stephens, M.A.P., & Franks, M.M. (1999). Intergenerational relationships in later-life families: Adult daughters and sons as caregivers to aging parents. In J.C. Cavanaugh & S.K. Whitbourne (Eds.), *Gerontology: An interdisciplinary perspective* (pp. 329–354). New York: Oxford University Press.

Stephens, M.A.P., & Townsend, A.L. (1997). (See References)

Acknowledgments—This research, titled "Multiple Roles of Middle-Generation Caregiving Women," was supported in part by Grant R01 AG11906 from the National Institute on Aging (Mary Ann Parris Stephens, principal investigator, and Aloen L. Townsend, co-principal investigator) and in part by Kent State University.

Note

1. Address correspondence to Mary Ann Parris Stephens, 118 Kent Hall, Department of Psychology, Kent State University, Kent, OH 44242-0001; e-mail: mstephen@kent.edu.

References

Barnett, R., & Baruch, G. (1985). Women's involvement in multiple roles and psychological distress. *Journal of Personality and Social Psychology, 49*, 135–145.

Brody, E.M. (1981). "Women in the middle" and family help to older people. The *Gerontologist, 25*, 19–29.

Franks, M.M., & Stephens, M.A.P. (1992). Multiple roles of middle generation caregivers: Contextual effects and psychological mechanisms. *Journal of Gerontology: Social Sciences, 47*, S123–S129.

Goode, W.J. (1960). A theory of role strain. *American Sociological Review, 25*, 483–496.

Marks, S.R. (1977). Multiple roles and role strain: Some notes on human energy, time and commitment. *American Sociological Review, 42*, 921–936.

Stephens, M.A.P., & Franks, M.M. (1995). Spillover between daughters' roles as caregiver and wife: Interference or enhancement? *Journal of Gerontology: Psychological Sciences, 50B*, P9–P17.

Stephens, M.A.P., Franks, M.M., & Atienza, A.A. (1997). Where two roles intersect: Spillover between parent care and employment. *Psychology and Aging, 12*, 30–37.

Stephens, M.A.P., Franks, M.M., & Townsend, A.L. (1994). Stress and rewards in women's multiple roles: The case of women in the middle. *Psychology and Aging, 9*, 45–52.

Stephens, M.A.P., & Townsend, A.L. (1997). Stress of parent care: Positive and negative effects of women's other roles. *Psychology and Aging, 12*, 376–386.

Stone, R., Cafferata, G.L., & Sangl, J. (1987). Caregivers of the frail elderly: A national profile. *The Gerontologist, 27*, 616–626.

This article has been reprinted as it originally appeared in *Current Directions in Psychological Science*. Citation information for this article as originally published appears above.

Parental School Involvement and Children's Academic Achievement: Pragmatics and Issues

Nancy E. Hill[1]
Duke University

Lorraine C. Taylor
University of North Carolina

Abstract

Developing collaborations between families and schools to promote academic success has a long-standing basis in research and is the focus of numerous programs and policies. We outline some of the mechanisms through which parental school involvement affects achievement and identify how patterns and amounts of involvement vary across cultural, economic, and community contexts and across developmental levels. We propose next steps for research, focusing on the importance of considering students' developmental stages, the context in which involvement takes place, and the multiple perspectives through which involvement may be assessed. Finally, we discuss enhancing involvement in diverse situations.

Keywords

parental involvement; academic achievement; family-school partnerships

Families and schools have worked together since the beginning of formalized schooling. However, the nature of the collaboration has evolved over the years (Epstein & Sanders, 2002). Initially, families maintained a high degree of control over schooling by controlling hiring of teachers and apprenticeships in family businesses. By the middle of the 20th century, there was strict role separation between families and schools. Schools were responsible for academic topics, and families were responsible for moral, cultural, and religious education. In addition, family and school responsibilities for education were sequential. That is, families were responsible for preparing their children with the necessary skills in the early years, and schools took over from there with little input from families. However, today, in the context of greater accountability and demands for children's achievement, schools and families have formed partnerships and share the responsibilities for children's education. Parental school involvement is largely defined as consisting of the following activities: volunteering at school, communicating with teachers and other school personnel, assisting in academic activities at home, and attending school events, meetings of parent-teacher associations (PTAs), and parent-teacher conferences.

It is well established that parental school involvement has a positive influence on school-related outcomes for children. Consistently, cross-sectional (e.g., Grolnick & Slowiaczek, 1994) and longitudinal (e.g., Miedel & Reynolds, 1999) studies have demonstrated an association between higher levels of parental school involvement and greater academic success for children and adolescents.

For young children, parental school involvement is associated with early school success, including academic and language skills and social competence (Grolnick & Slowiaczek, 1994; Hill, 2001; Hill & Craft, 2003). Head Start, the nation's largest intervention program for at-risk children, emphasizes the importance of parental involvement as a critical feature of children's early academic development because parental involvement promotes positive academic experiences for children and has positive effects on parents' self-development and parenting skills.

Most of the literature focuses on parental school involvement in elementary schools. Parental school involvement is thought to decrease as children move to middle and high school, in part because parents may believe that they cannot assist with more challenging high school subjects and because adolescents are becoming autonomous (Eccles & Harold, 1996). However, few parents stop caring about or monitoring the academic progress of their children of high school age, and parental involvement remains an important predictor of school outcomes through adolescence. For example, one study demonstrated that parental school involvement was associated with adolescents' achievement and future aspirations across middle and high school (Hill et al., in press). Moreover, although direct helping with homework declines in adolescence, parental school involvement during middle and high school is associated with an increase in the amount of time students spend on homework and with an increase in the percentage of homework completed (Epstein & Sanders, 2002).

HOW DOES PARENTAL SCHOOL INVOLVEMENT MAKE A DIFFERENCE?

There are two major mechanisms by which parental school involvement promotes achievement. The first is by increasing social capital. That is, parental school involvement increases parents' skills and information (i.e., social capital), which makes them better equipped to assist their children in their school-related activities. As parents establish relationships with school personnel, they learn important information about the school's expectations for behavior and homework; they also learn how to help with homework and how to augment children's learning at home (Lareau, 1996). When parents are involved in their children's schooling, they meet other parents who provide information and insight on school policies and practices, as well as extracurricular activities. Parents learn from other parents which teachers are the best and how difficult situations have been handled successfully. In addition, when parents and teachers interact, teachers learn about parents' expectations for their children and their children's teachers. Baker and Stevenson (1986) found that compared with parents who were not involved, involved parents developed more complex strategies for working with schools and their children to promote achievement.

Social control is a second mechanism through which parental school involvement promotes achievement. Social control occurs when families and schools work together to build a consensus about appropriate behavior that can be effectively communicated to children at both home and school (McNeal, 1999). Parents' coming to know one another and agree on goals—both behavioral and academic—serves as a form of social constraint that reduces problem behaviors. When children and their peers receive similar messages about appropriate behavior across settings and from different sources, the messages become clear and salient, reducing confusion about expectations. Moreover, when families do not agree with each other or with schools about appropriate behavior, the authority and effectiveness of teachers, parents, or other adults may be undermined. Through both social capital and social control, children receive messages about the importance of schooling, and these messages increase children's competence, motivation to learn, and engagement in school (Grolnick & Slowiaczek, 1994).

FAMILY AND SCHOOL CHARACTERISTICS
THAT INFLUENCE PARENTAL SCHOOL INVOLVEMENT

Parent-school relationships do not occur in isolation, but in community and cultural contexts. One of the biggest challenges schools have today is the increasing diversity among students (Lichter, 1996). Demographic characteristics, such as socioeconomic status, ethnicity, and cultural background, and other parental characteristics are systematically associated with parental school involvement. Overall, parents from higher socioeconomic backgrounds are more likely to be involved in schooling than parents of lower socioeconomic status. A higher education level of parents is positively associated with a greater tendency for them to advocate for their children's placement in honors courses and actively manage their children's education (Baker & Stevenson, 1986). In contrast, parents from lower socioeconomic backgrounds face many more barriers to involvement, including nonflexible work schedules, lack of resources, transportation problems, and stress due to residing in disadvantaged neighborhoods. Finally, because parents in lower-socioeconomic families often have fewer years of education themselves and potentially harbor more negative experiences with schools, they often feel ill equipped to question the teacher or school (Lareau, 1996). It is unfortunate that parents with children who would most benefit from parental involvement often find it most difficult to become and remain involved.

Involvement in school sometimes varies across ethnic or cultural backgrounds as well. Often, teachers who are different culturally from their students are less likely to know the students and parents than are teachers who come from similar cultural backgrounds; culturally different teachers are also more likely to believe that students and parents are disinterested or uninvolved in schooling (Epstein & Dauber, 1991). One study found that teachers believed that those parents who volunteered at school valued education more than other parents, and this belief about parents' values was in turn associated with the teachers' ratings of students' academic skills and achievement (Hill & Craft, 2003). Parental school involvement seems to function differently or serve different purposes in different ethnic and cultural groups. For example, African American parents often are more involved in school-related activities at home than at school, whereas Euro-American parents often are more involved in the actual school setting than at home (Eccles & Harold, 1996). This tendency to be more involved at home than at school may be especially true for ethnic minorities whose primary language is not English. Among African American kindergartners, parental involvement at school is associated with enhanced academic skills, perhaps reflecting the role of social capital

(Hill & Craft, 2003), and the influence of parental involvement in schooling on achievement is stronger for African Americans than Euro-Americans among adolescents (Hill et al., in press).

Apart from demographic factors, parents' psychological state influences parental school involvement. Depression or anxiety present barriers to involvement in schooling. Studies consistently show that mothers who are depressed tend to be less involved than nondepressed mothers in preparing young children for school and also exhibit lower levels of involvement over the early years of school.

Self-perceptions also affect parents' school involvement. Negative feelings about themselves may hinder parents from making connections with their children's schools. Parents' confidence in their own intellectual abilities is the most salient predictor of their school involvement (Eccles & Harold, 1996). A factor that may be especially important in this regard is the experience of poverty. Poverty exerts direct effects on parents' mental health and self-perceptions through increased stress resulting from the struggle to make ends meet. Poverty also has indirect effects on children's early school outcomes because its adverse effects on parents are in turn associated with lower parental involvement in school.

Parents' own experiences as students shape their involvement in their children's schooling. As a parent prepares a child to start school, the parent's memories of his or her own school experiences are likely to become reactivated and may influence how the parent interprets and directs the child's school experiences (Taylor, Clayton, & Rowley, in press). Memories of supportive school experiences are likely to enhance parents' involvement and comfort interacting with their children's school.

In addition to characteristics of the parent and family, the school's context and policies influence parental school involvement. Teachers' encouragement of such involvement is associated with greater competence among parents in their interactions with their children and more parental involvement in academic activities at home (Epstein & Dauber, 1991). There is increasing recognition of the importance of promoting *schools'* readiness for children (Pianta, Cox, Taylor, & Early, 1999). "Ready schools" (Pianta et al., 1999) reach out to families, building relationships between families and the school setting before the first day of school. The success of teachers' and schools' efforts to encourage parental school involvement suggests that parents want and will respond to information about assisting their children. For example, LaParo, Kraft-Sayre, and Pianta (2003) found that the vast majority of families were willing to participate in school-initiated kindergarten-transition activities. These practices were associated with greater involvement across subsequent school years, underscoring the importance of school-based activities that encourage family-school links.

KEY ISSUES FOR RESEARCH

The most significant advances in the research on parental school involvement have arisen from the recognition that context is important and there are multiple dimensions to parental school involvement. Whether parental school involvement occurs because a child is having problems in school or because of ongoing positive dialogue between parents and school makes a difference in how involvement influences children's academic outcomes (Hill, 2001). For example, a parent who volunteers in the classroom to learn more about the teacher's expectations for students and a parent who volunteers in the classroom to monitor the teacher's behavior toward her child are both involved in the school, but only the latter parent is likely to create distrust that may impact the children's attitudes toward the school and the teacher.

Parental school involvement does not reflect just one set of activities. Such diverse activities as volunteering in the classroom, communicating with the teacher, participating in academic-related activities at home, communicating the positive value of education, and participating in the parent-teacher relationship are all included in parental school involvement, and each is related to school performance (Epstein & Sanders, 2002; Hill & Craft, 2003). Research on parental school involvement is taking these diverse factors into account.

Despite the recent advances in conceptualizing and studying parental school involvement, there are still challenges. First, the multidimensional nature of parental school involvement has led to a lack of agreement about definitions and to measurement inconsistencies, making it difficult to compare findings across studies. In addition, whereas research typically examines the relations between types of parental involvement and achievement, the types of parental involvement may influence each other. For example, a high-quality parent-teacher relationship may strengthen the positive impact of a parent's home involvement on achievement. And volunteering at school may lead to an increase in the communicated value of education or change the way parents become involved at home. Issues concerning the reciprocal relations among different types of involvement have yet to be addressed.

The second research challenge is integrating various perspectives. Whom should we survey when assessing parental school involvement? Parents? Teachers? Students? Is one perspective more accurate than another perspective? In fact, multiple perspectives are important for understanding parental school involvement. Although few studies have examined the influence of different perspectives on our understanding of parental school involvement, some studies found that teachers', children's, and parents' reports of parental school involvement were only moderately correlated, but each was related to achievement, suggesting that each perspective is unique and important (Hill et al., in press). The vast majority of research on parental school involvement, like parenting research, in based on mothers' involvement. What are the roles of fathers and other relatives? Does involvement of other family members vary according to demographic background?

Some research suggests that teachers' or parents' perspectives may be biased. Teachers often evaluate African American and low-income families more negatively than Euro-American and higher-income families (Epstein & Dauber, 1991). Moreover, teachers who are not particularly supportive of parental school involvement may tend to prejudge minority or low-income parents (Epstein & Dauber, 1991). Such stereotyping often results in substandard treatment of students and of parents when they do become involved.

Much of our knowledge about parental school involvement is based on research in elementary schools. Parental school involvement declines as children grow up, and middle and high schools are less likely than elementary schools to encourage involvement (Eccles & Harold, 1996). Despite this decline, parental school involvement remains associated with academic outcomes in adolescence (Epstein & Sanders, 2002; Hill et al., in press). Thus, the third research challenge is to take into consideration developmental changes in parental school involvement. Parental school involvement may be different for a 7th-grade student selecting course tracks or 11th-grade student selecting colleges than for a 1st-grade student learning to read. Current measures of parental school involvement do not reflect these developmental variations. In fact, parents' involvement in schooling may not decline during middle and high school; rather, the research may show declining involvement only because the nature of involvement changes in ways that are not reflected in our measures.

FROM RESEARCH TO PRACTICE

Evidence strongly supports the potential benefits of policies and programs to increase parental school involvement across the school years and even before children start school. Most parents want information about how to best support their children's education, but teachers have little time or resources to devote to promoting parental school involvement, and some parents are simply "hard to reach." How do we help teachers facilitate parental school involvement? Most teacher training programs do not include courses on how to effectively involve parents. Linking research on parental school involvement to teacher training programs may go far to support family-school collaborations.

When parents cannot become involved, how can schools compensate for the loss of the benefits of involvement? Understanding the mechanisms through which involvement promotes academic achievement would point to logical targets for intervention. For example, if parental school involvement promotes achievement through its effects on the completion and accuracy of homework, then providing homework monitors after school might be an appropriate intervention strategy.

Impoverished families are less likely to be involved in schooling than wealthier families, and schools in impoverished communities are less likely to promote parental school involvement than schools in wealthier communities. Consequently, the children who would benefit most from involvement are those who are least likely to receive it unless a special effort is made. Promoting parental school involvement entails more in disadvantaged schools than in wealthier schools. Compared with more advantaged parents, parents in impoverished communities often need much more information about how to promote achievement in their children, are overcoming more of their own negative school experiences, and have less social capital. Thus, programs and policies designed to promote parental school involvement in advantaged districts may be ineffective in promoting parental school involvement in high-risk or disadvantaged communities. Understanding each community's unique barriers and resources is important for establishing and maintaining effective collaborations between families and schools.

Recommended Reading

Booth, A., & Dunn, J.F. (Eds.). (1996). *Family-school links: How do they affect educational outcomes?* Mahwah, NJ: Erlbaum.

Epstein, J.L., & Sanders, M.G. (2002). (See References)

National PTA. (2000). *Building successful partnerships: A guide for developing parent and family involvement programs.* Bloomfield, IN: National Education Service.

Note

1. Address correspondence to Nancy E. Hill, Department of Psychology, Duke University, Box 90085, Durham, NC 27708-0085; e-mail: nancy@duke.edu.

References

Baker, D.P., & Stevenson, D.L. (1986). Mothers' strategies for children's school achievement: Managing the transition to high school. *Sociology of Education, 59,* 156–166.

Eccles, J.S., & Harold, R.D. (1996). Family involvement in children's and adolescents' schooling. In A. Booth & J.F. Dunn (Eds.), *Family-school links: How do they affect educational outcomes?* (pp. 3–34). Mahwah, NJ: Erlbaum.

Epstein, J.L., & Dauber, S.L. (1991). School programs and teacher practices of parent involvement in inner-city elementary and middle schools. *The Elementary School Journal, 91,* 289–305.

Epstein, J.L., & Sanders, M.G. (2002). Family, school, and community partnerships. In M.H. Bornstein (Ed.), *Handbook of parenting: Vol. 5. Practical issues in parenting* (pp. 407–437). Mahwah, NJ: Erlbaum.

Grolnick, W.S., & Slowiaczek, M.L. (1994). Parents' involvement in children's schooling: A multidimensional conceptualization and motivation model. *Child Development, 65,* 237–252.

Hill, N.E. (2001). Parenting and academic socialization as they relate to school readiness: The role of ethnicity and family income. *Journal of Educational Psychology, 93,* 686–697.

Hill, N.E., Castellino, D.R., Lansford, J.E., Nowlin, P., Dodge, K.A., Bates, J., & Pettit, G. (in press). Parent-academic involvement as related to school behavior, achievement, and aspirations: Demographic variations across adolescence. *Child Development.*

Hill, N.E., & Craft, S.A. (2003). Parent-school involvement and school performance: Mediated pathways among socioeconomically comparable African-American and Euro-American families. *Journal of Educational Psychology, 95,* 74–83.

LaParo, K.M., Kraft-Sayre, M., & Pianta, R.C. (2003). Preschool to kindergarten transition activities: Involvement and satisfaction of families and teachers. *Journal of Research in Childhood Education, 17*(2), 147–158.

Lareau, A. (1996). Assessing parent involvement in schooling: A critical analysis. In A. Booth & J.F. Dunn (Eds.), *Family-school links: How do they affect educational outcomes?* (pp. 57–64). Mahwah, NJ: Erlbaum.

Lichter, D.T. (1996). Family diversity, intellectual inequality, and academic achievement among American children. In A. Booth & J.F. Dunn (Eds.), *Family-school links: How do they affect educational outcomes?* (pp. 265–273). Mahwah, NJ: Erlbaum.

McNeal, B., Jr. (1999). Parental involvement as social capital: Differential effectiveness on science achievement, truancy, and dropping out. *Social Forces, 78,* 117–144.

Miedel, W.T., & Reynolds, A.J. (1999). Parent involvement in early intervention for disadvantaged children: Does it matter? *Journal of School Psychology, 37,* 370–402.

Pianta, R.C., Cox, M.J., Taylor, L.C., & Early, D.M. (1999). Kindergarten teachers' practices related to the transition into school: Results of a national survey. *Elementary School Journal, 100,* 71–86.

Taylor, L.C., Clayton, J.D., & Rowley, S.J. (in press). Academic socialization: Understanding parental influences on children's school-related development in the early years. *Review of General Psychology.*

This article has been reprinted as it originally appeared in *Current Directions in Psychological Science.* Citation information for this article as originally published appears above.

Family Factors and Adolescent Substance Use: Models and Mechanisms

Thomas Ashby Wills[1]

Department of Epidemiology and Population Health,
Albert Einstein College of Medicine, Bronx, New York (T.A.W.)

Alison M. Yaeger

Kaiser-Permanente Medical Center, Santa Rosa, California (A.M.Y.)

Abstract

This article considers the relation of family factors to adolescent substance use, with a focus on the specific pathways by which family factors have their effects. We review findings on four types of variables (family substance use, parental support and monitoring, parent-child conflict, and family life events) and discuss theoretical models of how family risk and protective factors are related to adolescents' outcomes. The evidence favors a transactional model in which family factors have largely mediated effects on adolescent substance use through relations to adolescents' self-control, life events, and peer affiliations; interactions between variables are also prominent. We discuss the implications of mediated effects for theoretical models of human development and consider how the transactional approach opens avenues for preventive intervention.

Keywords

family factors; substance use; adolescents; self-control; mediation

Adolescents' use of tobacco, alcohol, and marijuana is of interest to psychologists for several reasons. One reason is that the prevalence of substance use can be appreciable in early adolescence even though several types of substances have known harmful effects on health; in later adolescence, at least 10% of teenagers have a level of substance use problems sufficient to meet diagnostic criteria for alcohol or marijuana abuse (Harrison, Fulkerson, & Beebe, 1998). Another reason is that adolescent substance use has multiple predictors, being related to factors that span a range from biological to personality, family, and peer variables. In addition, variables from these different domains are substantially intercorrelated, so it is necessary for psychologists to consider why these correlations exist. For these reasons, it is important to have theoretical approaches that help to explain this complex phenomenon.

Research has shown that family factors are one of the major predictors of adolescent substance use (Jacob & Johnson, 1999). In this article, we discuss these research findings from the perspective of a theoretical model that addresses multiple predictors and pathways for adolescent substance use (Wills, Sandy, & Yaeger, 2000). The question is not so much whether family variables are related to adolescents' substance use. Rather, our focus is on explicating a theoretical approach for understanding the relations among family factors, other variables, and adolescents' outcomes.

WHAT ARE THE RISK AND PROTECTIVE FACTORS?

We begin by briefly discussing several types of family variables that have been shown to be related to adolescent substance use.

Family Substance Use and History

Smoking or alcohol use in the home is correlated with adolescents' substance use, and a family history of substance abuse (e.g., having a first-degree relative who is alcoholic) is related to the likelihood of offspring becoming substance abusers (Jacob & Johnson, 1999; McGue, 1999). At the same time, the magnitude of the correlations of family substance use with adolescents' use is modest, so modeling explanations (i.e., adolescents simply imitate their parents' behavior) are not sufficient to fully explain the phenomenon. Also, adoption studies show that the majority of adult alcoholics—up to 70% in some studies—do not have a family history of substance abuse (Windle, 1999). Thus, other predictors should be considered.

Family Support and Communication

Emotional support, the perception that parents will listen with sympathy and understanding when the teen has a problem, is a protective factor, consistently related to lower likelihood of adolescent substance use (Wills & Cleary, 1996). Open and frequent communication among family members is also protective. Parental support and communication are found to have a wide impact on other variables that are related to adolescent substance use, including adolescents' self-control, competence, and peer affiliations (Wills, Cleary, et al., 2001).

Discipline and Monitoring

Measures of these parenting practices index whether adolescents receive consistent and reasonable discipline, and the extent to which parents are aware of where their adolescents are (outside of school) and what they are doing. These variables are also protective factors and are correlated with, but not identical to, support and communication (Jacob & Johnson, 1999).

Parent-Child Conflict

A pattern of family interaction based on destructive arguing and adolescents' feelings that their interactions with their parents are often negative (e.g., teens report that "I often feel my parent is giving me a hard time") has substantial positive correlations with substance use. Several studies have linked parent-child conflict to adolescents' disengagement from the family and entry into deviant peer networks (i.e., having several friends who are engaging in smoking, drinking, or antisocial behavior; Blackson, Tarter, Loeber, Ammerman, & Windle, 1996; Wills, Sandy, Yaeger, & Shinar, 2001).

Family Life Events

Some studies of adolescent substance use assess negative events that occur directly to parents, such as parental unemployment, accidents, or illness. These events are essentially outside the control of the adolescent though they probably have repercussions within the family. Analyses controlling for demographic characteristics have shown that such negative life events are a risk factor for adolescent substance use and are correlated with adolescents' affiliating with deviant peers (Wills, Cleary, et al., 2001; Wills, Sandy, et al., 2001).

Intercorrelations

We have discussed the family factors separately, but in fact they are correlated with each other, so they do not represent independent processes. Parental substance use is correlated with other risk factors, such as negative family life events and parent-child conflict. Parental support and monitoring tend to be inversely related to parental substance use and positively correlated with adolescent characteristics such as good self-control. The theoretical task is to understand these correlations and their implications.

MODELS OF THE RELATION BETWEEN PREDICTORS AND SUBSTANCE USE

The correlations among the predictors of adolescent substance use can be understood using transactional models, which derive from the traditions of developmental psychology, behavior genetics, and personality-social psychology (Wills, Sandy, & Yaeger, 2000). Transactional models differ from previous approaches in considering several types of relations between predictors and outcomes. This theoretical approach incorporates two major concepts: mediated effects and buffering effects.

Indirect Effects and Mediation Pathways

Transactional models make a distinction between *direct effects* and *indirect effects*. In principle, a risk factor such as family history of substance abuse could be related to adolescent outcomes directly, without involving any intermediate processes. This would be termed a direct effect, and an example of a direct-effect model is diagrammed in Figure 1a, which shows a direct path from family history of substance use, the predictor, to adolescent substance use, the outcome. Figure 1b outlines an extended direct-effect model in which other variables are correlated with family history but are not closely involved in the effects of this predictor on the outcome. These other variables could include a confounder, a variable that is correlated with the predictor but has no causative effect itself on the outcome. The simple direct-effect model would be tested by determining whether correlations or odds ratios indicate that a significant relation exists between the predictor and the outcome. The extended model would be tested using multiple regression to determine whether the family factor makes a significant contribution to substance use and does so independently of plausible confounder variables.

It is possible, however, that the effects of a family factor are transmitted through intermediate processes (Tarter & Vanyukov, 1994). That is, a risk factor may affect the levels of intermediate variables, which in turn affect the outcome of substance use. These intermediate variables may be causally remote from the

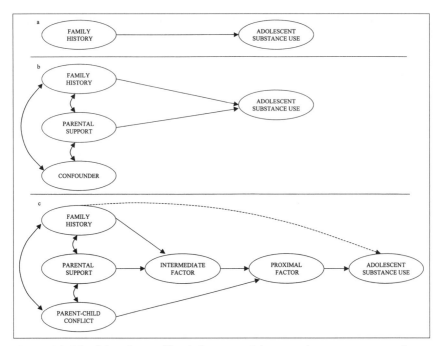

Fig. 1. Models of the relation of family factors to adolescent substance use: a strict direct-effect model with family history as a risk factor (a), a direct-effect model with a second family factor and a confounder (b), and an indirect-effect model with family history related to other family variables, an intermediate factor such as an adolescent's self-control, and a proximal factor such as peers' substance use (c). In the indirect-effect model, family history might have a direct effect on adolescent substance use (dashed line).

outcome (distal factors) or causally close to the outcome (proximal factors). Such a model is outlined in Figure 1c, which portrays a pathway from family history to distal and proximal variables, which then are related to the outcome. This is an example of an indirect-effect model or a *mediated model*. Statistical procedures can test indirect-effect models by determining whether the relation between a predictor and an outcome is mediated through other variables and testing for pathways that are statistically significant (e.g., MacKinnon, 1994).

Note that a factor may have a significant direct path to the outcome even when mediators are also involved (e.g., the dashed line from family history to adolescent substance use in Fig. 1c). However, the direct effects and mediated effects would represent different types of processes. Behavior geneticists (e.g., McGue, 1999) have suggested the importance of considering indirect effects in mechanisms underlying the impact of genetic factors on substance-use outcomes.

Buffering Effects

Another important concept in transactional models is buffering. It is commonly observed that people exposed to similar adverse experiences do not all have the same outcomes. Thus, some variables must operate to reduce the impact of risk factors, particularly for persons experiencing high levels of adversity. This is termed a *buffering effect* or a resilience effect (Wills, Sandy, et al., 2001).

Recent research on substance use has shown that buffering processes of several types are at work. For adolescents, emotional support from parents is a prominent buffering agent, shown in several studies to reduce the impact of life stress on adolescent substance use (e.g., Wills & Cleary, 1996). It has also been suggested that resilience effects help to explain why children of alcoholics do not all become substance abusers (Windle, 1999). Thus, models of family effects have given increasing attention to the interplay between risk factors and buffering processes, in order to account for the observation that some adolescents who are exposed to fairly adverse experiences have relatively low levels of substance use.

EVIDENCE FOR A TRANSACTIONAL MODEL

Recent studies of adolescent substance use have examined parental substance use together with a range of variables that are theoretically plausible as mediators (Blackson et al., 1996; Wills & Cleary, 1996). The results discussed here have been obtained in diverse samples of families and are independent of demographic characteristics such as ethnicity and socioeconomic status.

Studies show that family history of substance use is correlated with a range of other variables that are related to adolescent substance use. For example, parental substance use is correlated with difficult temperament of adolescents, and this personality characteristic is implicated in risk for substance use (Wills, Cleary, et al., 2001). Parental substance use also tends to be related to lower levels of parental support and to higher levels of parent-child conflict and negative family life events (Wills, Sandy, et al., 2001). These results indicate that part of the effect of family history occurs through an impact on family interaction processes.

Another consistent finding is that family factors are strongly related to self-control characteristics of adolescents. These characteristics include a planful, problem-solving orientation, noted as an important protective factor in several types of studies (Rutter et al., 1997; Wills & Stoolmiller, 2002), and poor self-control or impulsiveness, a significant risk factor for adolescent substance use (Wills et al., 2001). The findings suggest that two different processes connect family history with adolescent substance use. Protective family factors like support and communication are related to indices of good self-control, whereas (with relative independence) factors such as parent-child conflict are related to indices of poor self-control (Wills, Cleary, et al., 2001). Self-control variables, in turn, are related to proximal factors such as negative life events and deviant-peer affiliations, and these proximal factors are strongly linked to onset and escalation of adolescent substance use (Wills, Cleary, et al., 2001; Wills & Stoolmiller, 2002). Parental substance use tends to have primarily indirect effects on adolescent substance use because of pathways from family history to adolescent life events, peer affiliations, and motives for substance use. These findings are consistent with the model in Figure 1c, in which the effects of family factors on adolescent substance abuse are largely mediated by other variables.[2]

A second type of transactional process is indicated by a number of studies that have shown buffering effects. The impact of family risk factors on adolescent substance use is reduced, particularly among high-risk adolescents, by temperament attributes such positive mood and good control of attention (Wills, Sandy, et al., 2001). Family support reduces the impact of negative life events on adolescent substance use (Wills & Cleary, 1996), and both family factors and self-control characteristics reduce the impact of other variables on substance abuse, which is characterized by escalated use and inability to function in important life domains (Wills, Sandy, & Yaeger, 2002).

Thus, results have been consistent with the postulates of the transactional model because family risk factors have been linked with other variables, indirect effects have been demonstrated, and buffering effects have been observed. Longitudinal studies have shown that predictor variables at one point in time are related to subsequent change in mediators and outcomes. Researchers have analyzed data obtained from multiple sources (adolescents, parents, and teachers), and participant groups have included both general-population samples and clinical samples. Findings have generally been comparable across samples and data sources, so the evidential base is substantial.

WHERE DO RESEARCHERS GO FROM HERE?

Recent research on family factors has been conducted using a theoretical approach that compares a predictive model having only direct effects (from predictors to outcomes) with a model that can include direct and indirect effects. For the most part, results have favored the latter model. The effects of family factors tend to be mediated by relations to aspects of adolescent self-control, and pathways from these variables to proximal factors for substance use (Blackson et al., 1996; Wills, Cleary, et al., 2001; Wills & Stoolmiller, 2002).

The transactional approach can be a useful one for models of human development. Behavior geneticists have emphasized that genetic effects on complex behaviors may in some cases be indirect ones and that genetic characteristics can interact with environmental factors (Dick & Rose, 2002; Rutter et al., 1997). This position is wholly consistent with the transactional approach to adolescent substance use that we have summarized here, and analytic methods used in this research (as illustrated in Fig. 1) can be useful for testing how early factors influence later behaviors. Further research using this approach is needed to clarify the relations of family processes to changes in adolescent characteristics over time, and to evaluate the genetic and environmental contributions to intermediate factors that link family variables to adolescents' outcomes (McGue, 1999; Rutter et al., 1997).

From the standpoint of prevention, we note that the transactional approach opens avenues for prevention research. Research has repeatedly demonstrated that there are multiple pathways to adolescent substance use, which implies that there are many possible points for early intervention. The transactional model also delineates how variables recognized as final common pathways for risk, such as having friends who smoke and drink, themselves have antecedents in family factors and self-control processes; so prevention studies can develop methods to target more distal factors, such as adolescents' self-control processes, as well as proximal factors, such as peers' substance use. Prevention studies and etiological studies can proceed in partnership to develop better models for understanding and preventing substance abuse.

Recommended Reading

Glantz, M.D., & Hartel, C.R. (1999). *Drug abuse: Origins and interventions*. Washington, DC: American Psychological Association.

Johnston, L.D., O'Malley, P.M., & Bachman, J.G. (2000). *National survey results on drug use from the Monitoring the Future study, 1975–1999: Vol. 1. Secondary school students*. Rockville, MD: National Institute on Drug Abuse.

Rothbart, M.K., & Ahadi, S.A. (1994). Temperament and the development of personality. *Journal of Abnormal Psychology, 103*, 55–66.

Wills, T.A., Mariani, J., & Filer, M. (1996). The role of family and peer relationships in adolescent substance use. In G.R. Pierce, B.R. Sarason, & I.G. Sarason (Eds.), *Handbook of social support and the family* (pp. 521–549). New York: Plenum Press.

Zucker, R.A. (1994). Pathways to alcohol problems: A developmental account of the evidence for contextual contributions to risk. In R.A. Zucker, G.M. Boyd, & J. Howard (Eds.), *The development of alcohol problems* (pp. 255–289). Rockville, MD: National Institute on Alcohol Abuse and Alcoholism.

Acknowledgments—This work was supported by Research Scientist Development Award No. K02 DA00252 from the National Institute on Drug Abuse.

Notes

1. Address correspondence to Thomas Ashby Wills, Department of Epidemiology and Population Health, Albert Einstein College of Medicine, 1300 Morris Park Ave., Bronx, NY 10461.

2. The studies are not totally consistent: Parental support can show a direct effect (a path with a negative sign, indicating support is related to lower levels of adolescent substance use), and parental substance use sometimes has a direct effect (a path with a positive sign, indicating parental substance use is related to higher levels of adolescent substance use). The differences between studies may be attributable to the age of the participants and the models that are tested, and these possibilities need to be addressed in further research.

References

Blackson, T.C., Tarter, R.E., Loeber, R., Ammerman, R.T., & Windle, M. (1996). The influence of paternal substance abuse and difficult temperament on sons' disengagement from family to deviant peers. *Journal of Youth and Adolescence, 25*, 389–411.

Dick, D.M., & Rose, R.J. (2002). Behavior genetics: What's new, what's next? *Current Directions in Psychological Science, 11*, 70–74.

Harrison, P.A., Fulkerson, J.A., & Beebe, T.J. (1998). DSM-IV substance use disorder among adolescents based on a statewide school survey. *American Journal of Psychiatry, 155*, 486–492.

Jacob, T., & Johnson, S.L. (1999). Family influences on alcohol and other substance use. In P.J. Ott, R.E. Tarter, & R.T. Ammerman (Eds.), *Sourcebook on substance abuse* (pp. 165–174). Boston: Allyn and Bacon.

MacKinnon, D.P. (1994). Analysis of mediating variables in prevention studies. In A. Cazares & L.A. Beatty (Eds.), *Methods in prevention research* (pp. 127–153). Rockville, MD: National Institute on Drug Abuse.

McGue, M. (1999). The behavioral genetics of alcoholism. *Current Directions in Psychological Science, 8*, 109–115.

Rutter, M., Dunn, J., Plomin, R., Simonoff, E., Pickles, A., Maughan, B., Ormel, J., Meyer, J., & Eaves, L. (1997). Integrating nature and nurture: Implications of person-environment correlations and interactions. *Development and Psychopathology, 9,* 335–364.

Tarter, R.E., & Vanyukov, M. (1994). Alcoholism as a developmental disorder. *Journal of Consulting and Clinical Psychology, 62,* 1096–1107.

Wills, T.A., & Cleary, S.D. (1996). How are social support effects mediated: A test for parental support and adolescent substance use. *Journal of Personality and Social Psychology, 71,* 937–952.

Wills, T.A., Cleary, S.D., Filer, M., Shinar, O., Mariani, J., & Spera, K. (2001). Temperament related to early-onset substance use: Test of a developmental model. *Prevention Science, 2,* 145–163.

Wills, T.A., Sandy, J.M., & Yaeger, A. (2000). Temperament and adolescent substance use: An epigenetic approach. *Journal of Personality, 68,* 1127–1152.

Wills, T.A., Sandy, J.M., & Yaeger, A. (2002). Moderators of the relationship between substance use level and problems: Test of a self-regulation model. *Journal of Abnormal Psychology, 111,* 3–21.

Wills, T.A., Sandy, J.M., Yaeger, A., & Shinar, O. (2001). Family risk factors and adolescent substance use: Moderation effects for temperament dimensions. *Developmental Psychology, 37,* 283–297.

Wills, T.A., & Stoolmiller, M. (2002). The role of self-control in early escalation of substance use. *Journal of Consulting and Clinical Psychology, 70,* 986–997.

Wills, T.A., & Stoolmiller, M. (2002). The role of self-control in early escalation of substance use. *Journal of Consulting and Clinical Psychology, 70,* 986–997.

Windle, M. (1999). *Alcohol use among adolescents.* Thousand Oaks, CA: Sage.

This article has been reprinted as it originally appeared in *Current Directions in Psychological Science*. Citation information for this article as originally published appears above.

Peer Victimization in School: Exploring the Ethnic Context

Sandra Graham[1]
Department of Education, University of California, Los Angeles

Abstract

This article provides an overview of recent research on peer victimization in school that highlights the role of the ethnic context—specifically, classrooms' and schools' ethnic composition. Two important findings emerge from this research. First, greater ethnic diversity in classrooms and schools reduces students' feelings of victimization and vulnerability, because there is more balance of power among different ethnic groups. Second, in nondiverse classrooms where one ethnic group enjoys a numerical majority, victimized students who are members of the ethnic group that is in the majority may be particularly vulnerable to self-blaming attributions. The usefulness of attribution theory as a conceptual framework and ethnicity as a context variable in studies of peer victimization are discussed.

Keywords

peer victimization; attributions; ethnicity; ethnic diversity

A generation ago, if children and adolescents had been asked what they worried most about at school, they probably would have said passing their exams and being promoted to the next grade. Today, students' school concerns often revolve around safety, including the specter of peer victimization, as much as around achievement. Survey data indicate that anywhere from 40 to 80% of school-aged youth report that they personally have experienced victimization from peers, ranging from relatively minor instances of verbal abuse and intimidation to more serious forms of harassment, including assault, property damage, and theft (e.g., Nansel et al., 2001). Peer victimization is now recognized as a major public health concern, as the perpetrators of such abuse are perceived by many students as quite aggressive and the targets of their abuse report feeling quite vulnerable.

WHAT IS PEER VICTIMIZATION?

Peer victimization, also known as bullying or peer harassment (researchers tend to use these terms interchangeably), is defined as physical, verbal, or psychological abuse that takes place in and around school, especially in places where adult supervision is minimal. The critical features that distinguish victimization from simple conflict between peers are the intention to cause harm and an imbalance of power between perpetrator and victim (Olweus, 1993). Hitting, name calling, intimidating gestures, racial slurs, spreading of rumors, and exclusion from the group by powerful others are all examples of behaviors that constitute peer victimization. This definition of peer victimization does not include the more lethal sorts of peer-directed hostilities such as those seen in widely publicized school shootings. Although some of those shootings may have been precipitated by a history of peer abuse, they remain rare events. My focus here is on more typical and widespread types of peer harassment that affect the lives of many youth.

Research on the consequences of peer victimization confirms why it is a public health concern: A growing literature has documented that victims tend to have low self-esteem and to feel more lonely, anxious, and depressed than their nonvictimized peers do (see Juvonen & Graham, 2001). Victims also are disliked by their peers, particularly during the middle-school years. In general, early adolescents appear unsympathetic toward victims, who are often perceived to be responsible for their plight. Although studies linking victim status to academic achievement are fewer, there is evidence that victimization is associated with negative attitudes toward school or with poor performance as early as kindergarten and extending into the adolescent years (e.g., Schwartz, Gorman, Nakamoto, & Tobln, 2005). It is not difficult to imagine the chronic victim who becomes so anxious about going to school that she or he tries to avoid it at all costs.

THE ETHNIC CONTEXT OF PEER VICTIMIZATION

Most research on peer victimization has been conducted at the level of the individual. A common strategy involves first identifying students classified by peers as victims, as well as other behavior subtypes such as bullies and bully/victims, and then examining how those classifications map onto particular adjustment difficulties (e.g., Juvonen, Graham, & Schuster, 2003; Perry, Kusel, & Perry, 1988). Largely missing from that research is a focus on context, or the broader sociocultural milieu in which victimization unfolds. Contexts are the physical and social settings in which individuals develop, and some contextual factors include peer groups, ethnic groups, and classrooms. A good deal of peer-victimization research is conducted in urban schools where multiple ethnic groups are represented, but very little of that research has examined ethnicity-related context variables. This is disappointing because the factors that exacerbate or protect against peer victimization are likely influenced by such context factors as the ethnic composition of schools and neighborhoods, as well as the social and ethnic identities that are most significant to youth. In our research, we have attempted to bring the ethnic context to the study of peer victimization. Figure 1 shows our conceptual model. We examine peer victimization from a social-cognitive perspective, which focuses on an individual's thoughts, perceptions, and interpretations of victimization as determinants of subsequent behavior. We are particularly interested in youth who make self-blaming attributions for victimization and how such attributions relate to specific adjustment outcomes. Attributions are answers to "why" questions: Why did I get picked on? Why doesn't anyone like me? (See Weiner, 1986.) We also examine the ways in which attributional processes are shaped by the ethnic context, specifically the ethnic composition of classrooms and schools. We do this in two ways. First, we investigate the ethnic context as an antecedent to both peer victimization and to related adjustment outcomes (paths a and b in Fig. 1). Second, we examine the ethnic context as a moderator of the relations between both victimization and adjustment (path c) and between victimization

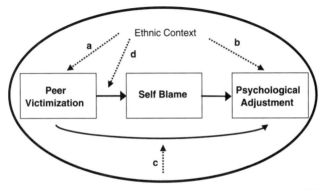

Fig. 1. Conceptual model of the relations between peer victimization, self-blame attributions, and psychological adjustment as moderated (paths a, b, c, and d) by the ethnic composition of schools and classrooms.

and self-blame (path d). Our model underscores the importance of causal beliefs as a theoretical framework and of ethnicity as a central context variable for understanding the dynamics of peer victimization.

Ethnicity and the Antecedents of Peer Victimization

How might the ethnic context shed light on the factors that can increase or decrease perceived victimization and vulnerability? We hypothesized that greater diversity would lessen experiences with victimization and feelings of vulnerability because in diverse settings students belong to one of many ethnic groups who share a balance of power. We based this hypothesis on the definition of peer victimization as conflict that involves an imbalance of power between perpetrator and victim. Asymmetric power relations take many forms, as when stronger youth harass weaker classmates or when older students pick on younger peers. At the group level, an imbalance of power can also exist when members of majority ethnic groups (more powerful in the numerical sense) harass members of minority ethnic groups (less powerful in the numerical sense). When multiple ethnic groups are present and represented evenly, the balance of power is less likely to be tipped in favor of one ethnic group over another.

We examined how victimization and feelings of vulnerability vary as a function of school and classroom ethnic diversity (Juvonen, Nishina, & Graham, 2006). A large sample of 2,000 sixth-grade students was recruited from 99 classrooms in 11 different middle schools in metropolitan Los Angeles. The students self-identified as Latino (46%), African American (29%), Asian American (9%), Caucasian (9%), or multiethnic (7%). The middle schools that these students attended were carefully selected to vary in ethnicity such that five schools were predominantly Latino (more than 50%), three were predominantly African American, and three were ethnically diverse, with no single ethnic group constituting a 50% majority. Students reported on experiences with victimization and indicators of vulnerability using well-validated rating scales.

Ethnic diversity in the 99 classrooms and 11 schools was measured with an instrument adapted from the ethology literature, known as Simpson's index

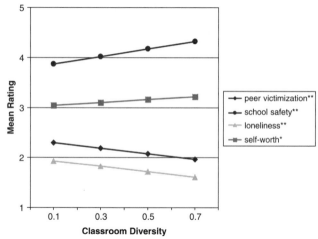

Fig. 2. Effects of classroom-level diversity on ratings of self-reported peer victimization, loneliness, self-worth, and perceived safety during spring of sixth grade (*$p < .05$, **$p < .001$; data from Juvonen, Nishina, & Graham, 2006).

(Simpson, 1949); it is a measure that captures both the number of different groups in a setting and the relative representation of each group. With scores ranging from 0 to approximately 1, Simpson's index was used to calculate the probability that any two students randomly selected from the same classroom or school will be from a different ethnic group. Higher scores reflected greater diversity (i.e., more ethnic groups that are relatively evenly represented, or a higher probability that two randomly selected students will be from different ethnic groups).

Figure 2 shows how students' self-reported victimization and feelings of vulnerability in the spring of sixth grade varied as a function of classroom diversity (the data on school-level diversity were almost identical). Plotted in the figure are the slopes predicting levels of vulnerability at high and low levels of classroom diversity. As diversity increased, self-reported victimization and loneliness decreased, whereas self-worth and perceived school safety increased. Thus, when there was a shared balance of power, students felt less vulnerable at school. Although a few studies in the literature have examined peer victimization in different ethnic groups (e.g., Hanish & Guerra, 2000), to my knowledge this is the first study to document the buffering effects of greater ethnic diversity.

Ethnicity and the Consequences of Peer Harassment

In the next set of analyses, we examined how the ethnic context influences the consequences of peer victimization (paths c and d in Fig. 1). Juvonen et al. (2006) revealed that as ethnic diversity decreased, students felt more vulnerable. In non-diverse contexts there are both a majority ethnic group and one or more minority ethnic groups. Is one group more vulnerable to the consequences of peer harassment than the other? It seems reasonable to think that members of the numerical-minority ethnic groups would be more vulnerable. That would be consistent with conventional wisdom, the way in which we think about an imbalance of power, and the reality that minority-group victims may have fewer same-ethnicity friends to either ward off potential harassers or buffer the consequences of victimization.

Yet, consider what it must be like to be both a victim and a member of a numerical-majority group. Having a reputation as a victim when one's ethnic group holds the numerical balance of power might be especially debilitating because that person deviates from what is perceived as normative for his or her group. Social psychologists have used the term *social misfit* to describe the negative outcomes of an individual whose problem social behavior deviates from group norms (Wright, Giammarino, & Parad, 1986).

Guided by the social-misfit analysis, we developed a two-part hypothesis. First we proposed that the relations between victim reputation and psychological adjustment would be stronger for students in our sample who were members of the ethnic majority group (path c in Fig. 1). That hypothesis was supported (Bellmore, Witkow, Graham, & Juvonen, 2004). As the number of same-ethnicity peers in one's classroom increased, the relations between victim status and the outcomes of social anxiety and loneliness increased.

In the second part of our hypothesis we turned to attributions as mediators of the relations between victimization and adjustment. When someone is a member of the majority ethnic group, repeated encounters with peer harassment, or even an isolated yet particularly painful experience, might lead that victim to ask, "Why me?" In the absence of disconfirming evidence, such an individual might come to blame him- or herself—concluding, for example, that "I'm the kind of kid who deserves to be picked on." Self-blame can then lead to many negative outcomes, including low self-esteem and depression. In the literature on causal explanations for adult rape (another form of victimization), attributions that imply personal deservingness—called characterological self-blame—are especially detrimental (Janoff-Bulman, 1979). From an attributional perspective, characterological self-blame is internal and therefore reflects on the self; it is stable and therefore leads to an expectation that harassment will be chronic; and it is uncontrollable, suggesting an inability to prevent future harassment. Attributions for social failure to internal, stable, and uncontrollable causes lead individuals to feel both hopeless and helpless. Several researchers have documented that individuals who make characterological self-attributions for negative outcomes cope more poorly, feel worse about themselves, and are more depressed than are individuals who attribute outcomes to their own actions (as opposed to character) (see Anderson, Miller, Riger, Dill, & Sedikides, 1994).

In earlier research we documented that victims of harassment were more likely than were nonvictims to endorse characterological self-blame and that they also felt more lonely and anxious at school (Graham & Juvonen, 1998). In the present multiethnic sample, we examined the mediating role of self-blame attributions and the possibility that relations between victim reputation, self-blame, and maladjustment would be moderated by classroom ethnic composition. We hypothesized that victims whose behavior deviated from local norms (i.e., victim status when one's group holds the numerical balance of power) would be particularly vulnerable to self-blaming attributions ("It must be me"). As the number of same-ethnicity peers increases in one's social milieu, external attributions that protect self-esteem become less plausible. On the other hand, being a victim and a member of the minority group should facilitate external attributions to the prejudice of others ("It could be them"). For minority ethnic-group members, we therefore expected weak relations between victim status, self-blaming tendencies, and adjustment. Finally, in ethnically diverse contexts, with a greater balance of power, we expected the most attributional ambiguity ("It might be me, but it could be them").

We identified groups of students who were members of the majority ethnic group in their classroom, who were members of a minority group, or who were in diverse classrooms with no majority group. Separately in each group, structural-equation modeling was performed to test relations between victimization, self-blame, and the maladjustment outcomes of depression and low self-esteem (Graham, Bellmore, Nishina, & Juvonen, 2006). As predicted, the strongest evidence for the relation between victim status and self-blame was documented for students who were members of the majority ethnic group, the weakest evidence was found for minority-group members, and students who were in ethnically diverse classrooms fell between these extremes.

CONCLUSION

The research presented here suggests that ethnicity is an important context variable for understanding the experiences of students who are victimized by their peers. Our sample included Latino, African American, Asian American, Caucasian, and multiracial students. Yet ethnic-group membership per se was less relevant than ethnicity within a particular school context. No one ethnic group is more or less at risk for being the target of peer abuse. Rather, a more critical variable is whether an ethnic group does or does not hold the numerical balance of power. If one's ethnic group is the numerical majority that holds that balance of power, then one's construals about the causes of victimization are more likely to implicate the self. Being both a victim and a member of the ethnic majority group has its own unique vulnerability.

In contrast, ethnic diversity in context—where no one group holds the numerical balance of power—may have particular psychological benefits. We propose that ethnic diversity creates enough attributional ambiguity to ward off self-blaming tendencies while allowing for attributions that have fewer psychological costs. Attributional ambiguity has a somewhat different meaning in social-psychology research on stigma. Such research highlights the threats to self-esteem when individuals stigmatized due to the prejudice of others are unsure about whether to attribute negative outcomes to that prejudice or to their own personal shortcomings (e.g., Major, Quinton, & McCoy, 2002). But in social contexts where multiple social cues are present and multiple causal appraisals of social predicaments are possible, attributional ambiguity can be adaptive if it allows the perceiver to draw from a larger repertoire of causal schemes.

Although I focus on an attributional explanation, there surely are other factors that can explain the positive effects of classroom ethnic diversity. For example, perhaps teachers in more diverse classrooms do something different (e.g., addressing equity issues or promoting more cultural awareness) than teachers in nondiverse classrooms do. Or it could be that diversity fosters strong ethnic identity, which then acts as a buffer against general feelings of vulnerability. No doubt there are many other psychological benefits of multiethnic school environments, just as there are some contexts in which being a part of the ethnic-majority group has self-enhancing functions. These are questions for the future. For now, I hope that the conceptual analysis and research presented here will stimulate new ways to think about ethnicity in context, ethnic diversity, and coping with peer victimization. With creative ways to measure ethnic diversity, today's multiethnic urban schools provide ideal settings for studying the social-cognitive mediators and contextual moderators of the linkages between victimization and adjustment.

Recommended Reading

Juvonen, J., & Graham, S. (Eds). (2001). (See References)
Olweus, D. (1993). (See References)
Sanders, C., & Phye, G. (Eds.). (2004). *Bullying: Implications for the classroom*. San Diego, CA: Elsevier.

Note

1. Address correspondence to Sandra Graham, Department of Education, University of California, Los Angeles, CA; e-mail: shgraham@ucla.edu.

References

Anderson, C., Miller, R., Riger, A., Dill, J., & Sedikides, C. (1994). Behavioral and characterological attributional styles as predictors of depression and loneliness: Review, refinement, and test. *Journal of Personality and Social Psychology, 66*, 549–558.

Bellmore, A., Witkow, M., Graham, S., & Juvonen, J. (2004). Beyond the individual: The impact of ethnic diversity and behavioral norms on victims' adjustment. *Developmental Psychology, 40*, 1159–1172.

Graham, S., Bellmore, A., Nishina, A., & Juvonen, J. (2006). Ethnic context and attributions for victimization. Manuscript submitted for publication.

Graham, S., & Juvonen, J. (1998). Self-blame and peer victimization in middle school: An attributional analysis. *Developmental Psychology, 34*, 587–599.

Hanish, L.D., & Guerra, N.G. (2000). The roles of ethnicity and school context in predicting children's victimization by peers. *American Journal of Community Psychology, 28*, 201–223.

Janoff-Bulman, R. (1979). Characterological and behavioral self-blame: Inquiries into depression and rape. *Journal of Personality and Social Psychology, 37*, 1798–1809.

Juvonen, J., & Graham, S. (Eds). (2001). *Peer harassment in school: The plight of the vulnerable and the victimized*. New York: Guilford Press.

Juvonen, J., Graham, S., & Schuster, M. (2003). Bullying among young adolescents: The strong, the weak, and the troubled. *Pediatrics, 112*, 1231–1237.

Juvonen, J., Nishina, A., & Graham, S. (2006). Ethnic diversity and perceptions of safety in urban middle schools. *Psychological Science, 17*, 393–400.

Major, B., Quinton, W., & McCoy, S. (2002). Antecedents and consequences of attributions to discrimination: Theoretical and empirical advances. In M. Zanna (Ed.), *Advances in experimental social psychology* (Vol. 34, pp. 251–330). San Diego, CA: Academic Press.

Nansel, T., Overpeck, M., Pilla, R., Ruan, W., Simons-Morton, B., & Scheidt, P. (2001). Bullying behaviors among U.S. youth: Prevalence and association with psychosocial adjustment. *JAMA: The Journal of the American Medical Association, 285*, 2094–2100.

Olweus, D. (1993). *Bullying at school*. Malden, MA: Blackwell Publishers.

Perry, D., Kusel, S., & Perry, L. (1988). Victims of peer aggression. *Developmental Psychology, 24*, 807–814.

Schwartz, D., Gorman, A., Nakamoto, J., & Tobin, R. (2005). Victimization in the peer group and children's academic functioning. *Journal of Educational Psychology, 97,* 425–435.

Simpson, E. (1949). Measurement of diversity. *Nature, 163,* 688.

Weiner, B. (1986). *An attributional theory of motivation and emotion.* New York: Springer.

Wright, J., Giammarino, M., & Parad, H. (1986). Social status in small groups: Individual-group similarity and the "social misfit." *Journal of Personality and Social Psychology, 50,* 523–536.

Children of Lesbian and Gay Parents

Charlotte J. Patterson[1]

University of Virginia

Abstract

Does parental sexual orientation affect child development, and if so, how? Studies using convenience samples, studies using samples drawn from known populations, and studies based on samples that are representative of larger populations all converge on similar conclusions. More than two decades of research has failed to reveal important differences in the adjustment or development of children or adolescents reared by same-sex couples compared to those reared by other-sex couples. Results of the research suggest that qualities of family relationships are more tightly linked with child outcomes than is parental sexual orientation.

Keywords

sexual orientation; parenting; lesbian; gay; child; socialization

Does parental sexual orientation affect child development, and if so, how? This question has often been raised in the context of legal and policy proceedings relevant to children, such as those involving adoption, child custody, or visitation. Divergent views have been offered by professionals from the fields of psychology, sociology, medicine, and law (Patterson, Fulcher, & Wainright, 2002). While this question has most often been raised in legal and policy contexts, it is also relevant to theoretical issues. For example, does healthy human development require that a child grow up with parents of each gender? And if not, what would that mean for our theoretical understanding of parent–child relations (Patterson & Hastings, in press)? In this article, I describe some research designed to address these questions.

EARLY RESEARCH

Research on children with lesbian and gay parents began with studies focused on cases in which children had been born in the context of a heterosexual marriage. After parental separation and divorce, many children in these families lived with divorced lesbian mothers. A number of researchers compared development among children of divorced lesbian mothers with that among children of divorced heterosexual mothers and found few significant differences (Patterson, 1997; Stacey & Biblarz, 2001).

These studies were valuable in addressing concerns of judges who were required to decide divorce and child custody cases, but they left many questions unanswered. In particular, because the children who participated in this research had been born into homes with married mothers and fathers, it was not obvious how to understand the reasons for their healthy development. The possibility that children's early exposure to apparently heterosexual male and female role models had contributed to healthy development could not be ruled out.

When lesbian or gay parents rear infants and children from birth, do their offspring grow up in typical ways and show healthy development? To address this question, it was important to study children who had never lived with heterosexual parents. In the 1990s, a number of investigators began research of this kind.

An early example was the Bay Area Families Study, in which I studied a group of 4- to 9-year-old children who had been born to or adopted early in life by lesbian mothers (Patterson, 1996, 1997). Data were collected during home visits. Results from in-home interviews and also from questionnaires showed that children had regular contact with a wide range of adults of both genders, both within and outside of their families. The children's self-concepts and preferences for same-gender playmates and activities were much like those of other children their ages. Moreover, standardized measures of social competence and of behavior problems, such as those from the Child Behavior Checklist (CBCL), showed that they scored within the range of normal variation for a representative sample of same-aged American children. It was clear from this study and others like it that it was quite possible for lesbian mothers to rear healthy children.

STUDIES BASED ON SAMPLES DRAWN FROM KNOWN POPULATIONS

Interpretation of the results from the Bay Area Families Study was, however, affected by its sampling procedures. The study had been based on a convenience sample that had been assembled by word of mouth. It was therefore impossible to rule out the possibility that families who participated in the research were especially well adjusted. Would a more representative sample yield different results?

To find out, Ray Chan, Barbara Raboy, and I conducted research in collaboration with the Sperm Bank of California (Chan, Raboy, & Patterson, 1998; Fulcher, Sutfin, Chan, Scheib, & Patterson, 2005). Over the more than 15 years of its existence, the Sperm Bank of California's clientele had included many lesbian as well as heterosexual women. For research purposes, this clientele was a finite population from which our sample could be drawn. The Sperm Bank of California also allowed a sample in which, both for lesbian and for heterosexual groups, one parent was biologically related to the child and one was not.

We invited all clients who had conceived children using the resources of the Sperm Bank of California and who had children 5 years old or older to participate in our research. The resulting sample was composed of 80 families, 55 headed by lesbian and 25 headed by heterosexual parents. Materials were mailed to participating families, with instructions to complete them privately and return them in self-addressed stamped envelopes we provided.

Results replicated and expanded upon those from earlier research. Children of lesbian and heterosexual parents showed similar, relatively high levels of social competence, as well as similar, relatively low levels of behavior problems on the parent form of the CBCL. We also asked the children's teachers to provide evaluations of children's adjustment on the Teacher Report Form of the CBCL, and their reports agreed with those of parents. Parental sexual orientation was not related to children's adaptation. Quite apart from parental sexual orientation, however, and consistent with findings from years of research on children of heterosexual parents, when parent–child relationships were marked by warmth and affection, children were more likely to be developing well. Thus, in this sample drawn from a known population, measures of children's adjustment were unrelated to parental sexual orientation (Chan et al., 1998; Fulcher et al., 2005).

Even as they provided information about children born to lesbian mothers, however, these new results also raised additional questions. Women who conceive children at sperm banks are generally both well educated and financially comfortable. It was possible that these relatively privileged women were able to protect children from many forms of discrimination. What if a more diverse group of families were to be studied? In addition, the children in this sample averaged 7 years of age, and some concerns focus on older children and adolescents. What if an older group of youngsters were to be studied? Would problems masked by youth and privilege in earlier studies emerge in an older, more diverse sample?

STUDIES BASED ON REPRESENTATIVE SAMPLES

An opportunity to address these questions was presented by the availability of data from the National Longitudinal Study of Adolescent Health (Add Health). The Add Health study involved a large, ethnically diverse, and essentially representative sample of American adolescents and their parents. Data for our research were drawn from surveys and interviews completed by more than 12,000 adolescents and their parents at home and from surveys completed by adolescents at school.

Parents were not queried directly about their sexual orientation but were asked if they were involved in a "marriage, or marriage-like relationship." If parents acknowledged such a relationship, they were also asked the gender of their partner. Thus, we identified a group of 44 12- to 18-year-olds who lived with parents involved in marriage or marriage-like relationships with same-sex partners. We compared them with a matched group of adolescents living with other-sex couples. Data from the archives of the Add Health study allowed us to address many questions about adolescent development.

Consistent with earlier findings, results of this work revealed few differences in adjustment between adolescents living with same-sex parents and those living with opposite-sex parents (Wainright, Russell, & Patterson, 2004; Wainright & Patterson, 2006). There were no significant differences between teenagers living with same-sex parents and those living with other-sex parents on self-reported assessments of psychological well-being, such as self-esteem and anxiety; measures of school outcomes, such as grade point averages and trouble in school; or measures of family relationships, such as parental warmth and care from adults and peers. Adolescents in the two groups were equally likely to say that they had been involved in a romantic relationship in the last 18 months, and they were equally likely to report having engaged in sexual intercourse. The only statistically reliable difference between the two groups—that those with same-sex parents felt a greater sense of connection to people at school—favored the youngsters living with same-sex couples. There were no significant differences in self-reported substance use, delinquency, or peer victimization between those reared by same- or other-sex couples (Wainright & Patterson, 2006).

Although the gender of parents' partners was not an important predictor of adolescent well-being, other aspects of family relationships were significantly associated with teenagers' adjustment. Consistent with other findings about adolescent development, the qualities of family relationships rather than the gender of parents' partners were consistently related to adolescent outcomes. Parents who reported having close relationships with their offspring had adolescents who reported more favorable adjustment. Not only is it possible for children and adolescents who are parented by same-sex couples to develop in healthy directions, but—even when studied in an extremely diverse, representative sample of American adolescents—they generally do.

These findings have been supported by results from many other studies, both in the United States and abroad. Susan Golombok and her colleagues have reported similar results with a near-representative sample of children in the United Kingdom (Golombok et al., 2003). Others, both in Europe and in the United States, have described similar findings (e.g., Brewaeys, Ponjaert, Van Hall, & Golombok, 1997).

The fact that children of lesbian mothers generally develop in healthy ways should not be taken to suggest that they encounter no challenges. Many investigators have remarked upon the fact that children of lesbian and gay parents may encounter anti-gay sentiments in their daily lives. For example, in a study of 10-year-old children born to lesbian mothers, Gartrell, Deck, Rodas, Peyser, and Banks (2005) reported that a substantial minority had encountered anti-gay sentiments among their peers. Those who had had such encounters were likely to report having felt angry, upset, or sad about these experiences. Children of lesbian and gay parents may be exposed to prejudice against their parents in some settings, and this may be painful for them, but evidence for the idea that such encounters affect children's overall adjustment is lacking.

CONCLUSIONS

Does parental sexual orientation have an important impact on child or adolescent development? Results of recent research provide no evidence that it does. In fact, the findings suggest that parental sexual orientation is less important than the qualities of family relationships. More important to youth than the gender of their parent's partner is the quality of daily interaction and the strength of relationships with the parents they have.

One possible approach to findings like the ones described above might be to shrug them off by reiterating the familiar adage that "one cannot prove the null hypothesis." To respond in this way, however, is to miss the central point of these studies. Whether or not any measurable impact of parental sexual orientation on children's development is ever demonstrated, the main conclusions from research to date remain clear: Whatever correlations between child outcomes and parental sexual orientation may exist, they are less important than those between child outcomes and the qualities of family relationships.

Although research to date has made important contributions, many issues relevant to children of lesbian and gay parents remain in need of study. Relatively few studies have examined the development of children adopted by lesbian or gay parents or of children born to gay fathers; further research in both areas would be welcome (Patterson, 2004). Some notable longitudinal studies have been reported, and they have found children of same-sex couples to be in good mental health. Greater understanding of family relationships and transitions over time would, however, be helpful, and longitudinal studies would be valuable. Future research could also benefit from the use of a variety of methodologies.

Meanwhile, the clarity of findings in this area has been acknowledged by a number of major professional organizations. For instance, the governing body of the American Psychological Association (APA) voted unanimously in favor of a statement that said, "Research has shown that the adjustment, development, and psychological well-being of children is unrelated to parental sexual orientation and that children of lesbian and gay parents are as likely as those of heterosexual parents to flourish" (APA, 2004). The American Bar Association, the American Medical Association, the American Academy of Pediatrics, the American Psychiatric Association, and other mainstream professional groups have issued similar statements.

The findings from research on children of lesbian and gay parents have been used to inform legal and public policy debates across the country (Patterson et al., 2002). The research literature on this subject has been cited in amicus briefs filed by the APA in cases dealing with adoption, child custody, and also in cases related to the legality of marriages between same-sex partners. Psychologists serving as expert witnesses have presented findings on these issues in many different courts (Patterson et al., 2002). Through these and other avenues, results of research on lesbian and gay parents and their children are finding their way into public discourse.

The findings are also beginning to address theoretical questions about critical issues in parenting. The importance of gender in parenting is one such issue. When children fare well in two-parent lesbian-mother or gay-father families, this suggests that the gender of one's parents cannot be a critical factor in child development. Results of research on children of lesbian and gay parents cast doubt upon the traditional assumption that gender is important in parenting. Our data suggest that it is the quality of parenting rather than the gender of parents that is significant for youngsters' development.

Research on children of lesbian and gay parents is thus located at the intersection of a number of classic and contemporary concerns. Studies of lesbian- and gay-parented families allow researchers to address theoretical questions that had previously remained difficult or impossible to answer. They also address oft-debated legal questions of fact about development of children with lesbian and gay parents. Thus, research on children of lesbian and gay parents contributes to public debate and legal decision making, as well as to theoretical understanding of human development.

Recommended Reading

Golombok, S., Perry, B., Burston, A., Murray, C., Mooney-Somers, J., Stevens, M., & Golding, J. (2003). (See References)
Patterson, C.J., Fulcher, M., & Wainright, J. (2002). (See References)

Stacey, J., & Biblarz, T.J. (2001). (See References)
Wainright, J.L., & Patterson, C.J. (2006). (See References)
Wainright, J.L., Russell, S.T., & Patterson, C.J. (2004). (See References)

Note

1. Address correspondence to Charlotte J. Patterson, Department of Psychology, P.O. Box 400400, University of Virginia, Charlottesville, VA 22904; e-mail: cjp@virginia.edu.

References

American Psychological Association (2004). Resolution on sexual orientation, parents, and children. Retrieved September 25, 2006, from http://www.apa.org/pi/lgbc/policy/parentschildren.pdf

Brewaeys, A., Ponjaert, I., Van Hall, E.V., & Golombok, S. (1997). Donor insemination: Child development and family functioning in lesbian mother families. *Human Reproduction, 12,* 1349–1359.

Chan, R.W., Raboy, B., & Patterson, C.J. (1998). Psychosocial adjustment among children conceived via donor insemination by lesbian and heterosexual mothers. *Child Development, 69,* 443–457.

Fulcher, M., Sutfin, E.L., Chan, R.W., Scheib, J.E., & Patterson, C.J. (2005). Lesbian mothers and their children: Findings from the Contemporary Families Study. In A. Omoto & H. Kurtzman (Eds.), *Recent research on sexual orientation, mental health, and substance abuse* (pp. 281–299). Washington, DC: American Psychological Association.

Gartrell, N., Deck., A., Rodas, C., Peyser, H., & Banks, A. (2005). The National Lesbian Family Study: 4. Interviews with the 10-year-old children. *American Journal of Orthopsychiatry, 75,* 518–524.

Golombok, S., Perry, B., Burston, A., Murray, C., Mooney-Somers, J., Stevens, M., & Golding, J. (2003). Children with lesbian parents: A community study. *Developmental Psychology, 39,* 20–33.

Patterson, C.J. (1996). Lesbian mothers and their children: Findings from the Bay Area Families Study. In J. Laird & R.J. Green (Eds.), *Lesbians and gays in couples and families: A handbook for therapists* (pp. 420–437). San Francisco: Jossey-Bass.

Patterson, C.J. (1997). Children of lesbian and gay parents. In T. Ollendick & R. Prinz (Eds.), *Advances in clinical child psychology* (Vol. 19, pp. 235–282). New York: Plenum Press.

Patterson, C.J. (2004). Gay fathers. In M.E. Lamb (Ed.), *The role of the father in child development* (4th ed., pp. 397–416). New York: Wiley.

Patterson, C.J., Fulcher, M., & Wainright, J. (2002). Children of lesbian and gay parents: Research, law, and policy. In B.L. Bottoms, M.B. Kovera, & B.D. McAuliff (Eds.), *Children, social science and the law* (pp. 176–199). New York: Cambridge University Press.

Patterson, C.J., & Hastings, P. (in press). Socialization in context of family diversity. In J. Grusec & P. Hastings (Eds.), *Handbook of socialization.* New York: Guilford Press.

Stacey, J., & Biblarz, T.J. (2001). (How) Does sexual orientation of parents matter? *American Sociological Review, 65,* 159–183.

Wainright, J.L., & Patterson, C.J. (2006). Delinquency, victimization, and substance use among adolescents with female same-sex parents. *Journal of Family Psychology, 20,* 526–530.

Wainright, J.L., Russell, S.T., & Patterson, C.J. (2004). Psychosocial adjustment and school outcomes of adolescents with same-sex parents. *Child Development, 75,* 1886–1898.

This article has been reprinted as it originally appeared in *Current Directions in Psychological Science*. Citation information for this article as originally published appears above.

How U.S. Children and Adolescents Spend Time: What It Does (and Doesn't) Tell Us About Their Development

Reed W. Larson[1]

Department of Human and Community Development,
University of Illinois, Urbana, Illinois

Abstract

Young people develop as "the sum of past experiences," and data on their time use are one means of quantifying those experiences. U.S. children and adolescents spend dramatically less time than in the agrarian past in household and income-generating labor. Because such labor is usually repetitive and unchallenging, this reduction has probably not deprived youths of crucial developmental experience. The schoolwork replacing this time has a clearer relationship to developmental outcomes. American teens, however, spend less time on schoolwork than teens in other industrialized countries. American teenagers have more discretionary time, much spent watching television or interacting with friends; spending large amounts of time in these activities is related to negative developmental outcomes. Increasing amounts of young people's discretionary time, however, appear to be spent in structured voluntary activities, like arts, sports, and organizations, which may foster initiative, identity, and other positive developmental outcomes.

Keywords

time use; developmental experiences

Children's and adolescents' use of time, a topic of public debate since the 1920s, has reemerged as an issue of national concern. Alarm is voiced that American youths do too little homework, spend too little time with their parents, and spend too much time watching television and, now, playing computer games or surfing the Internet. The after-school hours have been identified as a time of risk, when unsupervised children are endangered and teenagers use drugs, commit crimes, and have sex. The underlying question is whether young people are spending their time in ways that are healthy and prepare them for adulthood in the competitive, global world of the 21st century. Another, related question is whether young people are being overscheduled and denied the creative, exploratory freedom of youth.

Time, as economists tell us, is a resource—one that can be used productively or squandered. For developmental psychologists, study of children's and adolescents' use of this resource offers a means to examine their portfolio of daily socialization experiences. Data on their time spent in different activities provide estimates of how much they are engaged with the information, social systems, developmental opportunities, and developmental liabilities associated with each context. Of course, information on time spent in specific activities is only a rough proxy for actual socialization experiences. The impact of watching TV for 2 hours depends on whom a child is with, what the child watches, and how the child interprets it. Even two siblings eating supper with their parents each night may have much different experiences of this time. Nonetheless, assessment of time spent in different activities provides a useful starting point for evaluating a population's set of developmental experiences.

A LIFTED BURDEN OF REPETITIVE DRUDGERY

If we look back over the past 200 years, the most striking historic change in young people's use of time is that youths spend much less time on labor activities today than they did in America's agrarian past. In current nonindustrialized agrarian settings, household and income-generating labor fills 6 hours a day by middle childhood and reaches full adult levels of 8 or more hours per day by the early teens. By comparison, in the contemporary United States, time spent on household chores averages 15 to 30 minutes per day in childhood and 20 to 40 minutes in adolescence; income-generating activities account for little or no time, except among employed older teenagers (Larson & Verma, 1999).

Has this dramatic reduction in labor taken away valuable developmental experiences? In a comprehensive review, Goodnow (1988) found remarkably little evidence that household chores foster development. Children gain activity-specific skills (e.g., cooking skills), and care of younger children, if well-supervised, may bring positive outcomes. But evidence for broader developmental gains is thin. In reality, much time spent on chores in traditional agrarian settings involved highly repetitive activities, like carrying water and weeding fields; likewise, in contemporary America, most chores are mundane, with little challenge or developmental content. Evidence on the developmental benefits of U.S. adolescents' employment is more positive but also mixed. Definitive longitudinal studies indicate that employment during adolescence increases likelihood of employment and wages in early adulthood; however, teen employment over 20 hours per week is associated with greater delinquency, school misconduct, and substance use (Mortimer, Harley, & Aronson, 1999). Except in atypical circumstances in which youths have intellectually challenging jobs, it is hard to argue that more than 15 to 20 hours of employment per week brings additional developmental gains. Certainly, spending some time in chores and, especially, employment may provide useful learning experiences, but the dramatic reduction in youths' time in these repetitive labor activities appears to be a developmental plus.

Historically, this large burden of labor has been replaced by schooling, and schooling has clearer benefits. Young people often feel bored and unmotivated while doing schoolwork, as they do during chores and employment, and many experience schoolwork, too, as drudgery. But unlike labor activities, schoolwork brings experiences of high challenge and concentration. Amount of time spent in education correlates with youths' knowledge, intelligence, and subsequent adult earnings (Ceci & Williams, 1997), and is related to growth of a society's economy. Thus, economically and in other ways, the displacement of labor by schoolwork is a positive change in young people's time use.

American youths, however, spend less time on schoolwork than youths in most industrialized nations. As with other activities, the largest cross-national differences occur in adolescence (Table 1). U.S. teens spend approximately

Table 1. *Average daily time use of adolescents in 45 studies*

Activity	Nonindustrial, unschooled populations	Postindustrial, schooled populations		
		United States	Europe	East Asia
Household labor	5–9 hr	20–40 min	20–40 min	10–20 min
Paid labor	0.5–8 hr	40–60 min	10–20 min	0–10 min
Schoolwork	—	3.0–4.5 hr	4.0–5.5 hr	5.5–7.5 hr
Total work time	6–9 hr	4–6 hr	4.5–6.5 hr	6–8 hr
TV viewing	*insufficient data*	1.5–2.5 hr	1.5–2.5 hr	1.5–2.5 hr
Talking	*insufficient data*	2–3 hr	*insufficient data*	45–60 min
Sports	*insufficient data*	30–60 min	20–80 min	0–20 min
Structured voluntary activities	*insufficient data*	10–20 min	1.0–20 min	0–10 min
Total free time	4–7 hr	6.5–8.0 hr	5.5–7.5 hr	4.0–5.5 hr

Note. The estimates in the table are averaged across a 7-day week, including weekdays and weekends. Time spent in maintenance activities like eating, personal care, and sleeping is not included. The data for nonindustrial, unschooled populations come primarily from rural peasant populations in developing countries. Adapted from Larson and Verma (1999).

three fifths the amount of time on schoolwork that East Asian teens do and four fifths the time that European teens do. These differences are mostly attributable to American teens doing less homework, estimated at 20 to 40 minutes per day, as compared with 2.0 to 4.0 hours in East Asia and 1.0 to 2.5 hours in Europe. These figures do not take into account national differences in length of the school year (it is shortest in the United States) and overlook differences between individual students and school districts—some U.S. schools and state legislatures have recently taken action to increase homework. These figures also overlook possible differences in quality of instruction: An hour of schoolwork may yield more learning in one country than in another. Nonetheless, they provide one explanation for American students' lower test scores and raise questions about whether American youths are being disadvantaged in the new competitive global marketplace.

THE EXPANSE OF FREE TIME

What American youths, especially adolescents, have in greater quantities than young people in other industrialized nations is discretionary time. Studies carried out since the 1920s have found that 40–50% of U.S. teenagers' waking time (not counting summer vacations) is spent in discretionary activities. Current estimates are 25–35% in East Asia and 35–45% in Europe. Whether this time is a liability or gives American youths an advantage depends largely on what they do with it.

Media Use

American teens spend much of their free time using media, particularly watching television. Studies indicate that TV viewing is American youths' primary activity for 1.5 to 2.5 hours per day on average. Curiously, the averages in other nations are quite similar. Within the United States, rates of viewing are found to be highest in late childhood and among boys, youths of low socioeconomic status (SES), and African Americans across income levels.

Current theories emphasize that viewers are active, not passive—they "use" media. Research indicates, however, that TV is rarely used for positive developmental experiences and that viewing is associated with developmental liabilities. A high amount of time watching entertainment TV—which constitutes most of youths' viewing—is associated with obesity and changed perceptions of sexual norms. Watching more than 3 to 4 hours per day is associated with lower school grades. Controlled longitudinal studies show that rates of viewing violence predict subsequent aggression (Strasburger, 1995). TV watching may sometimes be used for relaxation: Much viewing occurs in the late evening, when young people wind down before bed. But, on balance, TV time is developmentally unconstructive.

The new kid on the block, of course, is computer and Internet use, and we know little about developmental impacts of these new media. Rates of use in the United States are still small, but are increasing steadily. A recent national survey found recreational computer use to account for an average of 30 minutes per day for youths over age 8, with greater use among higher-SES youngsters (Roberts, Foehr, Rideout, & Brodie, 1999). Children spend more time playing computer games, whereas adolescents devote more time to e-mail and other Internet activities. As with television, there are important concerns: about effects of violent and pornographic content, commercial exploitation, participation in deviant Internet groups, and social isolation among frequent users. At the same time, computers and the Internet permit more active individualized use than television and thus have more developmental promise. Young people can use these media to obtain information, develop relationships with people different from themselves, learn job skills, and even start companies, irrespective of their age, gender, ethnicity, and physical appearance. The question of developmental benefits versus liabilities for this use of time is not likely to have a singular conclusion; answers are likely to differ across uses and users.

Unstructured Leisure

The largest amount of U.S. youths' free time is spent playing, talking, hanging out, and participating in other unstructured leisure activities, often with friends. Play is more frequent in childhood than in adolescence, accounting for 1.5 to 3.0 hours per day in the elementary years. It is gradually displaced by talking, primarily with peers. U.S. first graders appear to spend about as much time playing as first graders in Japan and Taiwan, but play falls off more quickly with age in East Asia (Stevenson & Lee, 1990).

Abundant theory and research suggest that play promotes positive development. Piaget viewed play as an arena for experimentation and adaptation of mental schemas (including concepts and strategies) to experience. Research substantiates that play has relationships to children's cognitive, linguistic, social, and emotional development (Fisher, 1992). McHale, Crouter, and Tucker (2000), however, found that among 10-year-olds, more time spent in outdoor play was associated with lower school grades and more conduct problems. Thus, more time playing does not necessarily facilitate more development.

Adolescents' talking, it can be argued, is play at a symbolic level. Social interaction is an arena for exploration and development of emotional, interpersonal, and moral schemas. Therefore, we might expect time spent interacting with peers to be associated with developmental gains similar to those for time spent playing. Little research has directly addressed this question, but longitudinal research shows that spending more time interacting with friends in unstructured contexts predicts higher rates of problem behavior (Osgood, Wilson, O'Malley, Bachman, & Johnston, 1996). This relationship is undoubtedly complex, depending on the content of interaction, individual dispositions, and numerous other factors. But these findings certainly contradict the argument that youths need large amounts of unstructured, free time.

Structured Leisure Activities

U.S. adolescents stand out from East Asian youths in time spent in voluntary structured activities, like sports, arts, music, hobbies, and organizations. (Insufficient comparative data exist for younger children.) Even so, the current media image of "overscheduled kids" is misleading. Among American teens, the average amount of time spent in these activities per day is measured in minutes, not hours (Table 1), although there is mixed evidence suggesting this time is increasing (Fishman, 1999; Zill, Nord, & Loomis, 1995).

What are the developmental benefits and costs of spending time in these activities? When participating, young people report experiencing high challenge, concentration, and motivation. This combination, which rarely occurs elsewhere in youths' lives, suggests they are engaged and invested in ways that provide unique opportunities for growth. Theory and a partial body of research suggest that these activities are associated with development of identity and initiative, reduced delinquency, and positive adult outcomes (Larson, 2000; Mahoney, 2000), although some studies have found sports participation increases alcohol use. More research is needed, but there is good reason to hypothesize that, under the right conditions, structured activities provide unique developmental experiences.

CONCLUSIONS

Are U.S. children and adolescents spending their time in ways consistent with optimal development? This question, I confess, makes me cringe. Taken to its logical conclusion, it suggests submitting every moment of youth to utilitarian "time and motion study." We know too well from current trends in education that when things can be measured—for example, by test scores—policy discussions focus on measures as ends in themselves, irrespective of more important harder-to-measure variables. Given our limited state of knowledge and the loose relationship between how time is spent and what youths actually experience, overemphasis on time allocation is certain to mislead. It also overlooks individual and cultural differences in learning processes and developmental goals. Human development is not a board game that can be won by having one's pieces spend the most time on selected squares. Developmental science needs models that conceptualize time as one among many variables affecting growth.

With these cautions firmly in mind, it seems important to consider quantities of time as part of the package when appraising young people's portfolio of developmental experiences. Should U.S. teenagers' schoolwork time be lengthened to match that of East Asian teens? In fact, East Asian societies are engaged in intense public debates about the stress and developmental costs associated with their adolescents' exclusionary focus on school achievement. Recent U.S. efforts to require more homework for all young people are probably justified, and there are empirical rationales for experiments with lengthening the school year and redistributing summer vacation throughout the calendar. But I think the most pressing issue for U.S. youths is not further increasing schoolwork time, but ensuring consistent quality in what happens during this time. My research shows that adolescents, including honor students, are frequently bored during schoolwork (this is also true in East Asia). It may be less important to pack more studying into the day than for researchers and practitioners to find ways to increase the quality of engagement for all students.

Are Americans' large quantities of discretionary time—40 to 50% of waking hours—a developmental asset or liability? A romantic view sees large blocks of unstructured time giving youths opportunities to explore, create structure on their own, learn to think outside the box, and perhaps "find themselves" in the existential ground zero of free choice. The underlying reality is that, left to them-selves, children and adolescents often choose to spend time in unchallenging activities, like hanging out with friends and watching TV. Although some social interaction and time for relaxation are undoubtedly useful, it seems unlikely that spending many hours in unchallenging contexts fosters development. The hypoth-esis that youths need and benefit from unstructured free time, nonetheless, remains worthy of creative research, especially if the time they spend on schoolwork increases.

The small but possibly growing amount of time children and adolescents spend in structured voluntary activities provides more developmentally promising use for some of these discretionary hours. In these activities, youths often experi-ence challenge and exercise initiative. When adult leaders give responsibility to youths, they may provide better contexts for learning to create structure and think outside the box than can be found in free play or social interaction (Heath, 1999). In the absence of better knowledge, however, the current rush to create activities for after-school hours is unwise. Research is needed to determine the features of these activities associated with positive outcomes and how to fit par-ticipation to individuals' developmental readiness. A fundamental question is how to create activities with enough structure to contain and channel behavior with-out compromising youths' sense of agency.

Ultimately, development is probably best served by combinations of comple-mentary activities, including those that shape good habits, teach literacy, build interpersonal relationships, foster initiative, and provide relaxation. The task of future research is to illuminate how quantities and qualities of experiences in dif-ferent activities act in combination to affect development. Certainly, development is much more than an additive "sum of past experiences." We need to consider how individuals interpret, synthesize, and grow from experiences. Evaluation of time allocation is a useful entry point for examining links between experience and development, but only one small piece of a much more complex inquiry.

Recommended Reading

Larson, R., & Verma, S. (1999). (See References)

Robinson, J., & Bianchi, S. (1997). The children's hours. *American Demographics, 19*(12), 20–24.

Stevenson, H.W., & Stigler, J.W. (1992). *The learning gap.* New York: Simon & Schuster.

Wartella, E., & Mazzarella, S. (1990). A historical comparison of children's use of leisure time. In R. Butsch (Ed.), *For fun and profit: The transformation of leisure into con-sumption* (pp. 173–194). Philadelphia: Temple University Press.

Note

1. Address correspondence to Reed W. Larson, Department of Human and Com-munity Development, University of Illinois, 1105 W. Nevada St., Urbana, IL 61801; e-mail: larsonr@uiuc.edu.

References

Ceci, S.J., & Williams, W.M. (1997). Schooling, intelligence, and income. *American Psychologist, 52,* 1051–1058.

Fisher, E.P. (1992). The impact of play on development: A meta-analysis. *Play & Culture, 5*, 159–181.

Fishman, C. (1999). The smorgasbord generation. *American Demographics, 21*(5), 55–60.

Goodnow, J.J. (1988). Children's household work: Its nature and functions. *Psychological Bulletin, 103*, 5–26.

Heath, S.B. (1999). Dimensions of language development: Lessons from older children. In A.S. Masten (Ed.), *The Minnesota Symposium on Child Psychology: Vol. 29. Cultural processes in child development* (pp. 59–75). Mahwah, NJ: Erlbaum.

Larson, R. (2000). Towards a psychology of positive youth development. *American Psychologist, 55*, 170–183.

Larson, R., & Verma, S. (1999). How children and adolescents spend time across cultural settings of the world: Work, play and developmental opportunities. *Psychological Bulletin, 125*, 701–736.

Mahoney, J.L. (2000). School extracurricular activity participation as a moderator in the development of antisocial patterns. *Child Development, 71*, 502–516.

McHale, S.M., Crouter, A.C., & Tucker, C.J. (2000, March). *Free time activities in middle childhood: Links with adjustment in early adolescence.* Paper presented at the biannual meeting of the Society for Research on Adolescence, Chicago.

Mortimer, J.T., Harley, C., & Aronson, P. (1999). How do prior experiences in the workplace set the stage for transitions to adulthood? In A. Booth, A.C. Crouter, & M.J. Shanahan (Eds.), *Transitions to adulthood in a changing economy: No work, no family, no future?* (pp. 131–159). Westport, CT: Praeger.

Osgood, D.W., Wilson, J.K., O'Malley, P.M., Bachman, J.G., & Johnston, L.D. (1996). Routine activities and individual deviant behavior. *American Sociological Review, 61*, 635–655.

Roberts, D.F., Foehr, U.G., Rideout, V.J., & Brodie, M. (1999). *Kids & media @ the new millennium.* Menlo Park, CA: Kaiser Family Foundation.

Stevenson, H.W., & Lee, S. (1990). Context of achievement. *Monographs of the Society for Research in Child Development, 55*(1–2).

Strasburger, V.C. (1995). *Adolescents and the media.* Thousand Oaks, CA: Sage.

Zill, N., Nord, C.W., & Loomis, L.S. (1995). *Adolescent time use, risky behavior, and outcomes: An analysis of national data.* Rockville, MD: Westat.

Section 1: Critical Thinking Questions

1. Define ecological systems theory and a transactional model (according to Wills and Yaeger). How does transactional modeling facilitate the study of ecological systems?

2. Most of the articles in this section relate to child development, adjustment, or well-being. According to the evidence in these articles, what risk and protective factors within the microsystems and mesosytems of youth are important for positive development?

3. According to Marshall, what exo- and macrosystem factors affect access to high-quality child care? What portions of the population are most constrained by these factors? What are implications for intervention?

4. How do socioeconomic, ethnic, or cultural factors influence parental school involvement according to Hill and Taylor? How can school policies overcome barriers to involvement?

5. Larsen notes that some studies have found participating in sports may increase substance use in youth. How might the coaching intervention by Smith and Smoll in Section 4 buffer this effect? How do Smith and Smoll's findings relate to the protective factors identified by Wills and Yaeger?

6. Graham measures "the balance of power" in the ethnic contexts of schools quantitatively. What qualitative aspects of ethnic contexts may affect peer victimization? What are the potential benefits of multiethnic school environments for individuals, communities, and society?

7. Why does Patterson's review of studies with different sampling strategies strengthen the conclusion that child adjustment and development is not significantly affected by parental sexual orientation? What additional study designs could contribute to research on this topic?

8. Larsen states, "A fundamental question is how to create activities with enough structure to contain and channel behavior without compromising youths' sense of agency." Why is fostering a sense of agency important for youth development?

This article has been reprinted as it originally appeared in *Current Directions in Psychological Science*. Citation information for this article as originally published appears above.

Section 2: Environmental Impact: Neighborhoods and Macrosystems

This section moves from the immediate environments of people's lives to larger social units, such as neighborhoods and communities, and to socio-economic and cultural contexts, dubbed macrosystems. These articles illustrate how research may be designed and synthesized to capture the complex interplay of neighborhood-level or societal-level factors on individuals and communities, with implications for interventions and policies that are *not* targeted solely at the individual-level (e.g. education, behavioral modification). Instead, these articles bring to the fore qualities of communities that may have positive impacts (e.g. social capital and ties, collective efficacy) or negative impacts (e.g. unsafe environments, insufficient resources) on their members. The former may be fostered, and the latter prevented, by neighborhood and macrosystem interventions.

The first article by Leventhal and Brooks-Gunn provides a conceptualization of neighborhoods' impact on youth development that helps to situate the other articles. Both experimental and non-experimental studies find that neighborhood characteristics influence the well-being of youth and other residents. The authors propose three theoretical models at multiple ecological levels—institutional resources, relationships and ties, norms and collective efficacy—to illuminate potential processes for *how* neighborhoods matter. The second article by Cutrona, Wallace, and Wesner contribute further to the examination of processes by showing how neighborhood-level factors, including structural and functional characteristics of neighborhoods and community members, relate to daily stressors, negative events, and interpersonal relationships, which in turn affect depression. This article concludes that improving mental health in impoverished neighborhoods would require improving neighborhood quality.

Both these articles review research that controlled for family factors, such as income, to understand neighborhood effects. However, the socio-economic status (SES) of households also affects health. In the third article, Chen proposes psychosocial pathways across multiple ecological systems that may contribute to understanding the pervasive relationship found between SES and health. She emphasizes how processes may differ at different points in children's developmental trajectories and that SES itself may fluctuate across people's life spans.

Leventhal and Brooks-Dunn also acknowledge the paucity of research that examines how cultural differences may moderate neighborhoods effects on well-being. The last articles examine different aspects of culture. Seybold and Hill explore the relationship between religion and spirituality and health. Echoing other articles within this section, they note that social networks and social support of religious communities may be important factors.

Children and Youth in Neighborhood Contexts

Tama Leventhal[1] and Jeanne Brooks-Gunn

National Center for Children and Families, Teachers College, Columbia University, New York, New York

Abstract

Neighborhoods are increasingly studied as a context where children and youth develop; however, the extent of neighborhoods' impact remains debatable because it is difficult to disentangle this impact from that of the family context, in part because families have some choice as to where they live. Evidence from randomized experiments, studies using advanced statistical models, and longitudinal studies that control for family characteristics indicates that neighborhoods do matter. In nonexperimental studies, small to moderate associations were found, suggesting that children and adolescents living in high-income neighborhoods had higher cognitive ability and school achievement than those living in middle-income neighborhoods, and children and adolescents living in low-income neighborhoods had more mental and physical health problems than those living in middle-income neighborhoods. The home environment has been shown to be partly responsible for the link between neighborhood and children's development. For adolescents, neighborhood effects are partially accounted for by community social control. Experimental studies in which families were randomly assigned to move to low-poverty neighborhoods from housing projects found larger neighborhood effects than nonexperimental research, particularly for boys' outcomes. Additional issues reviewed are relevant neighborhood characteristics, theoretical models explaining the pathways underlying neighborhood effects, methods for research assessing neighborhood processes, and policy implications.

Keywords

neighborhood; community; achievement; health; income/socioeconomic status; policy

Historical trends document the declining economic conditions in which children grow up. Compared with their predecessors, children today are more likely to be raised in poor families (i.e., those whose incomes fall below a federally established threshold), as well as to live in poor neighborhoods (i.e., 20% or more of residents poor). Almost half of poor families reside in urban neighborhoods that are increasingly marked by concentrated poverty. Both family and neighborhood poverty are rooted in demographic shifts in family composition and labor-force participation, changes in migration and residential patterns, declines in industrialization, and housing segregation (Massey & Denton, 1993; Wilson, 1987). Responding to these trends, both academic scholars and policymakers developed a rising interest in the contexts in which children are reared, including larger social environments beyond the family, notably neighborhoods. By the mid-1980s, questions such as the following were raised: Does neighborhood residence influence children's well-being? How do neighborhoods affect children and youth? What can be done to alleviate neighborhood disadvantage and its potentially harmful effects on children's development? In response to these questions, scholars from various disciplines—economics, epidemiology, demography, sociology, and psychology—launched a field of study that has become known as neighborhood research (Brooks-Gunn, Duncan, & Aber, 1997).

NONEXPERIMENTAL STUDIES OF NEIGHBORHOOD EFFECTS ON DEVELOPMENT

Most neighborhood research has used census-based measures of neighborhood structural or sociodemographic characteristics in conjunction with data collected on children and families, often from large national data sets (e.g., Panel Study of Income Dynamics, National Longitudinal Survey of Youth-Child Supplement), to examine associations among neighborhood residence and child and adolescent outcomes. Data from the U.S. Census come from the forms the population fills out on April 1 of the 1st year of every decade. Thus, census information is limited to structural characteristics, such as median household income, percentage of residents with a high school diploma, racial composition, and percentage of homeowners. The census tract is the most frequently used definition of "neighborhood" in these studies. Tract boundaries are identified by local communities working under Census Bureau guidelines and reflect salient physical and social features that demarcate neighborhoods, such as major streets, railroads, and ethnic divisions; census tracts contain approximately 3,000 to 8,000 individuals.

Neighborhood income or socioeconomic status (SES)—a combination of social and economic indicators—is the most commonly investigated neighborhood characteristic. In these studies, researchers often use two separate measures of SES, because the presence of poor and affluent neighbors may have differential associations with child and adolescent outcomes (Jencks & Mayer, 1990). High-SES/affluence measures may take into consideration indicators such as income, percentage professionals, and percentage of residents who are college educated; low-SES/poverty measures may take into consideration indicators such as percentage poor, percentage of households headed by females, percentage on public assistance, and percentage unemployed. Other structural characteristics frequently examined include racialethnic mix (e.g., percentage Black, percentage Latino, and percentage foreign-born) and residential instability (e.g., percentage moved in last 5 years, percentage of households in their current home less than 10 years, and percentage renters).

Studies investigating neighborhood effects on children's development also account for family characteristics, such as income, composition, and parents' education, age, and race or ethnicity, to demonstrate whether neighborhood effects go "above and beyond" family influences. Because families have some choice as to where they live, adjusting for these background factors also minimizes the possibility that unmeasured individual and family characteristics associated with neighborhood residence (i.e., selection bias) might account for observed neighborhood effects. Some researchers also have addressed selection problems by using various advanced analytic strategies, such as comparisons of siblings or first cousins, which hold family characteristics constant; instrumental variable analyses, which minimize unmeasured correlations between neighborhood characteristics and child outcomes; and behavior genetics models, which differentiate between genetic and environmental influences.

We recently conducted a large-scale review of the neighborhood research (Leventhal & Brooks-Gunn, 2000). Findings reported in that review as well as subsequent work revealed consistent patterns of neighborhood effects on children's and adolescents' development; comparable findings have been documented in U.S. and Canadian samples and in cross-sectional and longitudinal studies that control for family characteristics. Across these studies, neighborhood effects were small to moderate in size. For preschool and school-age children, the presence of affluent or high-income neighbors was positively associated with children's verbal ability, IQ scores, and school achievement. In contrast, the presence of low-income or low-SES neighbors was associated with children's mental health problems. For adolescents, living in a high-income neighborhood was also associated with high school achievement and educational attainment, particularly for males. Residence in low-income neighborhoods was associated with adverse mental health, criminal and delinquent behavior, and unfavorable sexual and fertility outcomes for adolescents. For both children and adolescents, these patterns of results also have been found in studies employing advanced statistical techniques, although effect sizes are typically reduced.

EXPERIMENTAL STUDIES OF NEIGHBORHOOD EFFECTS ON DEVELOPMENT

Although nonexperimental neighborhood research has yielded fairly consistent patterns of findings, it has been criticized on the grounds that families have some choice as to the neighborhoods in which they live, resulting in selection bias (even after accounting for family characteristics). Experimental and quasi-experimental studies that randomly assign families to live in certain types of neighborhoods overcome the selection problem in nonexperimental research. Although such designs may seem implausible, they have been possible in the context of housing programs that randomly select families for assistance in relocating from public housing to less poor neighborhoods (e.g., they may receive vouchers to rent housing in the private market or be offered public housing built in nonpoor neighborhoods).

The oldest and most well known quasi-experimental study is the Gautreaux Program, enacted following a court order to desegregate Chicago's public housing. Families were given vouchers to move, and assignment of families to neighborhoods was random, based on housing availability (see Rubinowitz & Rosenbaum, 2000, for a review). A 10-year follow-up found that youth who moved to more affluent suburban neighborhoods fared better academically than youth who moved to poor urban neighborhoods.

In 1994, partially in response to positive findings reported in the Gautreaux Program, the U.S. Department of Housing and Urban Development initiated the Moving to Opportunity Program in five cities across the country. Approximately 4,600 families were randomly assigned vouchers to move out of public housing in high-poverty neighborhoods into private housing of their choice or into private housing in low-poverty neighborhoods (with special assistance); a subset of families remained in public housing. Although initial evaluations were conducted independently in each city, there is some overlap in the outcomes examined in different cities, so that it is possible to draw some preliminary conclusions from this research (Goering, in press). Findings from these experimental studies revealed that several years into the program, children and youth who moved to less poor neighborhoods had higher educational achievement and superior physical and mental health compared with their peers who remained in high-poverty neighborhoods (Katz, Kling, & Liebman, 2001; Leventhal & Brooks-Gunn, 2002, in press). In addition, arrests for violent crime were lower among male youth who moved to less poor neighborhoods than among peers who stayed in high-poverty neighborhoods (Ludwig, Duncan, & Hirschfield, 2001). Neighborhood effects in these experimental studies were large. In addition, larger effects were generally seen for children and youth who moved to low-poverty neighborhoods than for those who moved to moderately poor neighborhoods, and effects were more pronounced for boys than girls.

THEORETICAL MODELS OF NEIGHBORHOOD EFFECTS

The experimental and nonexperimental studies we have reviewed illuminated specific neighborhood characteristics that were associated with particular outcomes. These studies, however, do not address the mechanisms through which neighborhood effects occur. We have proposed several theoretical models to explain potential pathways of neighborhood influences (Leventhal & Brooks-Gunn, 2000). These models highlight different underlying processes operating at various levels (individual, family, school, peer, and community). This work draws heavily from a review and analysis by Jencks and Mayer (1990); from research on family stress, economic hardship, and unemployment; and from literature on community social organization and urban sociology.

The first model, *institutional resources,* posits that neighborhood influences operate by means of the quality, quantity, and diversity of learning, recreational, social, educational, health, and employment resources in the community. The second model, *relationships and ties,* highlights families as a potential mechanism of neighborhood effects. Important variables in this model include parental attributes (e.g., mental and physical health, coping skills, and efficacy), social networks, and behavior (e.g., supervision-monitoring, warmth, and harshness), as well as characteristics of the home environment (e.g., learning and physical environments, family routines, and violence). The last model, *norms and collective efficacy,* hypothesizes that neighborhood influences are accounted for by the extent of formal and informal social institutions in the community and the degree to which they monitor or control residents' behavior in accordance with socially accepted practices and the goal of maintaining public order (Sampson, Raudenbush, & Earls, 1997). This model includes influences such as peer groups and physical threats in the neighborhood (e.g., violence, availability of illegal and harmful substances). The models are intended to be complementary rather than conflicting, with the utility of each model for explaining neighborhood effects on children's well-being depending on both the particular outcome studied and the age group examined.

An emerging body of research, focused largely on adolescent problem behavior, substantiates the norms-and-collective-efficacy model. At both the community and the individual levels, mechanisms of social control have been found to account, in part, for associations among neighborhood structure and rates of problem behavior among adolescents (e.g., Elliott et al., 1996; Sampson et al., 1997). There has been scant research relevant to the other models, although several studies of young children support the relationships-and-ties model; quality of the home environment was found to partially account for associations between neighborhood structure and children's achievement and behavioral outcomes (Klebanov, Brooks-Gunn, McCarton, & McCormick, 1998).

CONCLUSIONS AND IMPLICATIONS

Evidence from randomized experiments, studies employing advanced statistical models, and longitudinal studies controlling for family characteristics indicates that neighborhoods, and particularly their socioeconomic composition, do matter. The size of neighborhood effects reported in the nonexperimental literature has typically been small to modest (after background characteristics are accounted for). However, neighborhood effects reported in the limited set of experimental studies were large, likely because the changes in neighborhood conditions were substantial (when families initiate their own moves, the changes are usually not so large, particularly among low-income families). To determine whether nonexperimental research is underestimating neighborhood effects, it will be necessary to try to replicate the experimental findings by undertaking natural studies where radical changes in neighborhood economic conditions have occurred. In addition, suggestive evidence from nonexperimental studies reveals that neighborhood residence may be differentially associated with outcomes for Latinos compared with European and African Americans, pointing to acculturation as a potentially important and unexplored variable moderating the effects of neighborhood structure.

The impact of neighborhood residence is also likely to vary across development; however, because much of the neighborhood research is cross-sectional or based on neighborhood residence at a single point in time, this issue has not been adequately addressed. This relatively static view of neighborhood influences extends to neighborhood conditions. Researchers often ignore the fact that families move across neighborhoods and that even when families do not move, neighborhood structure changes, for example, through gentrification and immigration (Leventhal & Brooks-Gunn, 2001).

What else remains unclear is how neighborhoods matter. Our proposed models—institutional resources, relationships and ties, and norms and collective efficacy—provide a framework intended to aid empirical investigations of theoretically driven neighborhood research. To test theoretical models, it is necessary to move beyond census measures of SES and directly assess underlying processes. Alternative data sources are required to measure neighborhood-level processes, in particular. Useful data will come from (a) city, state, and federal records (e.g., vital statistics from health departments, crime reports from police departments, school records from education departments, and child abuse and neglect records from social service departments); (b) systematic social observations by trained observers using a structured format to characterize neighborhoods along a range of social and physical attributes; (c) community surveys in which non-study participants (i.e., an independent sample) are interviewed about their neighborhoods (usually about their neighborhoods' social organization); and (d) neighborhood-expert surveys in which key community leaders are interviewed about neighborhood political and social organization (see Leventhal & Brooks-Gunn, 2001, for additional details). Recent studies designed specifically with neighborhood influences in mind are collecting longitudinal and process-oriented data on children, families, and neighborhoods and are well suited for exploring mechanisms through which neighborhoods influence child well-being, as well as addressing dynamic models of neighborhood influences.

Several policy implications may be drawn from the existing neighborhood research. The research suggests that it would be beneficial to develop programs that foster moving poor families out of poor neighborhoods. In line with this goal are efforts to reduce housing discrimination in nonpoor neighborhoods. What Moving to Opportunity and other such programs have demonstrated is that without special assistance, poor families who are given vouchers do not necessarily move out of poor neighborhoods. A complementary approach is to build scattered-site public housing in nonpoor neighborhoods, as was done in Yonkers, New York. However, if the most advantaged poor families move out of poor neighborhoods, what remains are concentrations of poor families, and possibly of those with the most mental and physical health problems, poor coping skills, and low literacy— all barriers to economic self-sufficiency.

An alternative strategy is to move nonpoor families into poor neighborhoods to change the mix and reduce poverty concentration and segregation. Gentrification also typically entails providing services (e.g., good-quality schools) and jobs in these neighborhoods. It is still unclear if poor families (or which poor families) benefit from this transformation or if they are forced out.

In summary, future research will likely lead to better answers to the original questions posed by academic scholars and policymakers, as well as to the design of more effective policies.

Recommended Reading

Brooks-Gunn, J., Duncan, G.J., & Aber, J.L. (Eds.). (1997). (See References)
Burton, L.M., & Jarrett, R.L. (2000). In the mix, yet on the margins: The place of families in urban neighborhood and child development research. *Journal of Marriage and the Family, 62,* 1114–1135.
Goering, J. (Ed.). (in press). (See References)
Leventhal, T., & Brooks-Gunn, J. (2000). (See References)
Sampson, R.J., Raudenbush, S.W., & Earls, F. (1997). (See References)

Note

1. Address correspondence to Tama Leventhal, National Center for Children and Families, Teachers College, Columbia University, New York, NY 10027; e-mail: tl91@ columbia.edu.

References

Brooks-Gunn, J., Duncan, G.J., & Aber, J.L. (Eds.). (1997). *Neighborhood poverty* (2 vols.). New York: Russell Sage Foundation Press.

Elliott, D., Wilson, W.J., Huizinga, D., Sampson, R., Elliott, A., & Rankin, B. (1996). The effects of neighborhood disadvantage on adolescent development. *Journal of Research in Crime and Delinquency, 33*, 389–426.

Goering, J. (Ed.). (in press). *Choosing a better life? How public housing tenants selected a HUD experiment to improve their lives and those of their children: The Moving to Opportunity Demonstration Program.* Washington, DC: Urban Institute Press.

Jencks, C., & Mayer, S. (1990). The social consequences of growing up in a poor neighborhood. In L.E. Lynn & M.F.H. McGeary (Eds.), *Inner-city poverty in the United States* (pp. 111–186). Washington, DC: National Academy Press.

Katz, L.F., Kling, J.R., & Liebman, J.B. (2001). Moving to Opportunity in Boston: Early results of a randomized mobility experiment. *Quarterly Journal of Economics, 116*, 607–654.

Klebanov, P.K., Brooks-Gunn, J., McCarton, C., & McCormick, M.C. (1998). The contribution of neighborhood and family income to developmental test scores over the first three years of life. *Child Development, 69*, 1420–1436.

Leventhal, T., & Brooks-Gunn, J. (2000). The neighborhoods they live in: The effects of neighborhood residence upon child and adolescent outcomes. *Psychological Bulletin, 126*, 309–337.

Leventhal, T., & Brooks-Gunn, J. (2001). Changing neighborhoods: Understanding how children may be affected in the coming century. *Advances in Life Course Research, 6*, 263–301.

Leventhal, T., & Brooks-Gunn, J. (2002). *A randomized study of neighborhood effects on low-income children's educational outcomes.* Manuscript submitted for publication.

Leventhal, T., & Brooks-Gunn, J. (in press). Moving to Opportunity: An experimental study of neighborhood effects on mental health. *American Journal of Public Health.*

Ludwig, J., Duncan, G.J., & Hirschfield, P. (2001). Urban poverty and juvenile crime: Evidence from a randomized housing-mobility experiment. *Quarterly Journal of Economics, 116*, 655–679.

Massey, D.S., & Denton, N.A. (1993). *American apartheid: Segregation and the making of the underclass.* Cambridge, MA: Harvard University Press.

Rubinowitz, L.S., & Rosenbaum, J.E. (2000). *Crossing the class and color lines: From public housing to white suburbia.* Chicago: University of Chicago Press.

Sampson, R.J., Raudenbush, S.W., & Earls, F. (1997). Neighborhoods and violent crime: A multilevel study of collective efficacy. *Science, 277*, 918–924.

Wilson, W.J. (1987). *The truly disadvantaged: The innercity, the underclass, and public policy.* Chicago: University of Chicago Press.

This article has been reprinted as it originally appeared in *Current Directions in Psychological Science*. Citation information for this article as originally published appears above.

Neighborhood Characteristics and Depression: An Examination of Stress Processes

Carolyn E. Cutrona[1], Gail Wallace, and Kristin A. Wesner
Iowa State University

Abstract

Neighborhoods with poor-quality housing, few resources, and unsafe conditions impose stress, which can lead to depression. The stress imposed by adverse neighborhoods increases depression above and beyond the effects of the individual's own personal stressors, such as poverty and negative events within the family or workplace. Furthermore, adverse neighborhoods appear to intensify the harmful impact of personal stressors and interfere with the formation of bonds between people, again increasing risk for depression. Neighborhoods do not affect all people in the same way. People with different personality characteristics adjust in different ways to challenging neighborhoods. As a field, psychology should pay more attention to the impact of contextual factors such as neighborhoods. Neighborhood-level mental health problems should be addressed at the neighborhood level. Public housing policies that contribute to the concentration of poverty should be avoided and research should be conducted on the most effective ways to mobilize neighborhood residents to meet common goals and improve the context in which they live.

Keywords

neighborhood; community; depression; poverty

Most theories relating depression to stress focus on events that occur within peoples' immediate lives, such as relationship problems or work stressors. Recent research reveals that depression may be linked to characteristics of the neighborhoods in which people live. Research has only recently undertaken to understand the ways in which neighborhoods affect depression and other forms of mental illness. Much less has been written about how neighborhoods influence mental health compared to the large amount that has been written about how neighborhoods influence problem behaviors like delinquency, crime, drug use, and adolescent childbearing (Leventhal & Brooks-Gunn, 2000).

It is important to understand the role of neighborhoods in the development of depression for at least three reasons: (a) People often do not realize that they are affected by the context around them and thus mistakenly blame themselves for the invisible stressors that affect their well-being; (b) outsiders also fail to realize that residents of adverse neighborhoods are influenced by their surroundings (high rates of mental health problems in poor neighborhoods may be blamed on the personal characteristics or race of residents rather than on the neighborhoods themselves); and (c) when threats to public health are caused by characteristics of entire communities, it is more efficient to address these threats at the community level rather than to treat each affected individual separately. Thus, it is important to raise public awareness of the mental health risks that accompany adverse neighborhoods.

Issues of neighborhood quality have immediate practical implications. The New Orleans neighborhoods most severely damaged by Hurricane Katrina in 2005 were areas of concentrated poverty; if they are rebuilt as before, with poor-quality resources and little integration with more prosperous families, a wide range of social problems, including threats to mental health, will reappear. As we will describe in more detail, the hopelessness of individual poverty is compounded by community impoverishment.

The question addressed in this article is how psychological health, specifically depression, is affected by residence in a specific neighborhood, beyond the strains of low family income and other personal factors that heighten risk for depression. All of the studies summarized in this review examined the effects of neighborhood characteristics on depression after statistically eliminating the effects of individual and family characteristics, such as income, education, employment status, age, and race, that may increase personal vulnerability to depression.

WHAT IS A NEIGHBORHOOD?

Most often, neighborhoods are defined as census tracts. The U.S. Census works with local residents to identify meaningful neighborhood units when it decides on tract boundaries. A census tract typically has 4,000 to 6,000 people and includes approximately nine city blocks. Some researchers use smaller units, called block groups, which are smaller areas within census tracts. A few researchers use very small areas, called face blocks (both sides of the street for one block). The impact of neighborhood characteristics on mental health does not depend much on the neighborhood unit that is used in a particular study (Sampson, Morenoff, & Gannon-Rowley, 2002).

NEIGHBORHOOD CHARACTERISTICS

Physical features of neighborhoods, such as quality of housing and the presence or absence of basic resources, including hospitals, reliable public transportation, and retail stores, can be important determinants of well-being. More research has been conducted on the influence of the people who live in neighborhoods than on the physical characteristics of neighborhoods. Two types of "person" characteristics have received research attention: *structural* and *functional*. Aspects of the population makeup of a neighborhood are termed structural characteristics. They include, but are not limited to, the percent of neighborhood residents who are poor, jobless, well-educated, or members of an ethnic minority group. Information about structural aspects of neighborhoods is almost always derived from the U.S. Census.

Aspects of how people in a neighborhood behave are termed functional characteristics. Examples of negative functional characteristics include the extent to which neighborhood residents behave in an uncivil or threatening manner and tolerate or engage in unlawful behavior ("social disorder"). Although not everyone in the neighborhood may engage in a specific behavior, if the behavior is sufficiently prevalent and affects a large number of residents, it may be viewed as a functional characteristic of that neighborhood. Functional characteristics are assessed through surveys of neighborhood residents or by systematic observation by researchers (e.g., counting the number of teenagers who hang out on the street late at night).

THEORETICAL FRAMEWORK

Stress plays a central role in theories that link neighborhood characteristics and depression. Characteristics of the neighborhoods in which people live influence the stress process in three different ways (see Fig. 1). First, neighborhood characteristics influence the level of daily stress imposed upon residents. Second, neighborhood characteristics influence people's vulnerability to depression following negative events in their lives (Elliott, 2000). In a highly adverse neighborhood, the same event is more likely to trigger depression than in a good-quality neighborhood. Third, neighborhood characteristics interfere with the formation of bonds among people. In turn, disrupted bonds lead to depression through several different pathways including lower levels of informal social control, inadequate social support, and poor family-role performance.

Daily Level of Stress

Neighborhood stressors may be imposed by physical characteristics of the neighborhood (e.g., lack of resources and unpleasant physical surroundings) or by the people who inhabit the neighborhood (e.g., threats to physical safety).

Lack of Resources and Physical Stressors   Many physical features of high-poverty neighborhoods impose stress on the lives of their residents, including low-quality housing, high traffic density, and undesirable commercial operations (e.g., adult bookstores). Observer ratings of housing quality predicted depression beyond the effects of family income in a study of low- and middle-income rural women (Evans, Wells, Chan, & Saltzman, 2000). Furthermore, women who moved from poor-quality apartments to single-family homes through Habitat for Humanity showed significant decreases in depressive symptoms (Evans et al., 2000). Low-income neighborhoods lack many resources, including health care, retail stores, and recreational facilities. Lack of access to needed resources is demoralizing because of the extra effort required to meet daily needs (Sampson et al., 2002). Very few studies have quantified neighborhood resources. More refined measures that capture type, accessibility, and distance to community resources are needed.

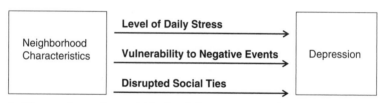

Fig. 1. Three pathways from neighborhood characteristics to depression.

The People in the Neighborhood   A potent source of stress is fear of victimization (Hill, Ross, & Angel, 2005). There is evidence that social disorder, not poverty per se, is the neighborhood characteristic that most directly causes depression (Ross, 2000). People who live in neighborhoods with high rates of crime must cope with anxiety over their safety and that of their possessions. Neighborhood social disorder is associated with depressive symptoms in both children and adults (Aneshensel & Sucoff, 1996; Hill et al., 2000). By contrast, neighborhood poverty without social disorder does not show a consistent effect on depression in adults (Cutrona, Russell, Hessling, Brown, & Murry, 2000), although its effects on children appear to be more consistent (Xue, Leventhal, Brooks-Gunn, & Earls, 2005).

Vulnerability to Depression Following Negative Events

A second way that adverse neighborhoods engender depression is by intensifying the harmful mental health impact of negative events in people's lives (Cutrona et al., 2005). Someone who experiences a negative event (e.g., job loss) in a poor neighborhood is more likely to become depressed than is one who experiences the same event in a more advantaged neighborhood. Among African American women, all of whom had experienced at least one severe negative life event in the past year, only 2% of those who lived in low-stress neighborhoods experienced the onset of a major depressive episode, as compared to 12% of those who lived in high-stress neighborhoods. Reasons for this heightened vulnerability may include lack of resources, the absence of role models who provide hope for personal success, and local norms that promote ineffective coping and negative interpretations of events (Elliott, 2000).

Neighborhood Effects on Interpersonal Relationships

Neighborhood characteristics influence the probability that people will form ties with each other (Sampson et al., 2002). When residential turnover is high, people are less likely to form relationships. Similarly, people do not tend to form relationships when they live in neighborhoods high in social disorder, because they mistrust their neighbors (Hill et al., 2005). Relationship disruption may have several different consequences relevant to depression, including lower levels of informal social control, inadequate social support, and poor family-role performance.

Informal Social Control   When people do not know each other, they do not monitor or control each others' behavior, and norms that permit antisocial or maladaptive behavior may arise (Sampson et al., 2002). When people engage in maladaptive behavior, problems often result, such as job loss or unintended pregnancy, which in turn lead to depression. By contrast, in neighborhoods where people know and trust one another, they are more likely to discourage problem behaviors that might lead to depression (e.g., through disapproval, telling parents, alerting authorities, or forming neighborhood-watch groups).

Social Support   People who live in high-social-disorder neighborhoods have fewer ties with their neighbors and perceive their relationships with their closest friends and relatives as being less supportive than do people in better neighborhoods

(Aneshensel & Sucoff, 1996), perhaps because support providers themselves are highly burdened. Residence in an economically disadvantaged neighborhood appears to weaken the protective power of social resources in people's lives. Among adolescents, a close supportive relationship with parents only protected against depression in higher-income neighborhoods, not in lower-income neighborhoods (Wickrama & Bryant, 2003). Similarly, among adults, frequent contact with friends and involvement in community organizations protected against depression in higher-but not in lower-income neighborhoods (Elliott, 2000).

Family-Role Performance Some neighborhoods provide few role models for competent fulfillment of family roles; thus marriages and parenting processes may suffer, resulting in depression among both adults and children (Cutrona et al., 2003; Wickrama & Bryant, 2003). Neighborhood poverty predicted lower-quality parenting behaviors, including lower observed warmth, in parents of adolescents (Wickrama & Bryant, 2003). Poor parenting, in turn, predicted depression among the adolescents. In another observational study, residents of high-poverty neighborhoods behaved less warmly toward their spouses than residents of low-poverty neighborhoods did (Cutrona et al., 2003). Low warmth may lead to marital problems, which have been widely shown to predict depression.

DIFFERENCES IN REACTIONS TO NEIGHBORHOODS

The impact of neighborhood characteristics on people's psychological adjustment varies noticeably, depending on people's personal traits and circumstances (Cutrona et al., 2000). In one study of women who lived in high-social-disorder neighborhoods, levels of distress were extremely high if the women were high on the personality trait of negative affectivity (a tendency to strong emotional reactions; see Fig. 2). By contrast, women who scored high on optimism and personal mastery were relatively immune to the negative mental health impact of neighborhood social disorder (Cutrona et al., 2000). Some people with particularly resilient personalities can cope successfully, even in dangerous and disorderly neighborhoods. However, other people are highly vulnerable to depression when they live in adverse surroundings. It may be that living in a disadvantaged and disorderly neighborhood eventually erodes optimism and replaces it with hopelessness and negativity.

CONCLUSIONS AND FUTURE DIRECTIONS

The field of psychology has paid insufficient attention to the impact of contextual factors on well-being. Neighborhood context affects important psychological processes, above and beyond personal and family stressors, by increasing stress load, intensifying reactivity to negative life events, and damaging the quality of interpersonal relationships. Furthermore, psychological characteristics appear to moderate the impact of neighborhoods on adjustment. Some people with particularly resilient personalities cope effectively with neighborhood stressors, but others appear to be significantly harmed psychologically. The influence of contexts on a wide range of psychological processes merits further study.

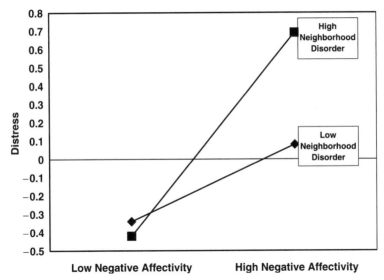

Fig. 2. Effect of neighborhood social disorder on distress for women high on negative affectivity versus for women low on negative affectivity. (Lines are plotted for 1 standard deviation above and one standard deviation below the sample mean on neighborhood social disorder; the y-axis is labeled in standard deviation units.) From "Direct and Moderating Effects of Community Context on the Psychological Well-Being of African American Women," by C.E. Cutrona, D.W. Russell, R.M. Hessling, & P.A. Brown, 2000, *Journal of Personality and Social Psychology, 79*, p. 1097. Copyright 2000 by the American Psychological Association. Reprinted with permission.

Better methods for separating the mental health impact of people's personal characteristics from those of their neighborhoods are needed. Social experiments in which low-income people are given rent subsidies and randomly assigned to live in different kinds of neighborhoods have shown that youth and adults show better mental health when they move from impoverished neighborhoods to middle-class neighborhoods (e.g., Rosenbaum & Harris, 2001). These studies demonstrate clearly that some of the problems associated with low-income people should actually be attributed to low-income environments.

Duncan and Raudenbush (2001) offered a number of suggestions for how to improve the design of survey-based neighborhood studies. These include analyzing family characteristics that might mistakenly be attributed to neighborhoods; examining the similarity between siblings, neighbors, and non-neighbors on mental health outcomes to sort out the contributions of family characteristics from those of neighborhood characteristics; and using separate samples of neighborhood residents to obtain information about the neighborhood (e.g., degree of social disorder) and outcome measures (e.g., level of depression).

The most efficient way to improve mental health in impoverished neighborhoods is to improve the quality of neighborhoods. A number of projects are currently underway around the country to help residents of impoverished inner-city neighborhoods organize to improve the quality of life in their neighborhoods (e.g., Jason, 2006). Research is needed to determine the best strategies for empowering local residents to take effective action. Techniques are needed to study processes of change in neighborhoods and the factors that facilitate change.

Decisions about where to build subsidized housing for low-income families are critically important. There is evidence that economically integrated neighborhoods are beneficial and that concentrating low-income housing in the poorest neighborhoods perpetuates problems of social disorder and resource deprivation. As noted earlier, rebuilding New Orleans presents the opportunity to avoid concentrations of poverty, which breed hopelessness and depression as well as other social problems. It is important that policymakers have access to empirical data that will help them make informed decisions about housing and economic-development issues. Greater collaboration across the disciplines of city planning, economics, sociology, and psychology are needed in generating such data.

Recommended Reading

Brooks-Gunn, J., Duncan, G.J., & Aber, J.L. (Eds.). (1997). *Neighborhood poverty, Vol. 1: Context and consequences for children.* New York: Russell Sage Foundation.

Jencks, C., & Mayer, S.E. (1990). The social consequences of growing up in a poor neighborhood. In L.E. Lynn & M.G.H. McGeary (Eds.), *Adolescents at risk: Medical and social perspectives* (pp. 19–34). Boulder, CO: Westview Press.

Massey, D.S., & Denton, N.A. (1993). *American apartheid: Segregation and the making of the underclass.* Cambridge, MA: Harvard University Press.

Pearlin, L. (1999). The stress process revisited: Reflections on concepts and their relationships. In C. Aneshensel & J. Phelan (Eds.), *Handbook of the sociology of mental health.* New York: Plenum Press.

Sampson, R.J. (2001). How do communities undergird or undermine human development? Relevant contexts and social mechanisms. In A. Booth & A.C. Crouter (Eds.), *Does it take a village? Community effects on children, adolescents, and families* (pp. 3–30). Mahwah, NJ: Erlbaum.

Note

1. Address correspondence to Carolyn E. Cutrona, Institute for Social and Behavioral Research, 2625 N. Loop Dr. Suite 500, Ames, IA 50010; e-mail: ccutrona@iastate.edu.

References

Aneshensel, C., & Sucoff, C.A. (1996). The neighborhood context of adolescent mental health. *Journal of Health and Social Behavior, 37*, 293–310.

Cutrona, C.E., Russell, D.W., Abraham, W.T., Gardner, K.A., Melby, J.N., Bryant, C., & Conger, R.D. (2003). Neighborhood context and financial strain as predictors of marital interaction and marital quality in African American couples. *Personal Relationships, 10*, 389–409.

Cutrona, C.E., Russell, D.W., Brown, P.A., Clark, L.A., Hessling, R.M., & Gardner, K.A. (2005). Neighborhood context, personality, and stressful life events as predictors of depression among African American women. *Journal of Abnormal Psychology, 114*, 3–15.

Cutrona, C.E., Russell, D.W., Hessling, R.M., Brown, P.A., & Murry, V. (2000). Direct and moderating effects of community context on the psychological well-being of African American women. *Journal of Personality and Social Psychology, 79*, 1088–1101.

Duncan, G.J., & Raudenbush, S.W. (2001). Neighborhoods and adolescent development: How can we determine the links? In A. Booth & A.C. Crouter (Eds.), *Does it take a village? Community effects on children, adolescents, and families* (pp. 105–136). Mahwah, NJ: Erlbaum.

Elliott, M. (2000). The stress process in neighborhood context. *Health & Place, 6*, 287–299.

Evans, G.W., Wells, N.M., Chan, H.Y.E., & Saltzman, H. (2000). Housing quality and mental health. *Journal of Consulting and Clinical Psychology, 68,* 526–530.

Hill, T.D., Ross, C.E., & Angel, R.J. (2005). Neighborhood disorder, psychophysiological distress, and health. *Journal of Health & Social Behavior, 46,* 170–186.

Jason, L.A. (2006). Benefits and challenges of generating community participation. *Professional Psychology: Research and Practice, 37,* 132–139.

Leventhal, T., & Brooks-Gunn, J. (2000). The neighborhoods they live in: The effects of neighborhood residence upon child and adolescent outcomes. *Psychological Bulletin, 126,* 309–337.

Rosenbaum, J.E., & Harris, L.E. (2001). Low-income families in their new neighborhoods. *Journal of Family Issues, 22,* 183–210.

Ross, C.E. (2000). Neighborhood disadvantage and adult depression. *Journal of Health and Social Behavior, 41,* 177–187.

Sampson, R.J., Morenoff, J.D., & Gannon-Rowley, T. (2002). Assessing "Neighborhood Effects": Social processes and new directions in research. *Annual Review of Sociology, 28,* 443–478.

Wickrama, K.A.S., & Bryant, C.M. (2003). Community context of social resources and adolescent mental health. *Journal of Marriage and Family, 65,* 850–866.

Xue, Y., Leventhal, T., Brooks-Gunn, J., & Earls, F.J. (2005). Neighborhood residence and mental health problems of 5- to 11-year-olds. *Archives of Genetic Psychiatry, 62,* 554–563.

This article has been reprinted as it originally appeared in *Current Directions in Psychological Science*. Citation information for this article as originally published appears above.

Why Socioeconomic Status Affects the Health of Children: A Psychosocial Perspective

Edith Chen[1]

University of British Columbia, Vancouver, British Columbia, Canada

Abstract

This article provides an overview of research on socioeconomic status (SES) and physical health in childhood. SES has a gradient relationship with children's health, such that for each incremental increase in SES, there is a comparable benefit in children's health. In this article, I discuss psychosocial mechanisms underlying this association and argue that it is important to utilize knowledge about how the relationship between SES and health changes with age to inform a developmentally plausible search for mediators of this relationship. Furthermore, SES at different points in a child's lifetime may have different effects on health. I advocate an interdisciplinary approach to searching for mediators that would allow researchers to understand how characteristics of society, the neighborhood, the family, and the individual child are involved in the processes linking SES and children's health.

Keywords

socioeconomic status; children's health; psychosocial

One of the most striking and profound findings in epidemiology is that individuals lower in socioeconomic status (SES) have poorer health than individuals higher in SES. This relationship holds true whether health is measured as the prevalence rate of illness, the severity of illness, or the likelihood of mortality, and it is true for most types of diseases, as well as for many risk factors for diseases. This finding has been reported for many countries, including those with and those without universal health care. And it has been demonstrated across the life span, from childhood to older adulthood (Adler et al., 1994; Anderson & Armstead, 1995; Chen, Matthews, & Boyce, 2002).

One of the most intriguing aspects of the relationship between SES and health is that it exists as a gradient. That is, it is not just that poor people have poorer health than rich people. Rather, each step increase in SES is accompanied by incremental benefits in health. This gradient makes the search for underlying mechanisms a challenge for researchers. Obvious mechanisms, such as inadequate nutrition, housing, or health insurance, cannot explain why upper-middle-class individuals have slightly poorer health than upper-class individuals. In this article, I discuss psychosocial explanations for the SES-health relationship, with an emphasis on children's health. I focus here on physical health; however, other researchers have explored these issues for children's mental health and well-being (see Leventhal & Brooks-Gunn and McLoyd under Recommended Reading).

POSSIBLE PSYCHOSOCIAL PATHWAYS

Researchers have suggested many explanations for the effect of SES on health. For example, the effect may be due to genetic influences, environmental exposures to toxins, quality of medical care, and psychological-behavioral factors, just to name a few possibilities (Anderson & Armstead, 1995). Here I provide a brief overview of some of the primary psychological-behavioral factors. Research in this area has focused on individual characteristics that fall into four main categories: stress, psychological distress, personality factors, and health behaviors (Adler et al., 1994; Anderson & Armstead, 1995).

With respect to stress, lower-SES children and adults experience more negative life events (stressors) than higher-SES individuals; in addition, they perceive greater negative impact from any given event (stress appraisal). In turn, a large body of literature has linked stress to a wide variety of negative biological and health outcomes in both children and adults. Evidence has documented that stress is one plausible mediator linking SES to health (Cohen, Kaplan, & Salonen, 1999). Thus, one theory is that as one moves down in SES, the amount of stress one experiences increases, which in turn takes a physiological toll on the body, putting one at greater risk for a variety of diseases.

A second possibility is that psychological distress plays a role. Because of the social environments in which they grow up, lower-SES individuals may be more prone to experiencing negative emotional states than higher-SES individuals are, and if the experience of negative emotions has biological consequences, this could also lead to poorer health. Previous research has found support for the notion that lower-SES individuals are more likely to experience negative emotions such as depression and anxiety, and that these negative emotions are linked to illnesses, such as cardiovascular disease, as well as to mortality rates (Gallo & Matthews, 2003).

A third hypothesis is that lower-SES individuals are likely to possess personality traits that are detrimental to health. That is, lower-SES individuals may be more likely than higher-SES individuals to possess certain dispositional traits that are adaptive in the social environments in which they live, but have negative health consequences. For example, living in a dangerous neighborhood may make lower-SES individuals likely to mistrust others and to hold cynical attitudes toward others. Thus, one might expect lower-SES individuals to be more hostile and less optimistic about their future than higher-SES individuals are. In turn, such personality traits have been found to place individuals at increased risk for illnesses (Adler et al., 1994).

Finally, compared with individuals of higher SES, those of lower SES may be less likely to engage in healthy behaviors, such as exercising, eating a healthy diet, and not smoking. In part, this may be because of available resources. For example, the availability of healthy products in grocery stores varies by the SES of neighborhoods (Williams & Collins, 2001); people with reduced access to healthy products in their neighborhood grocery stores will have increased difficulty maintaining a healthy diet. Lower-SES neighborhoods also are more dangerous than higher-SES neighborhoods, and less likely to have public parks and venues for exercise (Williams & Collins, 2001); thus, decreases in SES increase the barriers to engaging in regular exercise.

These factors are promising possibilities for clarifying the psychosocial reasons why decreases in SES are associated with decreases in health. However, most of these factors focus on the individual. In trying to understand the health of children, it is particularly important to consider the role of factors in the family and the larger environment. In addition, given the vast social, cognitive, emotional, and biological differences between young children and older adolescents, it is important to consider whether the relevance of the various factors depends on the individual's age.

DEVELOPMENTAL TRAJECTORIES

Exploring the strength of the SES-health relationship during different periods of childhood may provide insight into pathways linking SES with health. My colleagues and I have argued that the relationship between SES and health may be stronger in certain periods of childhood than others. In trying to understand why this is so, one should consider developmental factors that are important during each period of childhood.

Previously, we proposed three models of how the relationship between SES and health may change across childhood (Chen et al., 2002). The childhood-limited model states that relationships between SES and health are strongest in early childhood, and weaken with age. This suggests that factors that are particularly important during early childhood may play a role in explaining health outcomes. For example, the quality of child care, attachment to parents, and housing conditions may be important factors during this period. Research has shown, for example, that injuries are strongly correlated with SES early in childhood, but not during adolescence (West, 1997). It may be the case that unsafe housing conditions are most relevant to young children, who do not have the ability to recognize and avoid danger in their homes, but that as children age and improve in cognitive abilities, they more easily recognize and avoid dangers at home, so the strength of the relationship between SES and injury decreases.

The adolescent-emergent model states that relationships between SES and health are weak early in life, but strengthen with age. According to this model, factors that become important during adolescence, such as peer influence or certain personality characteristics, may play a role in the SES-health relationship. For example, physical activity is more strongly correlated with SES during adolescence than earlier in childhood (Chen et al., 2002). One explanation may be that earlier in life, health behaviors are shaped strongly by parents as role models, but as a child ages, peers begin to exert influence on his or her health behaviors. The combination of parent plus peer influence may lead to stronger relationships between SES and health behaviors during adolescence than earlier in childhood.

Finally, the persistence model states that relationships between SES and health are similar throughout childhood and adolescence. In such cases, factors that would not be expected to change with children's age may be important. For example, the correlation between severity of asthma and SES is similar across childhood and adolescence (Chen et al., 2002). One possible explanation for this correlation is that asthma severity is in part determined by a family's trust in their health care provider. Compared with higher-SES families, lower-SES families may have greater mistrust of the medical community, which in turn may lead to poorer adherence to instructions and advice regarding medications and behaviors for managing asthma. If this psychosocial factor does not change significantly as a child ages, then one would expect to see the relationship between SES and asthma severity follow a persistence model.

LONGITUDINAL RELATIONSHIPS

In addition to considering the relationship between SES and health at different points during childhood, it is important to understand how SES may change over children's lives, and what impact these changes have on children's health. Family SES can fluctuate dramatically from year to year, and a child's history of SES may affect health differently than current SES does. For example, current SES may affect the quality of health care a family has access to, as well as how they are treated in medical settings. In contrast, history of SES may play a role in the development of health problems.

For example, SES effects may accumulate over time. Previous research has shown that amount of time spent in low SES is an important predictor of adult mortality rates (McDonough, Duncan, Williams, & House, 1997), young adults' self-reported health (Power, Manor, & Matthews, 1999), and cognitive development and behavioral problems in children (Duncan, Brooks-Gunn, & Klebanov, 1994). These findings suggest that it takes time for SES to have effects on health.

Some researchers have suggested that there may be critical periods in childhood when SES has its biggest effect. For example, early childhood experiences may program a pattern of biological and behavioral responses that has prolonged effects across the life span. Research has demonstrated that SES early in life is a predictor of adult health behaviors (Lynch, Kaplan, & Salonen, 1997), and that early childhood environments predict adult cardiovascular disease (Barker, 1992). In addition, these relationships persist even after accounting for the effect of adult SES. These findings suggest that it may be important to understand the characteristics of a child's environment during critical windows in order to understand health consequences later in life.

LEVELS OF EXPLANATIONS

Explanations for how SES affects children's health are not likely to be limited to pathways involving individual psychological characteristics. For example, there could be SES differences in societal-level factors, neighborhood-levels factors, and family factors that also contribute to health disparities in children.

Societal factors could include social policies, such as ones that affect how access to and quality of health care vary across SES. Also, some researchers have argued that different societies have different levels of trust and cohesion among community members, and of investment in the community (social capital). Those communities that have low levels of social capital may have access to fewer public goods (such as community-organized group transportation) and find day-today life more stressful (e.g., difficulty getting to health care clinics) than those that have high levels of social capital. The communities of lower-SES families are likely to have lower levels of social capital than the communities of higher-SES families, and, in turn, social capital has been found to mediate the relationship between SES and health (Kawachi, Kennedy, Lochner, & Prothrow-Stith, 1997).

At the neighborhood level, there are several factors that may contribute to the SES-health relationship. A neighborhood that is dangerous creates barriers to engaging in positive health behaviors such as participating in sports or exercising. Lower-SES neighborhoods also are characterized by more toxic environments (greater pollution, more lead paint, etc.) than higher-SES neighborhoods. Finally, neighborhoods vary in terms of their degree of segregation. Neighborhoods that are segregated tend to receive less investment in public services than integrated neighborhoods do. More segregated neighborhoods tend to be lower in SES and to have higher mortality rates (Williams & Collins, 2001).

In addition, when studying children's health, it is important to consider the role of the family. Factors at this level include the quality of relationships within the family, such as whether they are characterized by conflict and aggression, as well as the degree of supportiveness in the home. Researchers have documented that families with high levels of conflict and with cold, unsupportive relationships are more likely than other families to have children who experience health problems throughout life, and have dysregulated biological systems (Repetti, Taylor, & Seeman, 2002).

At the individual level, as I have already described, factors such as stress, psychological distress, personality traits, and health behaviors are likely to play a role. In addition, certain psychological factors may buffer low-SES individuals from poor health outcomes. For example, one study found that individuals who were low in SES but believed they had a high degree of control over their lives had health profiles that were more similar to those of high-SES individuals than to those of low-SES individuals who did not believe that they had control over their lives (Lachman & Weaver, 1998).

CONCLUSIONS

Research has documented an intriguing gradient relationship between SES and children's health. Future research that addresses two main themes is needed. First, the field will achieve a more integrated understanding of the mechanisms behind the SES-health relationship by utilizing interdisciplinary collaborations to determine the extent to which societal-level variables (e.g., social capital), neighborhood-level variables (e.g., residential segregation), family-level variables (e.g., relationship quality), and individual-child factors (e.g., stress) contribute to this relationship. Methods from epidemiology, sociology, psychology, and medicine, among other disciplines, could be used not only to develop state-of-the-art assessments of factors at each of these levels, but also to determine how factors at one level interact with factors at another level to influence health. For example, thus far, studies have rarely examined the extent to which the neighborhood environment affects an individual child's personality development, or, conversely, the extent to which the personality of an individual child or adult contributes to the characteristics of a whole neighborhood; neither have many studies investigated how individual and neighborhood factors synergistically combine to affect health. Studies that take a broad view and consider factors at multiple levels would provide researchers and the public with greater knowledge about important contributors to health, and help society learn to effectively implement health-enhancing interventions.

The second important theme for future research is to more extensively explore dynamic effects of SES on physical health. It is important to understand whether each type of health outcome is more strongly shaped by early childhood SES, fluctuations in SES, or current SES. An understanding such as this would be critical for determining the timing of health interventions. That is, interventions should be targeted toward early childhood if SES early in life turns out to be critical; in contrast, if cumulative SES turns out to be important, intervention at any stage in life (to reduce the total amount of time spent in low SES) would be beneficial. Such effective targeting of health interventions could help tremendously in maximizing the long-term health of society.

Recommended Reading

Adler, N.E., Boyce, W.T., Chesney, M.A., Folkman, S., & Syme, S.L. (1993). Socio-economic inequalities in health: No easy solution. *Journal of the American Medical Association, 269,* 3140–3145.

Chen, E., Matthews, K.A., & Boyce, W.T. (2002). (See References)

Duncan, G.J., & Brooks-Gunn, J. (1997). *Consequences of growing up poor.* New York: Russell Sage Foundation.

Leventhal, T., & Brooks-Gunn, J. (2000). The neighborhoods they live in: The effects of neighborhood residence on child and adolescent outcomes. *Psychological Bulletin, 126,* 309–337.

McLoyd, V.C. (1998). Socioeconomic disadvantage and child development. *American Psychologist, 53,* 185–204.

Acknowledgments—I thank Gregory Miller for his helpful comments on this manuscript.

Note

1. Address correspondence to Edith Chen, University of British Columbia, Department of Psychology, 2136 West Mall, Vancouver, B.C. V6T 1Z4, Canada.

References

Adler, N.E., Boyce, T., Chesney, M.A., Cohen, S., Folkman, S., Kahn, R.L., & Syme, S.L. (1994). Socioeconomic status and health: The challenge of the gradient. *American Psychologist, 49,* 15–24.

Anderson, N.B., & Armstead, C.A. (1995). Toward understanding the association of socioeconomic status and health: A new challenge for the biopsychosocial approach. *Psychosomatic Medicine, 57,* 213–225.

Barker, D.J.P. (1992). *Fetal and infant origins of adult disease.* London: British Medical Journal.

Chen, E., Matthews, K.A., & Boyce, W.T. (2002). Socioeconomic differences in children's health: How and why do these relationships change with age? *Psychological Bulletin, 128,* 295–329.

Cohen, S., Kaplan, G.A., & Salonen, J.T. (1999). The role of psychological characteristics in the relation between socioeconomic status and perceived health. *Journal of Applied Social Psychology, 29,* 445–468.

Duncan, G., Brooks-Gunn, J., & Klebanov, P. (1994). Economic deprivation and early childhood development. *Child Development, 65,* 296–318.

Gallo, L.C., & Matthews, K.A. (2003). Understanding the association between socioeconomic status and physical health: Do negative emotions play a role? *Psychological Bulletin, 129,* 10–51.

Kawachi, I., Kennedy, B.P., Lochner, K., & Prothrow-Stith, D. (1997). Social capital, income inequality, and mortality. *American Journal of Public Health, 87,* 1491–1498.

Lachman, M.E., & Weaver, S.L. (1998). The sense of control as a moderator of social class differences in health and well-being. *Journal of Personality and Social Psychology, 74,* 763–773.

Lynch, J.W., Kaplan, G.A., & Salonen, J.T. (1997). Why do poor people behave poorly? Variation in adult health behaviors and psychosocial characteristics by stages of the socioeconomic lifecourse. *Social Science and Medicine, 44,* 809–819.

McDonough, P., Duncan, G.J., Williams, D., & House, J. (1997). Income dynamics and adult mortality in the United States, 1972 through 1989. *American Journal of Public Health, 87,* 1476–1483.

Power, C., Manor, O., & Matthews, S. (1999). The duration and timing of exposure: Effects of socioeconomic environment on adult health. *American Journal of Public Health, 89,* 1059–1065.

Repetti, R.L., Taylor, S.E., & Seeman, T. (2002). Risky families: Family social environments and the mental and physical health of offspring. *Psychological Bulletin, 128,* 330–366.

West, P. (1997). Health inequalities in the early years: Is there equalisation in youth? *Social Science and Medicine, 44,* 833–858.

Williams, D.R., & Collins, C. (2001). Racial residential segregation: A fundamental cause of racial disparities in health. *Public Health Reports, 116,* 404–416.

This article has been reprinted as it originally appeared in *Current Directions in Psychological Science*. Citation information for this article as originally published appears above.

The Role of Religion and Spirituality in Mental and Physical Health

Kevin S. Seybold[1] and Peter C. Hill

Department of Psychology, Grove City College,
Grove City, Pennsylvania

Abstract

An increased interest in the effects of religion and spirituality on health is apparent in the psychological and medical literature. Although religion in particular was thought, in the past, to have a predominantly negative influence on health, recent research suggests this relationship is more complex. This article reviews the literature on the impact of religion and spirituality on physical and mental health, concluding that the influence is largely beneficial. Mechanisms for the positive effect of religion and spirituality are proposed.

Keywords

religion; spirituality; health

It is not surprising that religion and spirituality remain important to the vast majority of individuals in a society such as the United States, which can be characterized as fragmented, disconnected, and increasingly aging (Thoresen, 1999). In response, the literature from a variety of disciplines (e.g., psychology, medicine, sociology, gerontology, and education) contains an increasing number of studies examining the role of religion and spirituality in physical as well as mental health.

When considering this role, researchers must take care to properly conceptualize the multifaceted nature of religion and spirituality. These constructs cannot be defined strictly in terms of a specific set of beliefs or behaviors. The multidimensional nature of both religion and spirituality was recently underscored by a working group of experts commissioned by the Fetzer Institute and the National Institute on Aging (NIA). This group identified 10 dimensions of religion and spirituality (religious-spiritual history, preference affiliation, social participation, private practices, coping styles, beliefs and values, commitment, experiences, sense of support, and motivation for regulating and reconciling relationships) that have been addressed by research in recent years and that hold promise for future research, especially in relation to health care (Fetzer Institute/ NIA, 1999).

Many characteristics common to religion may also be found in spirituality, and vice versa (Hill et al., 2000). For example, spirituality (like religion) may involve a personal transformation, an encounter with transcendence, or a search for ultimate truth or an ultimate reality that is sacred to the individual. What is religious may also include stipulated behavior patterns and encouragement of adherence to certain religious practices or forms of expression, characteristics that some forms of contemporary spirituality may resist. Still, there is much overlap between these phenomena.

Measurement of religion and spirituality must also take into account their multidimensional nature. A recent review of 125 measures of religion and spirituality (Hill & Hood, 1999), with a copy of each measure included and accompanied by a brief summary, suggests not only a surprising breadth in the measurement of religion and spirituality, but also the multidimensional approach researchers have taken. For example, in addition to 15 multidimensional measures, the book includes scales of more specific dimensions of religion and spirituality, such as beliefs and practices, attitudes, religious orientation, religious development, commitment and involvement, religious coping, mysticism, and views of death and afterlife. Perhaps the most thorough and widely standardized single multidimensional measure is the instrument constructed by the Fetzer/NIA (1999) working group. The 38-item short form, designed to measure the 10 dimensions of religion and spirituality identified by the group, was embedded in the 1997–1998 General Social Survey (GSS), a random national survey of the National Data Program for the Social Sciences. Initial analyses from the GSS data "support the theoretical basis of the measure and indicate it has the appropriate reliability and validity to facilitate further research" (Fetzer/NIA, 1999, p. 89).

In addition to careful conceptualization and measurement of religion and spirituality, a proper measure of the health variable is needed in studies evaluating the effect of religion and spirituality on health. Both specific indices of health (e.g., blood pressure in the case of physical health; delinquency and drug and alcohol abuse in the case of mental health) and more general, subjective measures are used. Some ambiguous and conflicting findings have been due, in part, to inconsistencies in defining or measuring religion and spirituality, as well as measuring health. In recent studies, researchers have therefore attempted to use multidimensional measures of religion or spirituality (or measures of specific dimensions of either construct) and specific behavioral indices of physical and mental health (Larson, Swyers, & McCullough, 1998).

HELPFUL AND HARMFUL EFFECTS OF RELIGION

Studies on the influence of religion on physical health suggest that religion usually, but not always, plays a positive role. A positive influence has been found in research involving subjects of all ages, both genders, and a variety of religions (i.e., Protestants, Catholics, Jews, Buddhists, and Muslims). Respondents from a number of regions (North America, Asia, Africa) and ethnic groups have been used in a broad range of research designs (seldom, however, experimental) that measured religiosity in a variety of ways (e.g., church attendance, prayer, various subjective measures). The salutary effects of religion and spirituality are summarized in Table 1 (see Larson et al., 1998; Levin & Vanderpool, 1992).

The positive effects of religious and spiritual experience on health are based on the assumption that the experience itself is positive and healthy. Of course, religion and spirituality can also be pathological: authoritarian or blindly obedient, superficially literal, strictly extrinsic or self-beneficial, or conflict-ridden and fragmented. Indeed, such unhealthy religion or spirituality can have serious implications for physical health, having been associated with child abuse and neglect, intergroup conflict and violence, and false perceptions of control, with

Table 1. *Salutary effects of religion and spirituality on physical health*

Health measure	Effect of religion-spirituality
Heart disease	Lowers rate
Systolic blood pressure	Lowers
Diastolic blood pressure	Lowers
Cirrhosis	Lowers rate
Emphysema	Lowers rate
Myocardial infarction	Lowers rate
Chronic pain	Decreases
Cholesterol levels	Lowers
Stroke	Lowers rate
Kidney failure	Lowers rate
Cancer mortality	Lowers rate
Cardiac surgery mortality	Lowers rate
Overall mortality	Lowers rate
Surgery-related stress	Lowers
Positive health habits	Increases
Longevity	Increases

Note. See Larson, Swyers, and McCullough (1998); Levin and Vanderpool (1992).

resulting medical neglect (see Paloutzian & Kirkpatrick, 1995). Such unhealthy associations may be most likely when the individual believes that he or she has direct communication with God with little or no social accountability (e.g., "God told me . . .") or employs a deferral-to-God problem-solving strategy (e.g., "It is best to just leave this problem in God's hands"; Pargament, 1997).

Research investigating mental health indicates a similar protective effect of religion. In a review of 139 research studies using quantified measures of religious commitment, Larson et al. (1992) found that only 39% reported any associations at all, but of these, 72% were positive. Measures of the religious variable in these studies included prayer, social support (e.g., fellowship, companionship), relationship with God, participation in religious ceremonies, and meaning (e.g., values, beliefs, ethics). Gartner (1996) reviewed the literature and found positive associations between religion-spirituality and well-being, marital satisfaction, and general psychological functioning; he found negative associations with suicide, delinquency, criminal behavior, and drug and alcohol use.

Religion has also been associated with some forms of psychopathology, including authoritarianism, rigidity, dogmatism, suggestibility, and dependence (Gartner, 1996). In addition, harmful as well as helpful forms of religious coping have been identified, and the harmful forms (e.g., discontentment or anger with God, clergy, or a congregation) correlated with impaired mental health and poorer resolution of negative life events (Pargament, 1997). Taken as a whole, however, the literature suggests a general salutary effect of religion on mental health, a finding at odds with some previous positions, which held that depression and low self-esteem are not only more likely but perhaps inevitable in religious individuals (Watters, 1992).

PUTATIVE MECHANISMS

One mechanism through which religion and spirituality may have beneficial effects on health is via social networks (Hill & Butter, 1995). Religious and spiritual communities provide opportunities for fellowship, involvement in formal social programs (e.g., visiting shutins, providing meals to the poor), and companionship. This kind of support can have beneficial effects by reducing both psychological and physical stressors.

Lifestyle can also act as a mechanism through which religion and spirituality have their positive effects. For example, religious commitment can lead a person to adopt better health-related behaviors, such as abstinence from smoking, alcohol and drug use, and risky sexual behaviors. Indeed, religious groups that follow a strict behavioral lifestyle (e.g., Mormons, Old Order Amish, Orthodox Jews) tend to have a better health status than the population as a whole (Hill & Butter, 1995).

Psychological factors might also mediate the relationship between health and religion. Pargament (1997), in particular, discussed various coping strategies that may facilitate beneficial resolution of negative life events. Cognitive processes such as locus-of-control beliefs (i.e., perception of personal control over events in one's life), acceptance from other people or God, attributions of purpose and meaning to negative life events, and optimistic explanatory style (i.e., perceiving negative events in life as externally caused and situation-specific, and positive events as internally caused and typical) have also been postulated as possible mechanisms and provide opportunities for future research.

For example, Sethi and Seligman (1993) found that people who hold fundamentalist religious beliefs are typically more optimistic, hopeful, and religiously involved than those who hold moderate religious beliefs, and moderates are more optimistic, hopeful, and religiously involved than those who hold liberal religious beliefs. Sethi and Seligman suggested that investigators need to reexamine the commonly held belief that fundamental religions negatively affect mental health. Given that the more behaviorally conservative religious groups tend to have a better health status than the population as a whole, this suggestion is sound.

Some researchers have postulated that religious and spiritual factors might positively affect various physiological mechanisms involved in health (Larson et al., 1998). Positive emotions (e.g., forgiveness, hope, contentment, love) might benefit the individual through their impact on neural pathways that connect to the endocrine and immune systems. Negative emotional states (e.g., anger and fear) can lead to arousal of the sympathetic nervous system (SNS) and the hypothalamic-pituitary-adrenal axis (HPA), systems involved in mobilizing the body's energy during stressful situations. Such excitability can produce a stress response in the body—excessive release of the neurotransmitter norepinephrine and of the endocrine hormone cortisol. The stress response, in turn, can lead over time to inhibition of the immune system, increased risk of infection, increased blood pressure, impaired healing response, and increased risk of stroke and heart attack.

Meditation, forgiveness, and certain religious and spiritual thoughts might reduce the arousal in the SNS and HPA (Thoresen, 1999), increasing immune competence and restoring physiological stability.

Uchino, Uno, and Holt-Lunstad (1999) reviewed the literature and found evidence suggesting that social support can influence health outcomes (e.g., cardiovascular and infectious diseases) via a number of physiological processes such as cardiovascular, neuroendocrine, and immune functions. The authors provided a model that emphasizes the importance of stress appraisal (i.e., how stressful an event is perceived to be), positive mood and self-esteem, and health behaviors as modulators of these physiological functions. This model is consistent with certain models developed specifically for the religion-health relationship (Levin & Chatters, 1998). These latter models emphasize the role of religion as a coping mechanism that works through social resources (e.g., fellowship), psychological mechanisms (e.g., worthiness), and meaning and belief systems. The empirical data not only suggest that religion is an important contributor to physical and mental health, but also support the models linking social support, such as the support religious communities provide, with positive health outcomes. Whether this support acts via the mechanisms detailed by Uchino et al. (i.e., health behaviors and psychological processes) is a subject of interest to researchers in this growing area of psychological science. What is clear, however, is that religiousness and spirituality have become important variables in the investigation of what contributes to people's physical and mental health.

CONCLUSION

Several research and clinical issues are raised by the literature on the relation between religion and health:

- To what extent do psychosocial factors such as social ties, psychological resources (e.g., sense of control), or personality charactersitics (e.g., optimism, hope) serve as possible mediators in the religion-health connection? Is religion only the context within which such mechanisms happen to play an important role, or is religion necessary for these positive effects?
- How do contextual factors such as race, culture, socioeconomic status, and religious preference affect the religion-health relationship?
- Can researchers better disaggregate the concepts of religion and spirituality to more systematically analyze the effects of specific dimensions on health?
- Can researchers develop general measures of religion and spirituality that cut across religious traditions without robbing those traditions of their distinctive and substantive characteristics?
- How can mental and physical health professionals be encouraged to consider a patient's religion or spirituality when taking a health history? Given the relationship between religion-spirituality and health, a patient's religious beliefs and practices should be taken into account in these clinical settings.

Approximately 50% of health professionals describe themselves as agnostic or atheist, compared with around 3% of the American public (Thoresen, 1999).

In addition, there is a long history of antagonism between pyschology and religion, a history that can be traced to fundamental differences between science and religion. It is important, therefore, that health researchers and health service providers not allow such barriers to limit their understanding of the crucial contributory roles of religion and spirituality in physical and mental health.

Recommended Reading

Ellison, C.G., & Levin, J.S. (1998). The religion-health connection: Evidence, theory, and future directions. *Health Education & Behavior, 25,* 700–720.
Koenig, H.G. (Ed.). (1998). *Handbook of religion and mental health.* San Diego: Academic Press.
Larson, D.B., Swyers, J.P., & McCullough, M.E. (Eds.). (1998). (See References)
Paloutzian, R.F., & Kirkpatrick, L.A. (Eds.). (1995). (See References)
Thoresen, C.E. (Ed.). (1999). Spirituality and health [Special issue]. *Journal of Health Psychology, 4*(3).

Note

1. Address correspondence to Kevin S. Seybold, Department of Psychology, Grove City College, 100 Campus Dr., Grove City, PA 16127-2104; e-mail: ksseybold@gcc.edu.

References

Fetzer Institute/National Institute on Aging. (1999). *Multidimensional measurement of religiousness/spirituality for use in health research: A report of the Fetzer Institute/National Institute on Aging working group.* Kalamazoo, MI: John E. Fetzer Institute.
Gartner, J. (1996). Religious commitment, mental health, and prosocial behavior: A review of the empirical literature. In E.P. Shafranske (Ed.), *Religion and the clinical practice of psychology* (pp. 187–214). Washington, DC: American Psychological Association.
Hill, P.C., & Butter, E.M. (1995). The role of religion in promoting physical health. *Journal of Psychology and Christianity, 14,* 141–155.
Hill, P.C., & Hood, W., Jr. (Eds.). (1999). *Measures of religiosity.* Birmingham, AL: Religious Education Press.
Hill, P.C., Pargament, K.I., Hood, R.W., McCullough, M.E., Swyers, J.P., Larson, D.B., & Zinnabauer, B.J. (2000). Conceptualizing religion and spirituality: Points of commonality, points of departure. *Journal for the Theory of Social Behaviour, 30,* 51–77.
Larson, D.B., Sherrill, K.A., Lyons, J.S., Craigie, F.C., Thielman, S.B., Greenwold, M.A., & Larson, S.S. (1992). Associations between dimensions of religious commitment and mental health reported in the *American Journal of Psychiatry* and *Archives of General Psychiatry:* 1978–1989. *American Journal of Psychiatry, 149,* 557–559.
Larson, D.B., Swyers, J.P., & McCullough, M.E. (Eds.). (1998). *Scientific research on spirituality and health: A consensus report.* Rockville, MD: National Institute for Healthcare Research.
Levin, J.S., & Chatters, L.M. (1998). Research on religion and mental health: An overview of empirical findings and theoretical issues. In H.G. Koenig (Ed.), *Handbook of religion and mental health* (pp. 33–50). San Diego: Academic Press.
Levin, J.S., & Vanderpool, H.Y. (1992). Religious factors in physical health and the prevention of illness. In K.I. Pargament, K.I. Maton, & R.E. Hess (Eds.), *Religion and prevention in mental health: Research, vision, and action* (pp. 83–103). New York: Haworth Press.
Paloutzian, R.F., & Kirkpatrick, L.A. (Eds.). (1995). Religious influences on personal and social well-being [Special issue]. *Journal of Social Issues, 51*(2).
Pargament, K.I. (1997). *The psychology of religion and coping.* New York: Guilford Press.
Sethi, S., & Seligman, M.E.P. (1993). Optimism and fundamentalism. *Psychological Science, 4,* 256–259.

Thoresen, C.E. (1999). Spirituality and health: Is there a relationship? *Journal of Health Psychology,* 4, 291–300.

Uchino, B.N., Uno, D., & Holt-Lunstad, J. (1999). Social support, physiological processes, and health. *Current Directions in Psychological Science,* 8, 145–148.

Watters, W. (1992). *Deadly doctrine: Health, illness, and Christian God-talk.* Amherst, NY: Prometheus Books.

Section 2: Critical Thinking Questions

1. Leventhal and Brooks-Gunn and Cutrona explain that the studies they review examine neighborhood effects "above and beyond" the impact of family characteristics. Explain why controlling for family factors is important to understand the impact of neighborhood factors.

2. A number of articles identify housing-related factors that may affect youth well-being (see also Adams and Masten in Section 3). What are those factors? How have experimental housing studies empirically contributed to this body of literature? What are the implications for neighborhood-level interventions?

3. What is social capital? Why is it important for the well-being of community members?

4. Several articles in this section acknowledge that neighborhood or community conditions influence both the number of ties people have with their neighbors and also the protective power of these ties. Why might social support from friends or parents be less helpful in economically disadvantaged neighborhoods than in higher income areas?

5. Cutrona states, "Neighborhood-level mental health problems should be addressed at the neighborhood level." How would neighborhood-level interventions differ from ones at the individual-level?

6. Seybold and Hill identify social networks and social support as potential putative mechanisms for the relationship between religion and health. Explain how these factors may contribute to this relationship.

This article has been reprinted as it originally appeared in *Current Directions in Psychological Science*. Citation information for this article as originally published appears above.

Section 3: The Impact of Disparate Stressors

Community psychologists often study environmental stressors and the ways people manage them. Understanding stress processes is theoretically interesting in its own right, but also essential for designing prevention and intervention programs to reduce stressors or to help people cope with them. Some stressors stem from the physical environment, as in Kaniasty and Norris work on natural disasters (although research on global warming suggests that climate change and the incidence of extreme weather events have important behavioral antecedents). Disasters occur at a particular point in time but have radiating effects. As Kaniasty and Norris describe, they not only displace people and destroy property, but also have positive and negative effects on the help and support people receive from others. Kaniasty and Norris trace out the complex patterns of stressors, supports, and distress and show that people, who are already disadvantaged by reason of education or race, are further neglected in the aftermath of disasters.

Adam looks not just at the quality of a child's environment, but at its stability, finding that residential moves and separations from parents are associated with poor adjustment. Both forms of instability are more common for low-income than middle-class children. Homelessness can be thought of as an extreme form of residential instability. At a minimum, families move from some form of housing to shelter and then back into housing, and many families make multiple moves in an attempt to secure affordable housing before turning to shelters. Homelessness is often associated with separations from parents as well. Thus it is not surprising that Masten finds that homeless youth are worse off than other poor children, although both groups differ even more from middle class norms. She suggests that policies and programs must address poverty to prevent negative developmental outcomes.

Karney and Bradbury examine how stressful social contexts may affect marriages, including financial difficulties, lack of adequate employment, and insufficient social support. They suggest that stressors, not values, explain the low rates of stable marriages among low-income couples and that educational interventions to promote marriage may be misplaced. Financial stressors lead to delays in marriage (as individuals seek better economic circumstances before tying the knot), are associated with greater challenges within marriages, and also diminish partners' abilities to manage those challenges.

Luthar and Latendresse show that affluent children experience surprising levels of adjustment problems, including higher levels of substance use, anxiety, and depression than inner-city youth. Indeed, they found that youth at opposite extremes of the income distribution were more alike than different, and in some cases, such as substance abuse, the affluent youth showed more problems. This work, like the earlier work by Fuligini on the greater success of first generation immigrant children than native-born peers, or the work by Patterson on the generally high levels of well-being among children raised by gay and lesbian parents, show the importance of conducting careful research rather than relying on assumptions to understand different population groups.

Mobilization and Deterioration of Social Support Following Natural Disasters

Krzysztof Kaniasty[1]
Indiana University of Pennsylvania

Fran H. Norris
Georgia State University

When natural disasters strike, the victims face a double jeopardy: To cope with their threats and losses, they need to marshal social support at the time when their social networks are most likely to be disrupted and potentially unable to carry out their supportive roles. The stress that challenges victims of natural disasters, such as floods, hurricanes, tornadoes, or earthquakes, is multifaceted.[2] It often involves immediate trauma arising from exposure to death and injury, extreme physical force, and life-threatening situations. Disaster stress often entails the destruction or loss of tangible goods and possessions that are of substantial monetary value or symbolic and emotional significance. It threatens and shatters various valued resources needed to sustain physical and psychological health. Not surprisingly, then, research has documented reliable increases in physical and psychological symptomatology experienced by victims.[3]

Disasters engulf whole communities. Victimization is shared. At the extreme, a disaster evolves into a devastating collective trauma, "a blow to the tissues of social life that damages the bonds linking people together and impairs the prevailing sense of communality."[4] Almost every definition of disaster speaks of the disruption of social structure or sense of community. With equal consistency, however, empirical and lay reports use labels such as "altruistic" or "therapeutic" community and postdisaster "utopia" or "heroism" when describing higher than usual levels of solidarity, fellowship, and altruism that emerge immediately after the impact. Therefore, natural disasters pose an interesting paradox for researchers of social support. On the one hand, disasters elicit outpourings of immense mutual helping; on the other hand, disasters impede the exchange of support because they disrupt social networks through death or injury, relocation, changes in routine activities, and physical destruction of environments conducive for social interactions.[5]

This review of a growing area of interdisciplinary research investigating mutual helping following catastrophic events is an attempt to describe postdisaster processes that originate with an instant mobilization of supportive behaviors but often lead to deterioration of helping resources, leaving some victims with a perceived sense of loss in their social relationships at a time when they need these relationships the most. To understand this phenomenon, we must look more closely at the dynamic transactions between characteristics of the stressor and social support. Although disasters occur suddenly, the stress they cause is not only acute. Disasters create continuous challenges for victims and their communities. The literature distinguishes explicitly among several postimpact stages: The salient heroic phase, with its therapeutic features of increased cohesiveness and altruism, is soon replaced by the disillusionment and reconstruction phases.

It is then that the victims discover that the need for assistance far exceeds the availability of resources and realize that the increased sense of benevolence was short-lived. President Clinton, during his visit to the areas of the Great Flood of '93, appropriately remarked, "Folks are brave and good-humored and courageous. But then the reality of the losses sinks in and grief takes over."[6] Social support is not a static property of a person or the environment. Its quantity, quality, and functions depend on individuals and the stressor demands they face. As a "rise and fall of utopia," natural disaster is an excellent example of an event that moves across time from an initial rush of spontaneous helping to a long-term depletion of supportive resources.

POSTDISASTER MOBILIZATION OF SUPPORT

It is important to differentiate various manifestations of social support. We distinguish among three general categories: received support (actual receipt of help), perceived support (the belief that help would be available if needed), and social embeddedness (quantity and type of relationships with other people). It could be said that the instant mobilization of help following disaster is the domain of received support, whereas a lingering sense of deterioration and disruption of the indigenous social fabric is the domain of perceived support and embeddedness.

The mutual help in emergent postdisaster helping communities is not distributed equally or randomly. Priority is given to those victims who are most exposed to the disaster's destructive powers. In fall 1990, 1 year after Hurricane Hugo devastated large areas of North and South Carolina (September 22, 1989), we interviewed 1,000 victims and nonvictims.[7] Disaster exposure, operationalized as loss (of property and belongings) and harm (injury or threat to life), was strongly associated with the amount of help received. The between-group differences were pervasive: Victims received much more help than nonvictims, and high-exposure victims received more support than low-exposure victims. The importance of loss and harm in predicting the receipt of assistance is consistent with the *rule of relative needs*. Relative needs, most often operationalized as the severity of experienced stressor, serve as an impetus in mobilizing support from other people.

Kin networks are the most utilized sources of support to disaster victims. Nonkin informal networks, such as friends, neighbors, or religious congregations, also appear to play a vital role in assisting victims, particularly when kin ties are weak or absent.[5] In a study of widespread flooding that occurred in southeastern Kentucky in 1981 and 1984, we found that victims received more help from kin than nonkin sources.[8] Interestingly, the extent of loss significantly predicted help only from nonkin sources. Thus, helping among immediate family and relatives may not follow a rule of relative needs, and may be allocated somewhat irrespectively of the extent of losses experienced.

According to the contemporary models of stress, social support is an asset in that it promotes preservation or recovery of physical and psychological resources that are needed for successful coping. Studies that have examined the role of social support among victims of natural disasters generally show that inadequate levels of social support are associated with greater distress. [5,9,10] If social networks are to play their protective and restorative functions, they have to provide resources that are most challenged by stressful circumstances. Consequently, in the study of Hurricane Hugo, we found that the greatest difference in support received by victims and nonvictims was in the realm of tangible help.[7] Victims helped each other extensively by cleaning properties, doing household chores, sharing shelter, and lending needed tools, equipment, or money. They also received much more help than nonvictims in the form of guidance and information. Victims need to know how to assess their emotions, where to go for organized aid, and how to protect their properties. All these supportive acts are specific and well matched to the ecological demands of the event. This point is important because receipt of support should be most beneficial to psychological well-being if the specific demands of the stressor and supportive provisions are congruent with each other.

Of course, being surrounded by people who are loving and understanding is imperative for disaster victims, many of whom not only have lost valuables of material or symbolic significance but also have been exposed to death and injury. Not surprisingly, then, emotional help was, in absolute terms, the most frequently exchanged helping behavior among Hugo victims. However, victims were not as different from nonvictims in amount of emotional support received as they were in amount of tangible and informational support received. Analyses of the concomitants of support receipt indicated that the levels of emotional help were determined less by disaster impact and more by person characteristics than tangible and information help. Possibly, people desire emotional support at all times, whereas their need for tangible aid and advice is determined more by demands of the stressor.

Besides the rule of relative needs, the *rule of relative advantage* surfaced in the post-Hugo helping community: Female, younger, married, white, and more educated persons typically received more help than their male, older, unmarried, black, and less educated counterparts. Relative advantage (person characteristics) interacted with relative needs (stressor) to produce two patterns of differential mobilization of support. The first, a *pattern of neglect,* emerged among less educated persons and blacks, who received proportionately less help than equally affected victims who were more educated and white. These findings are not isolated incidents peculiar to the context of Hurricane Hugo. Bolin and Bolton,[11] based on the examination of four disasters that struck culturally and ethnically diverse sites, concluded that the poor and minorities had the greatest difficulties securing adequate assistance and recovering from disaster. Often-publicized examples of altruism and solidarity that the public can marshal in times of crisis should not obscure the fact that the pattern of neglect is equally real.

Fortunately, a few victims of Hurricane Hugo experienced a *pattern of concern*: The oldest respondents (over 70 years old), when faced with threats to their lives and health, received relatively more help than similarly affected victims from younger age groups. However, older victims did not experience such a pattern of concern when faced with property loss. Findings of other studies also point to the limits of this special regard for the elderly. Some researchers reported that older victims may, in fact, experience neglect and receive considerably less help from all sources than younger people.[12] The Kentucky floods elicited such a pattern: Elderly flood victims received very little help—much less than they had expected.[8] Evidently, when the need for support is not manifested as a threat to their health, older victims may be overlooked by altruistic communities.

POSTDISASTER DETERIORATION OF SUPPORT

Our study of the Kentucky floods had two unique features. First, pre- as well as postdisaster measures were available because the floods occurred in the midst of an ongoing panel study of older adults in the area. This afforded an excellent opportunity to examine changes in perceptions of social support as a direct result of disaster. Second, we operationalized disaster victimization at both individual and community levels because disasters are community events with potential psychological and social consequences even for people who incur no direct losses.

The results indicated that post-flood perceptions of social support declined from preflood levels. Personal losses (extent of damages at the household level) were associated with substantial declines in expectations of how much support would be available from kin and nonkin sources. Similarly, in other disaster contexts, Solomon and her colleagues found that some victims experienced a profound loss of perceived availability of support.[10] In the case of the Kentucky floods, the need for support may simply have exceeded its availability. Therefore, decline in postflood perceptions of support availability may have constituted a veridical assessment of temporary inability (most of these effects were limited to 3 to 6 months postdisaster) of social networks to provide adequate support. Interestingly, these declines were not limited to people personally affected by the disaster (i.e., primary victims). Natural disasters most often affect entire indigenous networks. Consequently, in the Kentucky floods study, we found that community destruction (extent of damages at the county level) was negatively associated with postdisaster perceptions of support, suggesting that declines in perceived availability of support were also experienced by secondary victims, that is, people who resided in the flooded areas but did not sustain personal losses.

There was also a strong communitywide tendency to experience declines in social embeddedness. Destruction of the physical environment may have disrupted activities, such as visiting, shopping, religious services, and recreation, that maintain a sense of social embeddedness and promote companionship. Our initial analyses of a sample of 400 Floridians interviewed about 6 months after Hurricane Andrew (August 1992) destroyed their neighborhoods in South Miami suggest that victims experienced disruption of routine social activities, loss of opportunities for fun and leisure, and less satisfaction with their social lives. Relocation or job loss removed relatives, friends, or neighbors from readily accessible social networks. Physical fatigue, emotional irritability, and scarcity of resources augmented the potential for interpersonal conflicts, isolation, and loneliness. In the most tragic cases, like after the Buffalo Creek dam collapse, the sense of community may be completely shattered—and with it "the power it gave people to care for one another in moments of need, to console one another in moments of distress, and to protect one another in moments of danger."[13] Small or great, annual or centennial, natural disasters impair the capacity of a community's naturally occurring support systems, making support exchanges difficult, strenuous, or even impossible.

The deterioration of perceived social support and sense of embeddedness is one path through which natural disasters exert their adverse effects on psychological well-being. We tested a theoretical model stipulating that victims experience the impact of the disaster both directly, through immediate loss and exposure to trauma, and indirectly, through deterioration of their social supports (see Fig. 1). Using data from the Kentucky floods,[8] we found convincing evidence for this mediating model: The disaster-induced erosion of social support to a great extent accounted for increased depressive symptomatology among both primary and secondary victims. The loss of social support has also mediated psychological consequences of Hurricanes Hugo and Andrew.[14]

This *deterioration model of social support* recognizes the potential of the stressor to curtail support and in this way is conceptually different from the more prominent stress-buffering model of social support. The model assumes that the changes in support contribute to the detrimental effects of stress rather than counteract them. In fact, declines in perceived social support may be the reason why stress-buffering processes are not operating, or are very limited, in the context of natural disasters.[9,10] After all, if the belief that support is available is undermined, how could it protect against the impact of the stressor? Of course, those victims whose initial high levels of support do not deteriorate, or even increase, could enjoy the benefits of perceived support as a buffer of stress.

Is the deterioration of perceived social support inevitable, or can it be counteracted by higher levels of received support? We addressed this question with the data from Hurricane Hugo, whose victims received relatively high levels of help.[15] Figure 2 depicts the *deterioration deterrence model,* which closely resembles more general stress-suppressor or support-mobilization models.[16] If postdisaster support mobilization has occurred, the disaster stress should be positively related to received support. This received support, in turn, should be positively related to perceived support. Thus, the receipt of support deters the otherwise negative relation between stress and perceived support. Structural equation modeling analyses provided quite strong support for this conceptualization. For all types of support examined—emotional, informational, tangible—the sign of the path coefficient from disaster stress to perceived support was negative (indicating

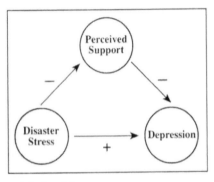

Fig. 1. Deterioration model of social support.

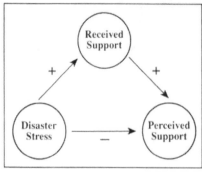

Fig. 2. Deterioration deterrence model.

deterioration), whereas the path from disaster stress to received support was positive (indicating mobilization). And, most important, there was a large positive coefficient for the path from received support to perceived support. Thus, when received support is low relative to needs, disaster victims' perceptions of support will deteriorate. However, when received support is adequate for those needs, disaster victims will maintain their expectations of available support.

SUMMARY MODEL

Figure 3 illustrates the processes linking the stress of natural disasters, person characteristics, social supports, and psychological distress. First, there is a deterioration process wherein disaster victims whose needs are unmet experience a decline in perceived support and a consequent increase in distress (see Paths a and b). Fortunately, the mobilization of received support may deter this deterioration and preserve victims' ongoing perceptions that support is available (see Paths c and d). These beliefs of being reliably connected to other people will shield victims from experiencing intense distress (Path b). Patterns of concern

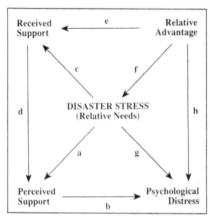

Fig. 3. Schematic framework depicting paths linking stress, person characteristics, social supports, and psychological distress.

and neglect may also emerge; that is, the mobilization of support may be influenced by victims' relative advantage (Path e) as well as their relative needs (Path c). As illustrated via Paths f, g, and h, other mechanisms operate as well.

We recognize that the processes we have described may not generalize easily to other stressful life events, especially those confined to lone individuals. However, these dynamics may apply to other community-level events in which the distinction between the victim and the supporter is just a matter of speech, not reality. Any time a resource is scarce, various rules that influence its distribution come into play. At best, the emergent altruistic community is insufficient to meet all the community needs; at worst, it may inadvertently exclude many citizens who are in need. Mobilizing indigenous support is a very difficult task. Therefore, we must explore ways to provide the resources that help people help each other.

Acknowledgments—Preparation of this review and some of the research reported in it were supported by Grant No. MH45069 (Hurricane Hugo) and Grant No. MH51278 (Hurricane Andrew) from the National Institute of Mental Health, Fran H. Norris, Principal Investigator.

Notes

1. Address correspondence to Krys Kaniasty, Department of Psychology, Indiana University of Pennsylvania, Indiana, PA 15705; e-mail: kaniasty@iup.bitnet.

2. The focus of this review is on helping behavior from indigenous social networks following natural disasters. In some cases, human-induced catastrophes (e.g., a collapse of a dam) share many features with natural disasters, and therefore could be included here. However, because of space limitations, we excluded from this review research on technological disasters that either do not have well-defined low points ("worst is over") and are not associated with immediate and clear damages (e.g., nuclear power plant accident, toxic waste spill) or are confined to relatively small groups of individuals (e.g., transportation disasters). For definitional issues, see, e.g., R. Gist and B. Lubin, Eds., *Psychosocial Aspects of Disaster* (Wiley, New York, 1989).

3. See, e.g., A. Rubonis and L. Bickman, Psychological impairment in the wake of disaster: The disaster-psychopathology relationship, *Psychological Bulletin, 109,* 384–399 (1991).

4. K. Erikson, Loss of communality at Buffalo Creek, *American Journal of Psychiatry, 133,* 302–305 (1976), p. 302.

5. See, e.g., T. Drabek and W. Key, *Conquering Disaster: Family Recovery and Long-Term Consequences* (Irvington Publishers, New York, 1984); S.D. Solomon, Mobilizing social support networks in times of disaster, in *Trauma and Its Wake: Vol. 2. Traumatic Stress Theory, Research, and Intervention,* C. Figley, Ed. (Brunner/Mazel, New York, 1986).

6. J. Adler, Troubled waters, *Newsweek* (July 26, 1993), p. 23.

7. K. Kaniasty and F. Norris, In search of altruistic community: Patterns of social support mobilization following Hurricane Hugo, *American Journal of Community Psychology* (in press).

8. K. Kaniasty, F. Norris, and S. Murrell, Received and perceived social support following natural disaster, *Journal of Applied Social Psychology, 20,* 85–114 (1990); K. Kaniasty and F. Norris, A test of the social support deterioration model in the context of natural disaster, *Journal of Personality and Social Psychology, 64,* 395–408 (1993).

9. See. e.g., J. Cook and L. Bickman, Social support and psychological symptomatology following a natural disaster, *Journal of Traumatic Stress, 3,* 541–556 (1990);

M. Cowan and S. Murphy, Identification of postdisaster bereavement risk predictors, *Nursing Research, 34,* 71–75 (1985).

10. S.D. Solomon. M. Bravo, M. Rubio-Stipec, add G. Canino, Effect of family role on response to disaster, *Journal of Traumatic Stress, 6,* 255–269 (1993).

11. R. Bolin and P. Bolton, *Race, Religion, and Ethnicity in Disaster Recovery* (University of Colorado, Boulder, 1966).

12. T. Kilijanek and T.E. Drabek, Assessing long-term impacts of a natural disaster: A focus on the elderly, *The Gerontologist, 19,* 555–566 (1979).

13. Erikson. note 3, p. 305.

14. C. Ironson, 0. Greenwood, C, Wynings, A. Baum, M, Rodriquez, C. Carver, C, Benight, J. Evans, M. Antoni, A. LaPerriere. M. Kumar, M. Fletcher, and N. Schneiderman, *Social support, neuroendocrine, and immune functioning during Hurricane Andrew,* paper presented at the annual meeting of the American Psychological Association, Toronto, Canada (August 1993); K. Kaniasty and F. Norris, *Social support from family and friends following catastrophic events: The role of cultural factors,* paper presented at the 7th International Conference on Personal Relationships, Groningen. The Netherlands (July 1994),

15. F. Norris and K. Kaniasty, *Receipt of help and perceived social support in times of stress: A test of the social support deterioration deterrence model,* manuscript submitted for publication (1994).

16. See M. Barrera. Models of social support and life stress: Beyond the buffering hypothesis, in *Life Events and Psychological Functioning.* L.H. Cohen, Ed. (Sage Publications. Newbury Park. CA, 1988).

Beyond Quality: Parental and Residential Stability and Children's Adjustment

Emma K. Adam[1]

School of Education and Social Policy, Northwestern University

Abstract

In identifying environmental factors affecting children's development, researchers have typically focused on the quality of children's home or family environments. Less attention has been paid to environmental stability as a factor influencing children's well-being. This is partially due to outdated notions of children's living arrangements and to the fact that children in the least stable environments are often the hardest to involve and retain in research. Recent research suggests that there are associations between the degree of environmental instability and difficulties in adjustment, such that children exposed to higher levels of family instability (e.g., more frequent separations from parent figures and more frequent residential moves) show worse adjustment across a variety of developmental domains. Although there is still uncertainty regarding the causal direction of these associations (does instability cause children's problems or do the problems cause instability?), the sources and consequences of family instability clearly deserve greater attention in future research on child and adolescent adjustment.

Keywords

parental separation; residential mobility; adjustment

Children's home or family lives have long been considered a primary environmental context influencing their cognitive, social, emotional, behavioral, and physical development. Although modern-day developmental theories also recognize the important influences of genetic factors and extrafamilial factors on children's outcomes, these variables have been found to have much of their effect through their influence on children's home environments (Collins, Maccoby, Steinberg, Hetherington, & Bornstein, 2000).

Many aspects of children's family environments have been studied. These variables include family structure or composition, family economic and learning resources, and the quality of parent-child relationships (Collins et al., 2000; Linver, Brooks-Gunn, & Kohen, 2002). Even when measured at multiple time points, however, these variables are typically treated as providing a "snapshot" of the quality of a child's home environment at each time. Rarely has the degree of change in children's home environments over time been treated as the primary variable of interest in research on child adjustment.

FAMILY INSTABILITY AS THE VARIABLE OF INTEREST

As many of us are aware from our own lives, family circumstances are not static. We move, change jobs, get sick, separate from romantic partners, and lose loved ones. For most people, these are relatively infrequent events. For others, change is a frequent and even defining feature of their home lives. Recent research has demonstrated that the degree of family instability children are exposed to is a strong predictor of their developmental adjustment (Ackerman, Kogos, Youngstrom, Schoff, & Izard, 1999; E.K. Adam & Chase-Lansdale, 2002).

Many family-instability variables can be studied, including changes in marital status and household composition, separations from parent figures, changes in physical residence, and episodes of antisocial behavior or mental or physical illness in the family. Because many of these events occur more often for low-income families than for families with more economic resources, family instability has been proposed as one mechanism explaining the associations between poverty and negative child outcomes (Ackerman et al., 1999; Linver et al., 2002).

In this review, I focus on two indicators of family instability that Chase-Lansdale and I investigated in a recent study of a sample of low-income adolescent girls: residential moves and separations from parent figures (E.K. Adam & Chase-Lansdale, 2002). *By residential moves,* I mean physical changes of residence, including moves that adolescents make either with their families or on their own. *By separations from parent figures,* I mean major separations[2] from any adults the child considers "parental."

Residential moves and separations from parent figures are both highly disruptive events in children's lives, and both are relatively easily quantified. These events are not uncommon, particularly in low-income populations. Among the girls in our study, 15% had experienced at least one separation from a mother figure, and 42% had experienced at least one separation from a father figure. They had lived with a range of 1 to 5 parent figures in their lifetime and had experienced from 0 to 6 major parental separations. The numbers of residential moves experienced in the past 5 years ranged from 0 to 10. Such events are not restricted to low-income families, however—16% of the U.S. population moved the year these data were collected (Faber, 1998).

SEPARATIONS FROM PARENT FIGURES AND CHILDREN'S ADJUSTMENT

Interest in separations from parent figures emerged from research on how loss of a parent affects children's mental health, as well as from research on the effects of divorce on children. In an early instability study, K.S. Adam, Bouckoms, and Streiner (1982) found that suicidal adolescents and adults were more likely to have experienced the loss of a parent through death, divorce, or separation, and to have experienced a generally disorganized, unpredictable home life, than were nonsuicidal individuals who were the same age and gender and similar in demographic background. Although early research treated divorce as a one-time event, later researchers noted that divorce is often associated with multiple changes in family structure, including the loss of the father from the home and subsequent remarriages and divorces of the mother. Studies found that multiple changes in a mother's partners have a cumulative negative effect on her children's social, emotional, educational, and behavioral outcomes (Capaldi & Patterson, 1991; Kurdek, Fine, & Sinclair, 1994).

Prior research has focused primarily on changes in children's contact with their fathers, rarely acknowledging that children experience major separations from their mothers as well. In our sample of adolescent girls, Chase-Lansdale and I found that as the number of separations from parent figures increased, adolescents showed higher levels of adjustment problems on an index measuring cognitive, emotional, academic, and behavioral functioning (E.K. Adam & Chase-Lansdale, 2002). (See Fig. 1.) Separations from mother figures and father figures were both significantly and independently related to the girls' adjustment. Separations from temporary (less than 2 years) and long-standing (more than 2 years) caregivers, and those occurring early in childhood, in middle childhood, and during adolescence, all had significant effects on adjustment. The effects of separations were independent of family demographics and the quality of current relationships with parents and peers, as well as neighborhood environments.

How and why might separations from parent figures have these effects? Attachment theorists have long argued that children's feelings of security are strongly determined by their internalized perceptions of the availability of their primary caregivers. Although threats to the availability of caregivers have their most visible effect in infants, such threats provoke profound feelings of anxiety, anger, and despair throughout childhood and adolescence, and therefore have implications for emotional health (Kobak, 1999). Kochanska (2003) also provided evidence that the internalized history of mutual positive emotion and trust between a parent and child ("mutually responsive orientation") is an important basis for conscience.

What happens when this internalized sense of emotional security and mutual trust is disrupted by a major separation from a parent? Negative implications for emotional health and behavior could be expected. What happens if a child experiences this kind of disruption repeatedly? An anecdote illustrates one possible answer. A child living in foster care, who had lived with five different

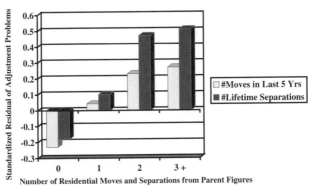

Fig. 1. Adolescents' adjustment problems as a function of two indicators of environmental instability: number of residential moves in the previous 5 years and number of separations from parent figures. The standardized residual measure of adjustment controls for household demographics and quality of the current environment, so that any effects of those variables are removed. Reprinted with permission from E.K. Adam and Chase-Lansdale (2002). Copyright 2002 by the American Psychological Association.

caregivers before the age of 6, was told: "You are a wonderful and special girl." She responded: "Then why does everybody leave me?" The violation of trust involved in the repeated loss of caregivers has implications not only for perceptions of other people, but also for perceptions of the self.

At the same time that the child is experiencing the emotional impact of a separation, he or she may also be losing an important source of social support. He or she may also experience dramatic changes in daily routines and reductions in the quality of care provided by the remaining adult or adults in the household.

RESIDENTIAL MOBILITY AND CHILDREN'S ADJUSTMENT

Sociological and epidemiological research on residential mobility has shown that a high rate of residential moves predicts social-emotional, behavioral, and educational problems, even when controlling for family characteristics contributing to a greater likelihood of moving (Pribesh & Downey, 1999; Wood, Halfon, Scarlata, Newacheck, & Nessim, 1993). In our study, the number of moves adolescents had experienced in the prior 5 years was positively associated with the number of adjustment problems they had (see Fig. 1), and this association was independent of the effects of separations from parent figures, family demographic characteristics, and the quality of the adolescents' current environments (E.K. Adam & Chase-Lansdale, 2002).

Researchers interested in explaining the effects of residential moves on children have proposed that these effects are due to the loss of familiar physical environments, activities, and routines; the loss of social-support networks; or decreases in parents' well-being and parenting quality. One study (Pribesh & Downey, 1999) found evidence that children's loss of prior social connections is indeed an important mechanism. Characteristics such as the age or sex of the child, family structure, and parental support have been found to moderate the effects of moves on children (Simmons, Burgeson, Carlton-Ford, & Blyth, 1987).

THE CAUSALITY PROBLEM

Clearly, the associations between family instability and children's and adolescents' adjustment problems can be explained in various ways. There is still considerable debate regarding the causal direction of these associations. Rather than family instability causing children's problems, children's adjustment problems may be the cause of family instability, or preexisting characteristics of families and communities may cause both family instability and adjustment problems. Evidence exists, for example, that children of couples who later divorce exhibit problematic behavior prior to the divorce (Cherlin, Chase-Lansdale, & McRae, 1998), that mothers who change partners tend to have preexisting personality attributes that contribute to unstable relationships (Capaldi & Patterson, 1991), and that families who move more frequently have more disadvantages than other families prior to their moves (Pribesh & Downey, 1999). Researchers strive to measure and statistically control for such possibilities, but adequate data have not always been available to rule out these alternative explanations. Experimental research on nonhuman primates, however, has shown that random assignment to high levels of social disruption results in an array of serious social, emotional, and physical health problems (Kaplan, 1983). At a minimum, the current findings indicate that high levels of separations from parent figures and residential moves are important markers that may be used to identify children at high risk for adjustment problems so that intervention efforts may be targeted toward them.

WHY HAS FAMILY INSTABILITY NOT RECEIVED MORE ATTENTION?

There are several reasons why family instability has not received much research attention thus far. First, there has been a reliance on cross-sectional studies, which are poor tools for studying change. Second, much psychological research has been conducted with middle-class families, who tend to have relatively low levels of instability. Third, studies often select traditional family types as a means of "control," thus automatically excluding children with unusual or changing family experiences. Fourth, narrowly worded questions about family, such as questions that ask about only biological parents rather than all potentially important adult figures, may fail to illuminate the complexity and changeability of children's family lives. Finally, families with the highest amount of instability are often the hardest to recruit, track, and retain in research.

CUMULATIVE INSTABILITY INDICES

In my research, the independent effects of residential moves and separations from parents on adolescent adjustment were assessed. Other researchers have added together multiple instability factors to form a single index (Ackerman et al., 1999) and tested the effect of this cumulative measure of instability. Whether it is more informative to cumulate or to separate different aspects of family instability remains to be determined. Arguments can be made for both approaches. Cumulative indices describe the total degree of instability children are exposed to, and may therefore produce stronger effects, but separate instability indicators could illuminate the processes by which particular instability factors relate to specific outcomes.

The cumulative perspective suggests that normative changes that take place during individual development, such as those associated with puberty, also are important aspects of instability and may increase the impact of external events. Simmons et al. (1987) found that early adolescents coping with several life changes concurrently (including normative changes and other less typical events) were at high risk for problematic outcomes. They suggested that adolescents need an "arena of comfort" involving continuity in at least some spheres of their lives. This notion of arena of comfort could be easily extended to explain the effects of instability on younger children and adults during periods of developmental transition.

FOCI FOR FUTURE RESEARCH

Numerous issues remain to be examined in future research on the effects of instability on children; the following recommendations should be considered. First, future studies should use prospective longitudinal data, preferably from representative samples including the full range of socioeconomic and family circumstances. Whether the effects of instability vary across different socioeconomic, racial-ethnic, and other subgroups needs to be explored. Second, a wider range of instability variables should be examined. Any variable contributing to disruption, unpredictability, or chaos in a child's life is a reasonable candidate. Such variables should be examined both independently and as part of a cumulative instability index, and the impact of the developmental timing of each instability event should be considered. Third, the interaction between the quality and stability of children's environments needs to be examined. Is a stable but low-quality environment better than a typically high-quality one punctuated by occasional disruption? Does previously having experienced a high-quality home environment buffer the individual from the effects of later disruption?

Fourth, physiological and physical health outcomes should be examined. Animal research and research on human stress physiology show that predictability and control are important variables determining the organism's ability to contain physiological stress responses, and that low predictability and control contribute to increases in physiological stress and worse health outcomes. Given the low control and predictability associated with family instability, its impact on physiological variables and health outcomes is of interest. Fifth, an experimental intervention approach, in which some children from unstable environments are randomly chosen to receive interventions that increase social stability, would help resolve the causality issue. For example, children in long-term foster care could be purposefully maintained in the same home, school, and neighborhood, so that they do not experience additional disruptions, or they could be provided a single case worker who would support them through any and all transitions. Studies of this nature could provide persuasive evidence that would bolster the argument for undertaking more widespread policy initiatives aimed at increasing the degree of stability in children's home lives.

In this review, I have suggested that in order to understand children's adjustment, researchers need to move beyond a focus on quality and also consider the degree of disruption or change children experience in their home environments. Although issues of causality remain to be clarified, family instability is a clear marker of risk for adjustment problems. In the past, developmental psychologists have encouraged practitioners and policymakers to ensure high quality in children's relationships and physical environments. If research continues to show that family instability is an important predictor of children's adjustment problems, ensuring high levels of stability in children's interpersonal relationships and physical environments will be an important additional policy recommendation, with implications for foster care, child custody, housing, and other child and family policies.

Recommended Reading

Ackerman, B.P., Kogos, J., Youngstrom, E., Schoff, K., & Izard, C. (1999). (See References)

Adam, E.K., & Chase-Lansdale, P.L. (2002). (See References)

Wood, D., Halfon, N., Scarlata, D., Newacheck, P., & Nessim, S. (1993). (See References)

Acknowledgments—This research was funded through support from the Carnegie Corporation of New York, the Ford Foundation, the Harrison Steans Foundation, the Social Sciences and Humanities Research Council of Canada, and the Alfred P. Sloan Foundation.

Notes

1. Address correspondence to Emma K. Adam, School of Education and Social Policy, Northwestern University, Evanston, IL 60208; e-mail: ek-adam@northwestern.edu.

2. Major separations are long-term separations that violate children's expectations for regular contact with their caregiver; they do not include short-term or predictable separations such as regular day-care experiences.

References

Ackerman, B.P., Kogos, J., Youngstrom, E., Schoff, K., & Izard, C. (1999). Family instability and the problem behaviors of children from economically disadvantaged families. *Developmental Psychology, 35,* 258–268.

Adam, E.K., & Chase-Lansdale, P.L. (2002). Home sweet home(s): Parental separations, residential moves and adjustment in low-income adolescent girls. *Developmental Psychology, 38,* 792–805.

Adam, K.S., Bouckoms, A., & Streiner, D. (1982). Parental loss and family stability in attempted suicide. *Archives of General Psychiatry, 39,* 1081–1085.

Capaldi, D.M., & Patterson, G.R. (1991). Relation of parent transitions to boys' adjustment problems: I. A linear hypothesis. II. Mothers at risk for transitions and unskilled parenting. *Developmental Psychology, 27,* 489–504.

Cherlin, A.J., Chase-Lansdale, P.L., & McRae, C. (1998). Effect of divorce on mental health through the life course. *American Sociological Review, 63,* 239–249.

Collins, W.A., Maccoby, E.E., Steinberg, L., Hetherington, E.M., & Bornstein, M.H. (2000). Contemporary research on parenting: The case of nature and nurture. *American Psychologist, 55,* 218–232.

Faber, C.S. (1998). *Geographic mobility: March 1996 to March 1997 (Update)* (Report No. P20-510). Washington, DC: U.S. Bureau of the Census.

Kaplan, J.R. (1983). Social stress and atherosclerosis in normocholesterolemic monkeys. *Science, 220,* 733–735.

Kobak, R. (1999). The emotional dynamics of disruptions in attachment relationships: Implications for theory, research, and clinical intervention. In J. Cassidy & P. Shaver (Eds.), *Handbook of attachment* (pp. 21–43). New York: Guilford.

Kochanska, G. (2002). Mutually responsive orientation between mothers and their young children: A context for the early development of conscience. *Current Directions in Psychological Science, 11,* 191–195.

Kurdek, L.A., Fine, M.A., & Sinclair, R.J. (1994). The relation between parenting transitions and adjustment in young adolescents: A multi-sample investigation. *Journal of Early Adolescence, 14,* 412–432.

Linver, M.R., Brooks-Gunn, J., & Kohen, D.E. (2002). Family processes as pathways from income to young children's development. *Developmental Psychology, 38,* 719–734.

Pribesh, S., & Downey, D.B. (1999). Why are residential and school moves associated with poor school performance? *Demography, 36,* 521–534.

Simmons, R.G., Burgeson, R., Carlton-Ford, S., & Blyth, D. (1987). The impact of cumulative change in early adolescence. *Child Development, 58,* 1220–1234.

Wood, D., Halfon, N., Scarlata, D., Newacheck, P., & Nessim, S. (1993). Impact of family relocation on children's growth, development, school function, and behavior. *Journal of the American Medical Association, 270,* 1334–1338.

Homeless Children in the United States: Mark of a Nation at Risk

Ann S. Masten[1]
University of Minnesota

One of the most disturbing images to emerge in public consciousness during the past decade is that of the homeless child. Public concern grew as stories of homeless families filled the media. Books like *Rachel and Her Children,* by Jonathan Kozol, roused the conscience of the nation. Clearly, emergency shelters and welfare hotels like New York City's Martinique, so vividly depicted by Kozol, were not fertile ground for child development.

Various attempts have been made to estimate the magnitude of the problem of homeless Americans, but, as the 1990 U.S. Census takers found, counting the homeless presents a host of definitional and methodological issues. Consequently, estimates varied. Nonetheless, data converged on three conclusions: (1) the number of homeless Americans increased during the 1980s, (2) the problem was significant (even by conservative estimates), and (3) the number of homeless families with children was increasing both in absolute terms and as a percentage of the total homeless population.

The estimate published in 1988 by the Institute of Medicine of the National Academy of Sciences represented a midrange figure: Nationwide, it was estimated that 100,000 children were homeless on any given night, excluding minors on their own. For 1989, the U.S. Conference of Mayors reported that 36% of the homeless population in their 27-city survey consisted of families and more than half of the family members were children. Approximately 25% of all the homeless Americans in this survey were minors.

Congress responded to the surge of homelessness by enacting in 1987 the Stewart B. McKinney Homeless Assistance Act. Homeless persons were defined as those who lack a "fixed, regular, and adequate nighttime residence" or who reside in emergency shelters and other places not intended to be homes. This legislation had the goal of coordinating government efforts and providing funds to meet the needs of the homeless. This law also stated the policy of Congress that each state ensure the access of each homeless child to a free and appropriate education.

Concerned scientists also responded to the alarming phenomenon of homeless children. Psychiatrist Ellen Bassuk and her colleagues were the first to publish much-needed data on the mental health problems of homeless mothers and their children. Their studies, suggesting significant developmental delays and psychological problems among homeless children in Massachusetts, influenced the McKinney legislation. Response by other investigators soon followed. The purpose of this review is to highlight the issues and findings emerging from research on the health, education, and psychological status of homeless children.

The focus of this review is children and adolescents living with their families. Minors on their own, "runaway" and "throwaway" children, are a distinctly different group of homeless individuals. Very little research has been done with unaccompanied minors, although limited data suggest high rates of mental illness, substance abuse, posttraumatic stress, suicidal behavior, trouble with the law, and histories of abuse among these adolescents, particularly among "street kids."[2]

HOMELESS FAMILIES: WHO ARE THEY?

Surveys of homeless families suggest that young families headed by mothers who are poor and unskilled have been particularly vulnerable to the macroeconomic and social trends that have led to the recent increase of homelessness among families. Nationwide, the majority of homeless families are headed by single mothers. These mothers tend to be young, and the age distribution of their children is correspondingly skewed, with more infants and preschoolers than school-age children.

The ethnic composition of homeless families appears to reflect in large part the ethnicity of very poor families in a given region. Among urban families, ethnic minorities are overrepresented in the homeless population. Beyond minority status, little is known about cultural factors that may influence shelter utilization. The prevalence and acceptability of "doubling up" families in a single apartment or of seeking public assistance may vary among communities and among cultural groups.

Income levels are very low among homeless families. Many depend on welfare supports that result in incomes well below the federal poverty level. Others, fleeing or abandoned by the family breadwinner, have no current income.

The immediate "cause" of living in an emergency shelter is typically a financial crisis characterized by too little money and no affordable alternative housing. However, pathways to this predicament appear to be diverse. Some families are migrating from one place to another, seeking a better job or life. In others, relationship conflicts have resulted in leaving a residence by choice or by force. In still others, economic hardships have gradually eroded family resources or came overnight when a parent lost a job, a building was condemned, or the rent went up. Many low-income families live from check to check and have no savings to buffer the costs of losing a job or moving, for whatever reason. Once lost, housing can be difficult to regain in a tight housing market, and up-front costs such as security deposits may be difficult to meet. There is a strong consensus among researchers as well as advocates that during the 1980s, the growing shortage of low-income housing, the recessionary economic forces early in the decade, and the falling value of economic assistance to poor families combined to squeeze more families into the ranks of the homeless.

Personal problems may also contribute to economic hardship or the necessity of moving. Deinstitutionalization and severe mental illness do not appear to be salient causal factors for family homelessness. Unwise choices, substance abuse, or mental health problems may play a role. Bad luck also may be a significant factor differentiating homeless families from other very poor, vulnerable families who retain housing. Systematic research on the risk factors and processes leading to homelessness remains very limited.

THE STRESSES OF HOMELESSNESS FOR CHILDREN

Concerns about homeless children stem in large part from the deprivations and adversities associated in the public mind with the image of "homelessness." Journalistic accounts of life in a welfare hotel like the Martinique would alarm any reasonable person about risks to the children. More systematic, if less dramatic, studies of shelter life and the experiences that precede home-lessness substantiate public concern. In a study of families residing in a Minneapolis shelter, homeless children had experienced significantly more stressful life events out of their control over the past year than a very similar comparison group of poor children living at home.[3] Events such as illness, injury or arrest of a parent, or separation of parents may have been causally related to the outcome of homelessness, although this could not be determined in the study.

By the time they arrive in a shelter, children may have experienced many chronic adversities and traumatic events. More immediately, children may have gone hungry and lost friends, possessions, and the security of familiar places and people at home, at school, or in the neighborhood. Children perceive the strain of frightened parents who do not know what is going to happen. Shelters, which may provide for basic needs of housing, food, and clothing, can be very stressful for parents and children. Locations are usually undesirable, particularly with respect to children playing outside. Moreover, necessary shelter rules may strain a child and family life. For example, it is typical for no visitors to be allowed and for children, including adolescents, to be required to be accompanied at all times by a parent. Some shelters separate fathers and adolescent males from the rest of their families. Children also may be humiliated by other children at school or on the bus knowing where they live. Health care, education, and other services may be difficult to access.

Based on demographic data and the circumstances of many homeless families, it is reasonable to predict that homeless children are at considerable risk for health problems and developmental delays, as well as academic, emotional, and behavioral problems. A small but growing number of studies corroborates the high-risk status of homeless children.

HEALTH

The elevated rate of health problems in homeless children has been documented with data from 16 cities participating in the National Health Care for the Homeless Program initiated by the Robert Wood Johnson Foundation, the Pew Memorial Trust, and the U.S. Conference of Mayors.[4] Compared with normative samples of urban children coming in for health care, homeless children had two to four times the rates of respiratory infections, skin problems, nutritional deficiencies, gastrointestinal disorders, and chronic illnesses. Several studies have found immunization delays to be more common among homeless children than among other poor children. A study in New York found much higher rates of a total lack of prenatal care among homeless women than poor, housed women.[5] Not surprisingly, rates of low birth weight and infant mortality were higher as well. These health problems could impair current functioning and compromise future development, particularly in the context of continuing poverty and inadequate health care.

EDUCATION

Homeless children miss more school, have repeated a grade more often, and receive fewer special educational services than other school-age children. Before advocates and the McKinney legislation focused national attention on the educational deprivation of homeless children, many of these children were effectively denied access to education by barriers such as residency requirements, lack of immunization or school records, and transportation. Although the 1987 McKinney Act required states to ensure that homeless children had access to public education, barriers remain.

Several studies have found significant learning delays in homeless children at all grade levels, including preschool. In a recent pilot study conducted in a Minneapolis shelter, the 8- to 12-year-old children ($N = 20$) were an average of 14 months behind their age levels on a standardized individual achievement test, significantly below national norms for this test.

DEVELOPMENT AND MENTAL HEALTH

Controlled studies of the cognitive, social, and emotional development or well-being of homeless children are few in number. Particularly little is known about the socioemotional status of homeless infants. Results are consistent in finding delays in development, but differences between homeless and other poor children are not found consistently. Studies of preschoolers indicate cognitive, social, and visual-motor delays in development. Language delays are particularly prominent. Two controlled studies of preschoolers found elevated rates of behavior problems among homeless compared with poor, housed comparison groups.[6,7] Similar results have been found using the same instrument for homeless school-age children in Boston,[8] Los Angeles,[9] Minneapolis,[3] and Philadelphia.[7] The Minneapolis study, for example, included 159 children ages 8 to 17 who lived in the largest shelter in the region. Homeless children and adolescents had significantly more behavioral and emotional problems than the general population, particularly for antisocial problems. The proportion of children with Total Problem scores in the clinical range on the Child Behavior Checklist was twice the normative rate. Although scores for homeless children tended to be higher than scores for the very low-income comparison group, the similarities among very poor children, whether housed or homeless, were more compelling than the differences.

Several findings in the Minneapolis study suggested other effects on these children. Compared with poor, housed children, more homeless children expected they might live in a shelter as adults. Fewer homeless children and adolescents reported having a close friend, and they had spent less time with friends over the past week. Compared with other Minneapolis elementary school children, homeless children had substantially lower job aspirations for the future. These differences may reflect the subtle but lasting tolls of long-term deprivation, as well as recent experiences.

There were other ways in which poor children, regardless of housing status, appeared to be more alike than different. Poor, housed boys, like homeless children, had low job aspirations. A comparison of 8- to 12-year-olds showed both the homeless and the housed poor had higher levels of fear than a control group of urban schoolchildren. Fears of deprivation, for example, such as fears of hunger and having no place to live, were salient in both groups of poor children.

IMPLICATIONS

Studies of homeless families strongly suggest that homeless status is a powerful marker of high cumulative vulnerability and risk for child development. The most alarming implication of the data, however, is that homeless children represent the plight of millions of American children being reared in poverty.[10] Homeless families typically arise from a vulnerable population of extremely poor families. Although the crisis of homelessness itself appears to add to the risks for problems in health, education, and development, the differences between homeless and other very poor children often are not so great as the differences between poor children and the general population.

Homeless children appear to represent the ominous tip of the iceberg of poverty threatening the course of this nation's future. Policies and programs to assist homeless families or prevent homelessness among families must address this problem in the larger context of poverty. Clearly, multiple strategies at many levels of intervention will be required to improve the odds for good developmental outcomes in these children.

Shifting the odds for favorable child development among the nation's poorest children will take time, even if this task becomes the top priority of every relevant national, state, and local agency in the country. The problem of homeless children is not going to disappear in the near future. Therefore, more immediate efforts to intervene on behalf of these children are needed.

Research indicates that many homeless children need direct health, educational, and mental health services. Access to available resources is a key problem. Schools and preschool programs may be able to play a critically important role as the access point to both family services and psychological support for children. Schools have diverse opportunities to help meet many of the basic needs of homeless children, including food and health care, stability, relationships with competent peers and adults, and extracurricular activities that build self-efficacy. Schools, however, cannot be expected to assist homeless and other highly mobile, disadvantaged children without added resources.

Researchers have an important role to play in providing information to guide policy and evaluate programs. Although a number of studies have been conducted and more are under way, there are major gaps in the knowledge base. Little is known about the processes leading to or out of homelessness or the factors that ameliorate risk and facilitate better outcomes for children and their families. Most studies include heterogeneous samples of homeless families that differ markedly in background and current status on many dimensions that may be crucial for understanding causes and outcomes and for developing strategies to reduce the risks of becoming homeless or ameliorate its effects on parents and children. There is also a great need for information on the welfare of unaccompanied minors and how homeless runaways and abandoned children differ from or resemble homeless adolescents who stay with their families.

In addition, there is a profound shortage of normative data on the development of ethnic minority children and of appropriately standardized measures for use with low-income or minority childen. Normative data on the development of ethnically and socioeconomically diverse populations of children would provide the context for understanding developmental problems among homeless and other high-risk populations.

Finally, it is clear that isolated efforts, whether in the domain of research, policy, or intervention, limited to one place, one discipline, or one perspective, are inadequate to meaningfully address the complex problem of homeless children. Coordinated, multifaceted efforts are required at each level in each domain of inquiry and action. Helping homeless children and preventing homelessness may also depend on national acceptance of the idea that poor children belong to all of us. Certainly, their development will affect all of our futures.

Recommended Reading

Institute of Medicine. (1988). *Homelessness, Health, and Human Needs* (National Academy Press, Washington, DC).

Rafferty, Y., and Shinn, M. (1991). The impact of homelessness on children. *American Psychologist, 46,* 1170–1179.

Acknowledgments—Support for the author's research on homeless children, partially described in this article, was provided by a McKnight Professorship and a Graduate School Grant-in-Aid award from the University of Minnesota.

Notes

1. Address correspondence to Ann S. Masten, University of Minnesota, 51 East River Rd., Minneapolis, MN 55455.

2. M.J. Robertson, *Characteristics and circumstances of homeless adolescents in Hollywood,* paper presented at the annual meeting of the American Psychological Association, Boston (August 1990).

3. A.S. Masten, D. Miliotis, S.A. Graham-Bermann, M. Ramirez, and J. Neemann, *Children in homeless families: Risks to mental health and development,* manuscript submitted for publication (1991).

4. J.D. Wright, Homelessness is not healthy for children and other living things, in *Homeless Children: The Watchers and the Waiters,* N.A. Boxhill, Ed. (Haworth Press, New York, 1990).

5. W. Chavkin, A. Kristal, C. Seabron, and P.E. Guigli, The reproductive experience of women living in hotels for the homeless in New York City, *New York State Journal of Medicine, 87,* 10–13 (1987).

6. J. Molnar, W.R. Rath, T.P. Klein, C. Lowe, and A.H. Hartmann, *III Fares the Land: The Consequences of Homelessness and Chronic Poverty for Children and Families in New York City* (Bank Street College of Education, New York, 1991).

7. L. Rescorla, R. Parker, and P. Stolley, Ability, achievement, and adjustment in homeless children, *American Journal of Orthopsychiatry, 61,* 210–220 (1991).

8. E.L. Bassuk and L. Rosenberg, Psychosocial characteristics of homeless children and children with homes, *Pediatrics, 85,* 257–261 (1990).

9. D.L. Wood, R.B. Valdez, T. Hayashi, and A. Shen, Health of homeless children and housed, poor children, *Pediatrics, 86,* 858–866 (1990).

10. C.M. Johnson, L. Miranda, A. Sherman, and J.D. Weill, *Child Poverty in America* (Children's Defense Fund, Washington, DC, 1991).

This article has been reprinted as it originally appeared in *Current Directions in Psychological Science*. Citation information for this article as originally published appears above.

Contextual Influences on Marriage: Implications for Policy and Intervention

Benjamin R. Karney[1]
RAND Corporation

Thomas N. Bradbury
University of California, Los Angeles

Abstract

Current proposals to promote and strengthen marriage among low-income populations focus on values and behavioral skills as primary targets of intervention. Marital research that examines contextual influences on marriage calls these emphases into question. Ethnographic and survey research reveal no evidence that populations experiencing higher rates of divorce value healthy marriages any less than other populations do. Longitudinal and observational research reveals two mechanisms through which the environment of a marriage may enhance or constrain effective relationship maintenance. First, some environments contain fewer sources of support and pose more severe challenges than others, presenting marriages in those environments with greater burdens than marriages in more supportive environments are faced with. Second, when demands external to the marriage are relatively high, even couples with adequate coping skills may have difficulty exercising those skills effectively. Together, such findings suggest that successful policies and interventions to strengthen marriages need to acknowledge the environments within which marriages take place.

Keywords

marriage; family policy; stress; relationship maintenance

To improve the well-being of low-income populations, federal policymakers have begun to emphasize the role of healthy marriages in shaping adult and child outcomes. The justification for this emphasis on marriage has been correlational research demonstrating that stable, fulfilling marriages are associated with improved physical and mental health and higher educational and economic achievement for parents and children and that the absence of such relationships is associated with poorer health and economic outcomes (e.g., Amato, 2001; Kiecolt-Glaser & Newton, 2001). Assuming that the parents' relationship plays a causal role in these associations, policymakers have proposed allocating over 1.5 billion dollars over the next 5 years to fund activities that support couples in forming and maintaining healthy marriages. Legislation currently being debated in the House and Senate specifies eight allowable activities for this funding, all of which involve some form of relationship education—e.g., teaching the value of stable marriages or teaching relationship and communication skills. Federal policy seems to be guided by two perspectives: one emphasizing values and another focusing on skills as primary determinants of marital outcome.

One challenge to applying educational interventions to low-income families stems from the fact that, although the target populations for these initiatives have been selected exclusively on the basis of their environment (i.e., low socioeconomic status), the models guiding educational interventions generally do not address the role of the environment in determining marital outcomes. Behaviorally oriented relationship education, for example, places the responsibility for marital success or failure squarely on the couple, without regard for how their relationship may be affected by the context within which their marriage takes place. Recent marital research that has directly examined the effects of context on couples' relationships calls this emphasis into question. Cross-sectional surveys and longitudinal studies of newlywed couples have begun to identify paths through which communication, problem solving, and other relationship processes may be constrained or enhanced by supports or demands present in a marriage's context. The emerging picture suggests that even skilled and relatively satisfied couples may have difficulty interacting effectively under conditions of stress or diminished resources. Thus, current research on contextual influences on marriage suggests broadening the focus of interventions and policies designed to support healthy families among low-income populations.

FAMILY VALUES: WHO HAS THEM? WHO NEEDS THEM?

Marriages are unquestionably less frequent and less stable in low-income populations. Survey data reveal that, compared to those in high-income populations, women in low-income populations are half as likely to be married, twice as likely to divorce if married, and several times more likely to bear children outside of marriage (Bramlett & Mosher, 2002; Singh, Matthews, Clarke, Yannicos, & Smith, 1995). The case for offering values education to these individuals rests on the assumption that people in low-income populations do not appreciate the benefits of stable, healthy marriages as much as do people in high-income populations, in which marriage is more common and divorce less common.

In fact, there has been little research on attitudes toward family issues in low-income populations, but what research does exist indicates that members of these populations may value marriage more, not less, than members of middle- or high-income groups do. For example, Edin (2000) conducted lengthy interviews with unmarried mothers receiving welfare, asking them to describe their attitudes and intentions toward marriage. Far from minimizing the importance of marriage, these mothers reported strongly positive feelings about the institution and expressed their own intentions to marry. They described their decisions to postpone marriage as having little to do with their values and more to do with their belief that their current economic circumstances and available partners would be unlikely to lead to an enduring marriage over time. Thus, members of low-income populations may postpone marriage not because they value it too little but rather because they value it so much that they are unwilling to enter into a marriage that has a high risk of ending in divorce.

It is important to note that Edin's data exclude low-income men, who are notoriously underrepresented in family research. However, quantitative survey data from low-income men and women paint a similar picture. A recent survey commissioned by the state of Florida examined family structures and attitudes in a representative sample (Karney, Garvan, & Thomas, 2003). Over 6,000 residents

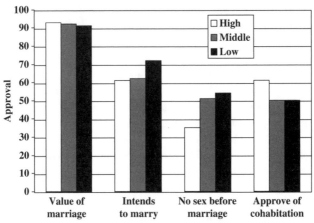

Fig. 1. Attitudes toward family issues by household income (high, middle, low). The low-income groups that report the highest rates of divorce, premarital sex, and cohabitation also express the lowest approval of them.

of Florida, Texas, California, and New York were asked in telephone interviews about their own experiences of marriage and families and about their opinions regarding marriage and family issues. Confirming the pattern in the broader census data, low-income respondents were far more likely than high-income respondents to be unmarried, to be divorced, and to be raising children outside of marriage. At the same time, however, compared to middle- or high-income respondents, members of low-income populations on average expressed the same or more positive attitudes toward traditional family structures (see Fig. 1). For example, when asked to rate their agreement with the statement "A happy, healthy marriage is one of the most important things in life," low-income respondents indicated that they agreed or strongly agreed at the same rate as did middle- and high-income respondents. When unmarried respondents were asked if they would like to be married someday, members of low-income households were substantially more likely than members of middle- or high-income households to say yes.

Existing research offers little justification for allocating limited resources toward values education for low-income populations. At least among women in this population, promarriage values appear to be in place already, and in any case such values may not be sufficient to bring about stable, fulfilling relationships.

CONTEXTUAL INFLUENCES ON MARRIAGE

Whereas there is little evidence that values are associated with decisions to enter into or postpone marriage, there is growing evidence to suggest that the quality of a couple's communication and problem solving is associated with marital outcomes over time (Heyman, 2001; Johnson et al., 2005). Furthermore, several studies provide evidence that premarital education programs focusing on communication can affect problem solving and that such programs may have long-term benefits for marriages (e.g., Halford, Sanders, & Behrens, 2001).

Despite this evidence, the existing research has been limited in two main ways. First, research on marital interaction and premarital education programs has addressed primarily white, college-educated, middle-class samples. In terms of their risk of experiencing marital dysfunction, the support available to them, and the demands they face outside of the marriage, such samples differ greatly from the low-income populations of interest to policymakers. It remains an open question whether programs developed within middle-class populations can be effective for improving the marriages of low-income couples. Second, when assessing relationship processes like problem solving and support, researchers have assumed that such processes are generally stable in the absence of intervention. Research on marital interactions in particular has treated the quality of a couple's communication as a stable, trait-like condition of the relationship that accounts for later marital outcomes. Far less frequent has been research on how marital interactions and relationship processes themselves may vary and develop over time. As a result, the conditions that encourage or discourage effective interactions in marriage remain poorly understood.

Current research on the effects of context and environmental stress on marital processes is beginning to illuminate both of these issues. Drawing from cross-sectional survey research, researchers have begun to examine relationship processes across a wide range of contexts and cultures, to understand how the predictors of marital success may differ depending on the context within which particular marriages form and develop. Using intensive longitudinal designs, researchers have begun to identify the correlates of variability in relationship processes within couples over time, in order to understand the forces that support or constrain couples in their efforts to maintain their relationships. Although it has long been known that marriages under stress report lower marital quality and are at increased risk of dissolution (e.g., Hill, 1949), research adopting these approaches has now elaborated on the mechanisms through which context affects marriage.

Context Shapes the Content of Marital Interactions

An emphasis on relationship skills reflects the assumption that the way couples communicate is more important than the specific issues they discuss. One reason that this assumption has gone unchallenged may be that studies have examined couples in a relatively narrow and privileged segment of the population whose problems are, on average, relatively mild. Surveying a broader range of the population, however, confirms that the couples in different contexts may face different sorts of marital problems. For example, when respondents rated the severity of potential relationship problems in the survey cited earlier (Karney et al., 2003), communication was rated as a relatively severe problem regardless of household income, although it was rated most severe in high-income households (see Fig. 2). Drugs and infidelity, in contrast, were rated as more severe problems by low-income households. Research on middle-class newlyweds indicates that spouses tend to report more severe relationship problems during periods of relatively high stress than they do during periods of relatively low stress (Neff & Karney, 2004). Not surprisingly, the more severe the problems discussed by a couple, the more negatively their communication is rated by objective observers (Vogel & Karney, 2002). Thus, independent of spouses' relationship skills, marriages taking place in more stressful contexts may be more challenging simply due to the

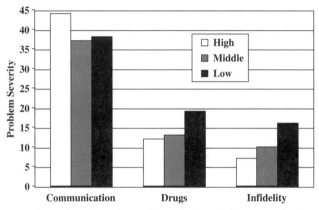

Fig. 2. Severity of specific relationship problems by household income (high, middle, low). Although couples at all income levels report problems with communication, low-income couples are more likely to report problems with drugs or infidelity.

increased severity of the obstacles that couples must face inside and outside of their marriages. Interventions that acknowledge those obstacles may prove more effective than interventions addressing communication skills alone.

Context Affects Spouses' Ability to Interact Effectively

When the context of a marriage contains many demands and few sources of support, spouses not only have more severe problems to cope with but may also have diminished ability to exercise the coping skills they possess. A 4-year study of 172 middle-class newlywed couples (Karney, Story, & Bradbury, 2005) revealed that couples experiencing relatively high levels of chronic stress (e.g., financial difficulties, lack of social support, inadequate employment) not only reported lower marital satisfaction overall but also seemed to have more difficulty maintaining their satisfaction over time. Relative to couples reporting better conditions, those reporting high levels of chronic stress experienced a steeper decline in marital satisfaction over the early years of marriage, a finding that held even after these couples' initially lower levels of satisfaction was controlled for. Moreover, for wives experiencing chronic stress, marital satisfaction was especially reactive to increases in acute stress, such that the same negative life events were associated with steeper declines in satisfaction for stressed wives than they were for less stressed wives.

Why would marital satisfaction be more difficult to maintain when conditions outside of the marriage are more adverse? The activities that maintain relationships take time and energy, so those activities should be harder to undertake under adverse conditions. Supporting this view is an independent study of 82 middle-class newlyweds that examined how spouses' willingness to forgive their partners' negative behaviors was associated with changes in their levels of stress over time (Neff & Karney, 2004). Within-couple analyses revealed that individuals who could excuse their partners' negative behaviors during intervals of relatively low stress were more likely to blame their partners for those same behaviors during periods of relatively high stress. In other words, spouses who are capable of making adaptive responses appear to be less likely to do so when facing challenges outside of their marriages.

It is worth noting that both of these studies sampled from a population experiencing a relatively narrow range of stress. In samples that included severely disadvantaged families, Conger and colleagues (e.g., Conger, Rueter, & Elder, 1999) also showed that economic strain inhibits effective relationship maintenance. Together, such studies begin to suggest how stressful environments come to be associated with negative marital outcomes. Stressful environments not only present couples with more challenges, but they diminish those couples' ability to deal with their challenges effectively.

IMPLICATIONS FOR MARITAL INTERVENTIONS AND POLICIES

Given what is currently known about the effects of context on marriage and marital processes, there are two reasons to expect that, by themselves, interventions developed for middle-class couples may not be adequate to support marriages among the low-income couples of interest to policymakers. First, the skills relevant to solving the problems faced by middle- and upper-income couples may not be relevant to the types of problems (e.g., substance abuse, domestic violence, infidelity) that low-income couples are more likely than other populations to face. Second, even if a set of valuable relationship skills could be identified and taught, those skills may be difficult or impossible to practice in the context of low-income marriage. Effective problem solving will matter little, for example, to couples who have few opportunities to interact together due to demands outside the marriage. Providing such couples with relationship skills training without also addressing the external forces that impede couples' ability to practice those skills may be akin to offering piano lessons to people with no access to a piano.

Providing a solid empirical foundation for interventions to promote and support low-income marriage requires basic research on marriage in this population, not only to identify the processes that make for successful relationships among low-income couples, but also to describe the circumstances that make those processes more or less likely. The unfortunate irony is that, just as this research is needed to inform policy, funding for research on marital outcomes has been explicitly removed from consideration at the National Institute of Mental Health, formerly the major source of support for marital research.

The drive to provide services that improve the lives of low-income families thus presents marital research with a challenge and an opportunity. The challenge is to find ways to specify the minimum conditions that must be met before behavioral skills training can have a positive impact on low-income marriages. The opportunity is the chance to reexamine what is known about the significant predictors of marital outcome in this new context, and thereby to establish which of those predictors are not only significant, but substantial.

Recommended Reading

Bradbury, T.N. & Karney, B.R. (2004). Understanding and altering the longitudinal course of marriage. *Journal of Marriage and Family, 66,* 862–879.

Edin, K., & Kefalas, M. (2005). *Promises I can keep: Why poor women put motherhood before marriage*. Berkeley: University of California Press.

Cherlin, A.J. (2004). The deinstitutionalization of American marriage. *Journal of Marriage and Family, 66*, 848–861.

Acknowledgments—Preparation of this article was supported by Grant R01MH59712 from the National Institute of Mental Health awarded to the first author, and Grant R01MH48764 from the National Institute of Mental Health awarded to the second author.

Note

1. Address correspondence to Benjamin R. Karney, RAND Corporation, 1776 Main Street, P.O. Box 2138, Santa Monica, CA 90407-2138; e-mail: bkarney@rand.org.

References

Amato, P.R. (2001). Children of divorce in the 1990s: An update of the Amato and Keith (1991) meta-analysis. *Journal of Family Psychology, 15*, 355–370.

Bramlett, M.D., & Mosher, W.D. (2002). *Cohabitation, marriage, divorce, and remarriage in the United States* (Vital and Health Statistics Series 23, No. 22). Hyattsville, Maryland: National Center for Health Statistics.

Conger, R.D., Rueter, M.A., & Elder, G.H. (1999). Couple resilience to economic pressure. *Journal of Personality and Social Psychology, 76*, 54–71.

Edin, K. (2000). What do low-income single mothers say about marriage? *Social Problems, 47*, 112–133.

Halford, W.K., Sanders, M.R., & Behrens, B.C. (2001). Can skills training prevent relationship problems in at-risk couples? Four-year effects of a behavioral relationship education program. *Journal of Family Psychology, 15*, 750–768.

Heyman, R.E. (2001). Observation of couple conflicts: Clinical assessment applications, stubborn truths, and shaky foundations. *Psychological Assessment, 13*, 5–35.

Hill, R. (1949). *Families under stress*. New York: Harper & Row.

Johnson, M.D., Cohan, C.L., Davila, J., Lawrence, E., Rogge, R.D., Karney, B.R., Sullivan, K.T., & Bradbury, T.N. (2005). Problem-solving skills and affective expressions as predictors of change in marital satisfaction. *Journal of Consulting and Clinical Psychology, 73*, 15–27.

Karney, B.R., Garvan, C.W., & Thomas, M.S. (2003). *Family formation in Florida: 2003 baseline survey of attitudes, beliefs, and demographics relating to marriage and family formation*. Gainesville, FL: University of Florida.

Karney, B.R., Story, L.B., & Bradbury, T.N. (2005). Marriages in context: Interactions between chronic and acute stress among newlyweds. In T.A. Revenson, K. Kayser, & G. Bodenmann (Eds.), *Emerging perspectives on couples' coping with stress* (pp. 13–32). Washington, DC: American Psychological Association.

Kiecolt-Glaser, J.K., & Newton, T.L. (2001). Marriage and health: His and hers. *Psychological Bulletin, 127*, 472–503.

Neff, L.A., & Karney, B.R. (2004). How does context affect intimate relationships? Linking external stress and cognitive processes within marriage. *Personality and Social Psychology Bulletin, 30*, 134–148.

Singh, G.K., Matthews, T.J., Clarke, S.C., Yannicos, T., & Smith, B.L. (1995). *Annual summary of births, marriages, divorces, and deaths: United States, 1994* (Monthly Vital Statistics Report, Vol. 43, No. 13). Atlanta, GA: National Center for Health Statistics.

Vogel, D.L., & Karney, B.R. (2002). Demands and withdrawal in newlyweds: Elaborating on the social structure hypothesis. *Journal of Social and Personal Relationships, 19*, 685–702.

This article has been reprinted as it originally appeared in *Current Directions in Psychological Science*. Citation information for this article as originally published appears above.

Children of the Affluent: Challenges to Well-Being

Suniya S. Luthar[1] and Shawn J. Latendresse
Teachers College, Columbia University

Abstract

Growing up in the culture of affluence can connote various psychosocial risks. Studies have shown that upper-class children can manifest elevated disturbance in several areas—such as substance use, anxiety, and depression—and that two sets of factors seem to be implicated, that is, excessive pressures to achieve and isolation from parents (both literal and emotional). Whereas stereotypically, affluent youth and poor youth are respectively thought of as being at "low risk" and "high risk," comparative studies have revealed more similarities than differences in their adjustment patterns and socialization processes. In the years ahead, psychologists must correct the long-standing neglect of a group of youngsters treated, thus far, as not needing their attention. Family wealth does not automatically confer either wisdom in parenting or equanimity of spirit; whereas children rendered atypical by virtue of their parents' wealth are undoubtedly privileged in many respects, there is also, clearly, the potential for some nontrivial threats to their psychological well-being.

Keywords

affluence; risk; contextual influences; socioeconomic status

Children of upper-class, highly educated parents are generally assumed to be at "low risk," but recent evidence suggests that they can face several unacknowledged pressures. In this article, we describe programmatic research relevant to this issue. We begin by characterizing the samples of youth we have studied across suburban communities in the Northeast. We then provide an overview of findings of problems in various spheres of adjustment and discuss associated implications for research, practice, and policy.

RESEARCH INVOLVING UPPER-CLASS SAMPLES

Since the late 1990s, our group has accumulated data on three cohorts of youth from high-income communities; characteristics of these cohorts are summarized in Table 1 (p. 122). The first, which we refer to as Cohort I, consisted of 264 tenth graders attending a suburban high school serving three contiguous towns.[2] These students were followed annually through their senior year, and as sophomores, we contrasted them with 224 tenth graders in an inner-city school.

Cohort II encompassed 302 middle school students from another high-income town, whom we studied when they were in the sixth and seventh grades (Luthar & Becker, 2002). Cohort III, subsequently recruited from the same community as Cohort II, incorporated all children attending the sixth grade during the 1998–1999 academic year, and these students were then followed annually (11th-grade assessments had been completed at the time of writing this report).

In parallel, we obtained annual assessments of an inner-city middle school sample, enabling further comparisons of youngsters from widely disparate socio-demographic settings.

EVIDENCE OF ADJUSTMENT DISTURBANCES

The first set of questions addressed with Cohort I was focused on substance use and related problems (Luthar & D'Avanzo, 1999), and descriptive analyses showed many signs of trouble among the suburban students. These youngsters reported significantly higher use of cigarettes, alcohol, marijuana, and hard drugs than did their inner-city counterparts, and also showed elevations in comparison with national norms. Suburban teens also reported significantly higher anxiety and somewhat higher depression than did inner-city youth. In comparison with normative samples, girls in the suburbs were three times more likely to report clinically significant levels of depression.

Also disturbing were findings on correlates of substance use. Among affluent (but not inner-city) youth, substance use was linked with depression and anxiety, suggesting efforts to self-medicate; this "negative affect" type of substance use tends to be sustained over time, rather than remitting soon after the teen years. In addition, among suburban boys (but not other subgroups in the study), popularity with classmates was linked with high substance use, suggesting that the peer group may endorse and even encourage substance use among affluent teenage boys.

In Cohort II, we saw no evidence of disturbance among the sixth graders, but among the seventh graders, some problems were beginning to emerge (Luthar & Becker, 2002). Among the older girls, for example, rates of clinically significant depressive symptoms were twice as high as those in normative samples. Whereas no boys in the sixth grade had used alcohol or marijuana, 7% of seventh-grade boys reported having drunk alcohol until intoxicated or using marijuana about once a month. Finally, results supported the earlier findings on correlates of substance use, which had significant links with depression and anxiety in this middle school sample, and with peer popularity among the seventh-grade boys.

In Cohort III, as well, preliminary data showed that suburban sixth graders scored below national norms on depression and anxiety, and also had lower scores than inner-city comparison youth. Once again, however, some signs of trouble began to emerge by the seventh grade, with popular students, for example, report-ing significantly higher levels of substance use than others (Luthar & Sexton, 2004). We are currently examining different developmental pathways to problems and to well-being from pre- through midadolescence.

WHY MIGHT "PRIVILEGED" YOUTH BE TROUBLED?

In exploring pathways to maladjustment in affluent suburbia, we considered two sets of potential antecedents in our study of Cohort II. The first encompassed *achievement pressures*. Statistical analyses showed, in fact, that children with very high perfectionist strivings—those who saw achievement failures as per-sonal failures—had relatively high depression, anxiety, and substance use, as did

Table 1. *Characteristics of the samples*

Source and sample	N	Minority ethnicity in sample (%)
Luthar & D'Avanzo (1999)		
Suburban Cohort I: 10th graders followed		
through high school	264	18
Comparison sample: inner-city 10th graders	224	87
Luthar & Becker (2002)		
Suburban Cohort II: 6th and 7th graders	302	8
Luthar & Latendresse (in press)		
Suburban Cohort III: 6th graders followed		
annually through high school (ongoing)	314	7
Comparison sample: inner-city 6th graders		
followed through 8th grade	300	80

those who indicated that their parents overemphasized their accomplishments, valuing them disproportionately more than their personal character (Luthar & Becker, 2002).

The second potential antecedent was *isolation from adults*, both literal and emotional. Among upper-middle-class families, secondary school students are often left home alone for several hours each week, with many parents believing that this promotes self-sufficiency. Similarly, suburban children's needs for emotional closeness may often suffer as the demands of professional parents' careers erode relaxed "family time" and youngsters are shuttled between various after-school activities. Again, results showed that both literal and emotional isolation were linked to distress as well as substance use.

We next sought to explore family functioning in greater depth among sixth graders in Cohort III and, simultaneously, their inner-city counterparts. A common assumption is that parents are more accessible to high- than to low-income youth, but our data showed otherwise (Luthar & Latendresse, in press). We considered children's perceptions of seven aspects of parenting, and average ratings on four of these dimensions were similar for the two sets of students: felt closeness to mothers, felt closeness to fathers, parental values emphasizing integrity, and regularity of eating dinner with parents. Inner-city students did fare more poorly than suburban students on two of the remaining three dimensions—parental criticism and lack of after-school supervision—but at the same time, they did significantly better than suburban students on the last dimension, parental expectations.

Results also revealed the surprising unique significance of children's eating dinner with at least one parent on most nights. Even after the other six parenting dimensions (including emotional closeness both to mothers and to fathers) were taken into account, this simple family routine was linked not only to children's self-reported adjustment, but also to their performance at school. Striking, too, were the similarities of links involving family dining among families ostensibly easily able to arrange for shared leisure time and those who had to cope with the sundry exigencies of everyday life in poverty.

Eligible for free or reduced lunch in school (%)	Median annual family income in region (census)	Adults with graduate or professional degrees in region (%; census)
1	$80,000–$102,000	24–37
86	$35,000	5
3	$120,000	33
3	$125,000	33
79	$27,000	6

Subsequent analyses with Cohort III students and their inner-city counterparts when they were in the seventh grade revealed similarities in peer-group influences as well (Luthar & Sexton, 2004). Early adolescents at both socioeconomic extremes showed admiration for classmates who openly flouted authority. In the suburban context, high peer status was linked with overt displays of low academic effort, disobedience at school, aggressiveness among girls, and substance use among boys, and in the urban context, high peer status was associated with aggression and substance use among both boys and girls. Also noteworthy were startlingly strong links between physical attractiveness and peer popularity among affluent girls. This variable alone explained more than half the variation in their popularity scores, suggesting particularly high emphasis on physical appearance among this subgroup of girls (the links between attractiveness and popularity were substantially weaker among inner-city girls and among both groups of boys). All in all, the substantive message was that affluent adolescents, just like their inner-city counterparts, valued some peer attributes that could potentially compromise overall competence or well-being.

DOES REBELLION AMONG AFFLUENT TEENS REALLY "MATTER"?

All adolescents might be drawn to overt forms of rebellion, but it is quite plausible that wealthy youth, unlike their poor counterparts, can dabble in drug use or delinquency without any substantive damage to their life prospects, given various safety nets (i.e., concerned adults and access to high-quality treatment services). To examine this possibility, we returned to our high school Cohort I data, as older teens reflect more variability on such forms of behavioral deviance than middle school students do. Once again, our findings showed that youth at the socioeconomic extremes were more similar than different (Luthar & Ansary, in press). In both settings, we found a distinct subgroup of teens who manifested multiple behavior problems—substance use, delinquency, poor interest in academics—and had school grades that were significantly lower than the average. Although the findings on urban adolescents were unsurprising in light of prior empirical evidence, the results on affluent youth were noteworthy in indicating that, despite the resources ostensibly available to them, nearly 1 of every 10 teenagers in this cohort exhibited high levels of behavior disturbances across multiple domains, and concurrently experienced significant risk for poor grades during the sophomore year of high school.

We also examined substance use among this subgroup of suburban sophomores annually through the remainder of high school (McMahon & Luthar, 2004). Twenty percent of these students showed persistently high substance use across time. Furthermore, across all three assessments, this group also showed relatively high levels of depression and physiologically manifest anxiety (e.g., nausea, difficulty breathing), as well as poor grades and negative teacher ratings. For as many as one in five of these affluent youth, therefore, high substance use, coexisting with depression, anxiety, and both behavioral and academic problems, was sustained up to the age of 18 years.

IMPLICATIONS FOR INTERVENTIONS

All is not necessarily well among children of the affluent. Across three suburban cohorts, a nontrivial proportion of youth reported diverse adjustment problems, and disconnectedness in families and pressured lifestyles constituted discernible challenges (for parallel evidence among adult samples, see Csikszentmihalyi, 1999; Kasser, 2002; Myers, 2000).

Why do affluent youth have these problems—despite all the mental health services ostensibly available? One possibility is that although high-income parents are generally willing to place overtly troubled youth in psychotherapy or on medication, they are less eager to delve into the less "conspicuous" problems in their children, in themselves, or in family processes more generally. Research has shown, for example, that parents in general tend to be aware when their children are depressed, but tend not to seek professional help unless symptoms include those that inconvenience adults, such as disobedience or asthma (Puura et al., 1998).

Upper-class parents can be particularly reluctant to seek help for the less visible problems because of privacy concerns, as well as embarrassment. Affluent adults are often very concerned about keeping family troubles private; this is not surprising, as misfortunes of the wealthy tend to evoke a malicious pleasure in people who are less well-off (a phenomenon called *schadenfreude;* see Feather & Sherman, 2002). Upper-class parents also can feel more compelled than most to maintain a veneer of well-being, feeling that "those at the top are supposed to be better able to handle their problems than those further down the scale" (Wolfe & Fodor, 1996, p. 80).

Then there are realities of everyday lives that impede change. In the subculture of affluent suburbia, overscheduled days are often the norm for young people, with high school students participating in numerous activities, which can then be logged on college applications. The careers of many parents, similarly, do in fact demand long work hours: Job sharing and flexible hours are not an option for chief executive officers or university presidents. At the same time, these careers do bring many personal rewards, including the gratification of mastering substantial professional challenges, and of providing well for stellar educations and leisure activities for the next generation. Few people would blithely repudiate such rewards.

Also relevant is practitioners' perseverance—or lack thereof—in pursuing nascent signs of trouble. School psychologists, for example, often hesitate to express concerns to high-income parents, anticipating resistance and sometimes even threats of lawsuits. Consequently (and paradoxically), wealthy youth can end up having less access to school-based counseling services than do students who are less well-off (Pollak & Schaffer, 1985). Clinicians may also minimize problems they see among the wealthy. The same symptoms are more often viewed as signs of mental illness among the poor than among the affluent; by corollary, the rich are more often dismissed as "not needing help" even when they report distress commensurate with that of others typically judged to be needing assistance (Luthar & Sexton, 2004).

Even if affluent youth do, in fact, receive high-quality psychiatric care, it should be emphasized that this is no substitute for strong attachments with parents. Decades of work on children's mental health policies have established that psychotherapy to address crystallized maladjustment is largely unproductive as long as the child's everyday life continues to present major challenges to adjustment (Knitzer, 2000).

In the future, an expedient first step toward addressing these issues would be to raise awareness of the potential costs of overscheduled, competitive lifestyles (Luthar & Sexton, 2004). This can be done effectively via books comprehensible to the lay public, such as those by Kasser (2002) and Myers (2000). Although obviously not panaceas, such dissemination efforts could begin to sensitize caregivers to risks in the context of affluence—risks that they (like developmental scientists) may have been only faintly aware of in the past.

Consideration of these issues is important not only for the families themselves, but also for society in general. Many children of highly educated, affluent parents will likely come to assume positions of influence in society, and their own equanimity of spirit may have far-reaching ramifications. Depression vastly impairs productivity. And people who are unhappy, with a fragile, meager sense of self, can be more acquisitive than philanthropic, focused more on gaining more for themselves than on improving the lot of others (Diener & Biswas-Diener, 2002).

CONCLUSIONS

Until the 1970s, developmental scientists had largely ignored children in poverty, and it is critical to correct the neglect of another group of youngsters heretofore invisible in psychological science: those in high-income families. Systematic research is needed on the generalizability of research results obtained thus far. Scientists need to establish, for instance, whether elevated distress or pressured lifestyles occur in wealthy metropolitan locations, and not just in suburban communities. It will also be important to determine whether these problems are discernible in nationally representative samples (assuming, of course, that high-income families are appropriately represented in them). Also critical are prospective studies that can indicate (a) whether problems such as depression or drug use generally represent temporary blips of adolescent angst among the wealthy or are early signs of continuing problems and, conversely, (b) if factors such as prolonged isolation and pressure within families do, in fact, set apart those teens who carry adolescent adjustment disturbances into adulthood. Finally, practitioners and parents must be alert to the risks potentially attached to wealth and status. The American dream spawns widespread beliefs that Ivy League educations and subsequently lucrative careers are critical for children's long-term happiness. In the sometimes single-minded pursuit of these goals, let us not lose sight of the possible costs to mental health and well-being of all concerned.

Recommended Reading

Csikszentmihalyi, M. (1999). (See References)
Kasser, T. (2002). (See References)
Luthar, S.S. (2003). The culture of affluence: Psychological costs of material wealth. *Child Development, 74*, 1581–1593.
Luthar, S.S., & Sexton, C. (2004). (See References)
Myers, D.G. (2000). (See References)

Acknowledgments—Preparation of this manuscript was supported by grants from the National Institutes of Health (RO1-DA10726, RO1-DA11498, RO1-DA14385), the William T. Grant Foundation, and the Spencer Foundation.

Notes

1. Address correspondence to Suniya S. Luthar, Teachers College, Columbia University, 525 West 120th St., Box 133, New York, NY 10027-6696.
2. We are currently examining effects of varying affluence across neighborhoods subsumed in wealthy townships.

References

Csikszentmihalyi, M. (1999). If we are so rich, why aren't we happy? *American Psychologist, 54*, 821–827.
Diener, E., & Biswas-Diener, R. (2002). Will money increase subjective well-being? *Social Indicators Research, 57*, 119–169.
Feather, N.T., & Sherman, R. (2002). Envy, resentment, Schadenfreude, and sympathy: Reactions to deserved and undeserved achievement and subsequent failure. *Personality and Social Psychology Bulletin, 28*, 953–961.
Kasser, T. (2002). *The high price of materialism*. Cambridge, MA: MIT Press.
Knitzer, J. (2000). Early childhood mental health services: A policy and systems development perspective. In J.P. Shonkoff & S.J. Meisels (Eds.), *Handbook of early childhood intervention* (2nd ed., pp. 416–438). New York: Cambridge University Press.
Luthar, S.S., & Ansary, N.S. (in press). Dimensions of adolescent rebellion: Risks for academic failure among high- and low-income youth. *Development and Psychopathology*.
Luthar, S.S., & Becker, B.E. (2002). Privileged but pressured: A study of affluent youth. *Child Development, 73*, 1593–1610.
Luthar, S.S., & D'Avanzo, K. (1999). Contextual factors in substance use: A study of suburban and inner-city adolescents. *Development and Psychopathology, 11*, 845–867.
Luthar, S.S., & Latendresse, S.J. (in press). Comparable "risks" at the SES extremes: Pre-adolescents' perceptions of parenting. *Development and Psychopathology*.

Luthar, S.S., & Sexton, C. (2004). The high price of affluence. In R.V. Kail (Ed.), *Advances in child development* (Vol. 32, pp. 126–162). San Diego, CA: Academic Press.

McMahon, T.J., & Luthar, S.S. (2004). *Substance use, psychopathology, and social competence: A longitudinal study of affluent, suburban, high school students.* Manuscript submitted for publication.

Myers, D.G. (2000). *The American paradox: Spiritual hunger in an age of plenty.* New Haven, CT: Yale University Press.

Pollak, J.M., & Schaffer, S. (1985). The mental health clinician in the affluent public school setting. *Clinical Social Work Journal, 13,* 341–355.

Puura, K., Almqvist, F., Tamminen, T., Piha, J., Kumpulainen, K., Raesaenen, E., Moilanen, I., & Koivisto, A.M. (1998). Children with symptoms of depression: What do adults see? *Journal of Child Psychology and Psychiatry and Allied Disciplines, 39,* 577–585.

Wolfe, J.L., & Fodor, I.G. (1996). The poverty of privilege: Therapy with women of the "upper classes." *Women & Therapy, 18,* 73–89.

Section 3: Critical Thinking Questions

1. Why is it difficult to be sure that associations between environmental circumstances and individual outcomes are causal? How do the authors in this section deal with this problem?

2. What is the paradox posed by natural disasters for research on social support?

3. How do Adam's findings on effects of family instability inform Masten's research on homelessness?

4. Masten states that "homeless children appear to represent the ominous tip of the iceberg of poverty." Elsewhere she describes homelessness as falling on one end of a "continuum of risk." Does the evidence suggest that homelessness is symptomatic of extreme poverty or that homeless children are categorically different from other children living in poverty?

5. Karney and Bradbury remark on the fact that people are targeted for interventions to promote healthy marriages on the basis of their environment (low socioeconomic status), but the interventions focus on education and skills and ignore the environment. What sort of intervention might be more appropriate?

6. Luthar and Latendresse hypothesize that "overscheduled competitive lifestyles" may be responsible for the adjustment problems of affluent children. Does Larsen's data on time use in Section 1 support this conjecture? Why or why not?

Section 4: Prevention and Promotion Programs

A central goal of community psychology is to prevent dysfunction and promote well-being of people in communities. Unlike clinical psychologists, who often wait for people to experience problems and seek out clinicians for help, community psychologists work with people to prevent problems before they arise, sometimes in special programs, but more often in the natural settings of their lives. And rather than seeing individuals one at a time in therapy, community psychologists endeavor to affect the health and welfare of groups of people.

Prevention and promotion programs have many forms. They may work with natural help-givers or modify schools, work organizations, and other social environments so that they are less stressful and more conducive to positive development. They may strengthen individual coping skills or support networks so that people can manage stressors and challenges better, or they may help to empower people to take more control of their environments. Often programs work on both individual and environmental levels simultaneously, and both reduce risk factors for adverse outcomes and increase protective factors that reduce risk.

Intervention strategies are based on theories and formative research about how personal and environmental factors combine to influence health and well-being and additional theories about how prevention and promotion programs work. Research on interventions, typically in randomized experiments, serves two functions: First, it tests the underlying theories (much as a laboratory psychologist manipulates experimental conditions to test theory). Second, in a more applied vein, it shows whether an intervention successfully improved the targeted aspect of people's lives.

The first two articles describe prevention and promotion efforts focusing on school settings. Olweus intervenes at the level of the school, the classroom, and individual students in a comprehensive effort to reduce bullying in schools. A number of studies conducted after he wrote this article have shown that his program is effective in American schools. Christenson and Thurlow summarize literature on interventions to prevent school dropout and promote completion; they suggest that additional research is needed to craft better programs to engage students.

The next two articles attempt to promote youth development by creating more positive relationships between young people and adults. Mentoring programs that provide youth with caring adult mentors are one of the most popular social interventions but not one that is universally effective. Rhodes and DuBois review characteristics of successful mentoring relationships, including how they come about and how they produce positive outcomes. Team sports are naturally occurring settings where youth develop relationships with adult coaches that are often similar to mentoring relationships. Smith and Smoll describe an intervention to train coaches to have more positive influences on their players.

Prevention programs need not focus only on youth. The last two articles in this section describe group-based interventions to prevent the spread of HIV and to prevent depression among adults who have lost jobs. Albarracín, Durantini, and Earl review over 350 interventions focused on preventing risky behaviors that can transmit HIV and abstract five general principles underlying program success. Price examines how job loss increases stress, family conflict, and risk for depression and shows that a short-term intervention can reduce the incidence of depression and help participants become re-employed in better jobs. Together, the articles in this section show important effects of prevention and promotion programs on health, mental health, and behavior for both youth and adults.

Bullying or Peer Abuse at School: Facts and Intervention

Dan Olweus[1]

University of Bergen, Norway

"For two years, Johnny, a quiet 13-year-old, was a human plaything for some of his classmates. The teenagers badgered Johnny for money, forced him to swallow weeds and drink milk mixed with detergent, beat him up in the rest room and tied a string around his neck, leading him around as a 'pet'. When Johnny's torturers were interrogated about the bullying, they said they pursued their victim because it was fun."[2]

Bullying among schoolchildren is certainly a very old and well-known phenomenon. Though many people are acquainted with the problem, it was not until fairly recently—in the early 1970s—that it became the object of systematic research.[3] For a number of years, these efforts were largely confined to Scandinavia. In the 1980s and early 1990s, however, bullying among schoolchildren began to attract attention also in other countries, such as Great Britain, Japan, the Netherlands, Australia, Canada, and the United States.

In my definition, a student is being bullied or victimized when he or she is exposed, repeatedly and over time, to negative actions on the part of one or more other students. Negative actions can include physical contact, words, making faces or dirty gestures, and intentional exclusion from a group. An additional criterion of bullying is an imbalance in strength (an asymmetric power relationship): The student who is exposed to the negative actions has difficulty defending himself or herself.

SOME PREVALENCE DATA

On the basis of surveys of more than 150,000 Norwegian and Swedish students with my Bully/Victim Questionnaire, I estimated that in the autumn of 1983, some 15% of the students in Grades 1 through 9 (roughly corresponding to ages 7 through 16) in Scandinavia were involved in bully-victim problems with some regularity.[4] Approximately 9% of the students surveyed were victims, and 7% bullied other students. Very likely, these figures underestimate the number of students involved in these problems during a whole year.

Bullying is thus a considerable problem in Scandinavian schools, a problem that affects a very large number of students. Recent data (in large measure collected with my Bully/Victim Questionnaire) from a number of other countries, including the United States,[5] indicate that this problem certainly exists also outside Scandinavia and with similar or even higher prevalence rates.[6] Applying the Scandinavian percentages to the school population in the United States would yield a estimate (conservatively) that some 5 million students in Grades 1 through 9 are involved in bully-victim problems during a school year.

There are many more boys than girls who bully other students, and boys are also somewhat more often victims of bullying. However, there occurs a good deal of bullying among girls as well, but girls typically use more subtle and indirect ways of bullying. Also, boys often bully girls, and older students often bully younger ones. There is a good deal of evidence to indicate that the behavior patterns involved in bully-victim problems are fairly stable over time.[7] Being a bully or a victim is something that is likely to continue for substantial periods of time unless systematic efforts are made to change the situation.

THREE COMMON MYTHS ABOUT BULLYING

Several common assumptions about the causes of bullying have received no support from empirical data. They include the hypotheses that bullying is a consequence of (a) large class or school size, (b) competition for grades and failure in school, and (c) differences in appearance (e.g., it is believed that students who are fat, are red haired, use glasses, or speak with an unusual dialect are particularly likely to become victims of bullying).

Because the empirical data do not support these hypotheses, one must look for other factors to find the origins of bully-victim problems. The research evidence collected so far suggests clearly that personality characteristics (i.e., typical reaction patterns, discussed in the next section), in combination with physical strength or weakness in the case of boys, are very important in the development of these problems in individual students. At the same time, other factors, such as teachers' attitudes, behavior, and routines, play a major role in determining the extent to which the problems will manifest themselves in a classroom or a school.

CHARACTERISTICS OF TYPICAL VICTIMS AND BULLIES

Briefly, the typical victims are more anxious and insecure than students in general. They are often cautious, sensitive, and quiet. Victims suffer from low self-esteem; they have a negative view of themselves and their situation. If they are boys, they are likely to be physically weaker than boys in general. I have labeled this type of victim the *passive or submissive victim,* as opposed to the far less common provocative victim.[3,4] It seems that the behavior and attitude of passive victims are a signal that they are insecure and worthless individuals who will not retaliate if they are attacked or insulted. In a nutshell, the typical victims are characterized by an anxious and submissive reaction pattern combined (in the case of boys) with physical weakness.

In a follow-up study, I found that the former victims of bullying at school tended to be more depressed and had lower self-esteem at age 23 than their non-victimized peers.[8] The results also clearly suggested that this was a consequence of the earlier, persistent victimization, which thus had left its scars on their minds.

A distinctive characteristic of the typical bullies is their aggression toward peers, implied in the definition of a bully. But bullies tend to be aggressive also toward adults, both teachers and parents. They are often characterized by impulsivity and strong needs to dominate other people. They have little empathy with victims of bullying. If they are boys, they are likely to be physically stronger than boys in general, and the victims in particular.

In several studies, and using various methods, I have tested the common assumption that bullies are basically insecure individuals under a tough surface. The empirical results did not support this hypothesis and pointed in fact in the opposite direction: The bullies had unusually little anxiety and insecurity, or were roughly average on such dimensions.

In summary, the typical bullies can be described as having an aggressive reaction pattern combined (in the case of boys) with physical strength. I have identified four child-rearing factors that are likely to be particularly important for the development of such a reaction pattern (in boys):[9] the basic emotional attitude of the primary caretaker(s) toward the child during early years (i.e., indifference, lack of warmth and involvement); permissiveness for aggressive behavior by the child (inadequate limit setting); use of power-assertive disciplinary techniques, such as physical punishment; and the temperament of the child (active, hotheaded).

As regards the possible psychological sources underlying bullying behavior, the pattern of empirical findings suggests at least three, partly interrelated motives (in particular in boys, who have been studied more extensively than girls). First, the bullies have strong needs for power and dominance; they seem to enjoy being in control and subduing other people. Second, in light of the family conditions under which many of them have been reared,[9] it is natural to assume that they have developed a certain degree of hostility toward the environment; as a result of such feelings and impulses, they may derive satisfaction from inflicting injury and suffering upon other individuals. Finally, there is clearly an instrumental component to their behavior. Bullies often coerce their victims to provide them with money, cigarettes, beer, and other things of value. In addition, it is obvious that bullying behavior is in many situations rewarded with prestige.

Bullying can also be viewed as a component of a more generally antisocial and rule-breaking (conduct-disordered) behavior pattern. In my follow-up studies, I have found strong support for this view. Approximately 35% to 40% of boys who were characterized as bullies in Grades 6 through 9 had been convicted of at least three officially registered crimes by the age of 24. In contrast, this was true of only 10% of the boys not classified as bullies. Thus, as young adults, the former school bullies had a fourfold increase in relatively serious, recidivist criminality.

A QUESTION OF FUNDAMENTAL DEMOCRATIC RIGHTS

The victims of bullying form a large group of students who tend to be neglected by their schools. For a long time, I have argued that it is a fundamental democratic right for a child to feel safe in school and to be spared the oppression and repeated, intentional humiliation implied in bullying. No student should be afraid of going to school for fear of being harassed or degraded, and no parent should need to worry about such things happening to his or her child!

Following up on an earlier proposal of mine (from 1981), the Swedish Parliament has recently passed a school law containing formulations that are very similar to the ideas just expressed. The law also places responsibility for realization of these goals, including development of an intervention program against bullying for the individual school, with the principal.

EFFECTS OF A SCHOOL-BASED
INTERVENTION PROGRAM

Against this background, it is appropriate to describe briefly the effects of the intervention program that I developed and evaluated in connection with a nationwide campaign against bully-victim problems in Norwegian schools.

Evaluation of the effects of the intervention program was based on data from approximately 2,500 students originally belonging to 112 classes in Grades 4 through 7 (modal ages: 11–14) in 42 primary and secondary/junior high schools in Bergen, Norway. The subjects of the study were followed over a period of 2.5 years. Because it was not possible to use a strictly experimental setup, a quasi-experimental design (usually called a selection cohorts design) was chosen, contrasting age-equivalent groups who had or had not been exposed to the intervention program.[10]

The main findings of the analyses can be summarized as follows:[4,10]

- There were marked reductions—by 50% or more—in bully-victim problems for the periods studied, with 8 and 20 months of intervention, respectively. By and large, the results applied to both boys and girls, and to students from all grades studied.
- There were also clear reductions in general antisocial behavior, such as vandalism, fighting, pilfering, drunkenness, and truancy.
- Various aspects of the social climate of the classroom registered marked improvement: improved order and discipline, more positive social relationships, and a more positive attitude to school-work and the school. At the same time, there was an increase in student satisfaction with school life.
- The intervention program not only affected already existing victimization problems; it also had a primary preventive effect in that it reduced considerably the number (and percentage) of new victims.

After a detailed analysis of the quality of the data and possible alternative interpretations of the findings, I concluded that it was very difficult to explain the results obtained as a consequence of (a) underreporting by the students, (b) gradual changes in the students' attitudes to bully-victim problems, (c) repeated measurement, or (d) concomitant changes in other factors, including general time trends. All in all, the changes in bully-victim problems and related behavior patterns were likely to be mainly a consequence of the intervention program and not of some other irrelevant factor. Self-reports, which were used in most of these analyses, are probably the best data source for the purposes of such studies.[11] At the same time, largely parallel results were obtained for two peer-rating variables and for teacher ratings of bully-victim problems at the class level; for the teacher data, however, the effects were somewhat weaker.

The reported effects of the intervention program must be considered quite positive, in particular because many previous attempts to systematically reduce aggressive and antisocial behavior in preadolescents and adolescents have been relatively unsuccessful. The importance of the results is accentuated by the fact that the prevalence of violence and other antisocial behavior in most industrialized societies has increased disturbingly in recent decades. In the Scandinavian countries, for instance, various forms of officially registered criminality, including criminal violence, have increased by 300% to 600% since the 1950s or 1960s. Similar changes have occurred in most Western, industrialized societies, including the United States.

BASIC PRINCIPLES

The intervention program is built on a limited set of key principles derived chiefly from research on the development and modification of the implicated problem behaviors, in particular, aggressive behavior. It is thus important to try to create a school (and, ideally, also a home) environment characterized by warmth, positive interest, and involvement from adults, on one hand, and firm limits to unacceptable behavior, on the other. Also, when limits and rules are violated, nonhostile, nonphysical sanctions should be applied consistently. Implied in the latter two principles is also a certain degree of monitoring and surveillance of the students' activities in and out of school.[12] Finally, adults both at school and at home should act as authorities, at least in some respects.

These principles have been translated into a number of specific measures to be implemented at the school, class, and individual levels. Table 1 lists the core components that are considered, on the basis of statistical analyses and experience with the program, to be particularly important.[13]

With regard to implementation and execution, the program is mainly based on utilization of the existing social environment: teachers and other school personnel, students, and parents. Non-mental health professionals thus play a major role in the desired restructuring of the social environment. Experts such as school psychologists, counselors, and social workers serve important functions planning and coordinating, counseling teachers and parents (groups), and handling relatively serious cases.

Table 1. *Overview of the core intervention program*

General prerequisites	
+ +	Awareness and involvement on the part of adults
Measures at the school level	
+ +	Questionnaire survey
+ +	School conference day
+ +	Better supervision during recess and lunch time
+	Formation of coordinating group
+	Meeting between staff and parents (PTA meeting)
Measures at the class level	
+ +	Class rules against bullying
+ +	Regular class meetings with students
Measures at the individual level	
+ +	Serious talks with bullies and victims
+ +	Serious talks with parents of involved students
+	Teacher and parent use of imagination

Note. + + indicates a core component; + indicates a highly desirable component.

Possible reasons for the effectiveness of this nontraditional intervention approach have been discussed in some detail.[14] They include changes in the opportunity and reward structures for bullying behavior (resulting in fewer opportunities and rewards for bullying). Also, bully-victim problems can be an excellent entry point for dealing with a variety of problems that plague today's schools. Furthermore, one can view the program from the perspective of planned organizational change (with quite specific goals) and in this way link it with the current lively work on school effectiveness and school improvement.

This antibullying program is now in use or in the process of being implemented in a considerable number of schools in Europe and North America. Though there have so far been few research-based attempts to evaluate the effects of the program, unsystematic information and reports indicate that the general approach is well received by the adults in the school society and that the program (with or without cultural adaptations or additions of culture-specific components) works well under varying cultural conditions, including ethnic diversity. In addition to the study in Bergen, there has been a recent large-scale evaluation of an implementation containing most of the core elements of the program.[15] This evaluation based on 23 schools (with a good deal of ethnic diversity) in Sheffield, United Kingdom, used a research design similar to that of the Bergen study and likewise showed results that were quite positive (though fewer behavioral aspects were studied). It can be argued that the success and possible generalizability of the program across cultures is not really surprising, because the existing evidence seems to indicate that the factors and principles affecting the development and modification of aggressive, antisocial behavior are fairly similar across cultural contexts, at least within the Western, industrialized part of the world.

FINAL WORDS

The basic message of these findings is quite clear: With a suitable intervention program, it is definitely possible to reduce dramatically bully-victim problems in school as well as related problem behaviors.

This antibullying program can be implemented with relatively simple means and without major costs; it is primarily a question of changing attitudes, behavior, and routines in school life. Introduction of the program is likely to have a number of other positive effects as well.

Acknowledgments—The research reported in this review was supported by grants from the William T. Grant Foundation, the Norwegian Research Council for Social Research, the Swedish Delegation for Social Research, and, in earlier phases, the Norwegian Ministry of Education. This support is gratefully acknowledged.

Notes

1. Address correspondence to Dan Olweus, Division of Personality Psychology, Oysteinsgate 3, N-5007 Bergen, Norway.

2. Newspaper clipping, quoted in D. Olweus, *Bullying at School: What We Know and What We Can Do* (Blackwell, Cambridge, MA, and Oxford, England, 1993), p. 7.

3. D. Olweus, *Hackkycklingar och översittare: Forskning om skolmobbning* (Almqvist & Wicksell, Stockholm, Sweden, 1973); D. Olweus, *Aggression in the Schools: Bullies and Whipping Boys* (Hemisphere Press, Washington, DC, 1978).

4. Olweus, note 1.

5. D.G. Perry, S.J. Kusel, and L.C. Perry, Victims of peer aggression, *Developmental Psychology, 24,* 807–814 (1988); D. Schwartz, K. Dodge, and J. Coie, The emergence of chronic peer victimization in boys' play groups, *Child Development, 64,* 1755–1772 (1993).

6. For references, see D. Olweus, Annotation: Bullying at school: Basic facts and effects of a school based intervention program, *Journal of Child Psychology and Psychiatry, 35,* 1171–1190 (1994); D. Farrington, Understanding and preventing bullying, in *Crime and Justice: A Review of Research,* Vol. 17, M. Tonry, Ed. (University of Chicago Press, Chicago, 1993).

7. D. Olweus, Stability of aggressive reaction patterns in males: A review, *Psychological Bulletin, 86,* 852–875 (1979); D. Olweus, Aggression and peer acceptance in adolescent boys: Two short-term longitudinal studies of ratings. *Child Development, 48,* 1301–1313 (1977); Olweus (1978), note 2.

8. D. Olweus, Victimization by peers: Antecedents and long-term outcomes, in *Social Withdrawal, Inhibition, and Shyness in Childhood,* K.H. Rubin and J.B. Asendorf, Eds. (Erlbaum, Hillsdale, NJ, 1993).

9. D. Olweus, Familial and temperamental determinants of aggressive behavior in adolescent boys: A causal analysis, *Developmental Psychology, 16,* 644–660 (1980); see also R. Loeber and M. Stouthamer-Loeber, Family factors as correlates and predictors of conduct problems and juvenile delinquency, in *Crime and Justice: A Review of Research,* Vol. 7, M. Tonry and N. Morris, Eds. (University of Chicago Press, Chicago, 1986).

10. For methodological details, see D. Olweus, Bully/victim problems among school-children: Basic facts and effects of a school based intervention program, in *The Development and Treatment of Child-hood Aggression,* D. Pepler and K.H. Rubin, Eds. (Erlbaum, Hillsdale, NJ, 1991); D. Olweus and F.D. Alsaker, Assessing change in a cohort longitudinal study with hierarchical data, in *Problems and Methods in Longitudinal Research,* D. Magnusson, L.R. Bergman, G. Rudinger, and B. Törestad, Eds. (Cambridge University Press, New York, 1991).

11. For a brief discussion of the validity of such self-report data, see Olweus, note 5, p. 1174, footnote.

12. G.R. Patterson, Performance models for antisocial boys, *American Psychologist, 41,* 432–444 (1986).

13. The package constituting the intervention program consists of the Bully/Victim Questionnaire (can be ordered from the author; will be published by Blackwell in 1996), a 20-min video cassette showing scenes from the everyday lives of two bullied children (with English subtitles; can be ordered from the author), and the book *Bullying at School: What We Know and What We Can Do,* note 1.

14. D. Olweus, Bullying among schoolchildren: Intervention and prevention, in *Aggression and Violence Throughout the Life Span,* R.D. Peters, R.J. McMahon, and V.L. Quincy, Eds. (Sage. Newbury Park, CA, 1992).

15. P.K. Smith and S. Sharp, *School Bullying: Insights and Perspectives* (Routledge, London, 1994).

This article has been reprinted as it originally appeared in *Current Directions in Psychological Science*. Citation information for this article as originally published appears above.

School Dropouts: Prevention Considerations, Interventions, and Challenges

Sandra L. Christenson[1] and Martha L. Thurlow
University of Minnesota

Abstract

Preventing school dropout and promoting successful graduation is a national concern that poses a significant challenge for schools and educational communities working with youth at risk for school failure. Although students who are at greatest risk for dropping out of school can be identified, they disengage from school and drop out for a variety of reasons for which there is no one common solution. The most effective intervention programs identify and track youth at risk for school failure, maintain a focus on students' progress toward educational standards across the school years, and are designed to address indicators of student engagement and to impact enrollment status—not just the predictors of dropout. To leave no child behind, educators must address issues related to student mobility, alternate routes to school completion, and alternate time lines for school completion, as well as engage in rigorous evaluation of school-completion programs.

Keywords

dropout; graduation; at-risk; engagement

No one questions the seriousness of the school-dropout problem in the United States. Attention to graduation and dropout rates has increased significantly, and is reflected in current federal priorities. Most recently, graduation rate has been targeted in Title I of No Child Left Behind (NCLB), which identifies schools as needing improvement if their overall performance does not improve from year to year or if subgroups, including students who need to learn English and youth with disabilities, do not make adequate yearly progress. Along with test performance, graduation rate, defined as the percentage of ninth graders receiving a standard diploma in 4 years, is a required indicator in calculations of adequate yearly progress for high schools.

Thousands of American youth are school dropouts, with an estimated 1 in 8 children never graduating from high school. In fact, high school graduation rates have not changed significantly since 1990 (National Educational Goals Panel, 2002). The startling statistic that one high school student drops out every 9 seconds illustrates the magnitude of the problem (Children's Defense Fund, 2002).

Most states are far from the 90% graduation rate that was targeted in the early 1990s (National Educational Goals Panel, 2002). Furthermore, students with disabilities are much more likely to drop out of school than their general-education peers. Also, dropout rates are disproportionately high for students from Hispanic, African American, Native American, and low-income backgrounds; students who live in single-parent homes; and those who attend large urban schools (National Center for Education Statistics, 2002). Dropout rates are highest among students with emotional and behavioral disabilities; half of these students dropped out of school in 1998–1999 (U.S. Department of Education, 2001). Although these marker variables identify students who may be at risk for dropout, predicting who will drop out is not foolproof. For example, in a study of middle and high school dropout-prevention programs for students with two or more risk factors, no single risk factor predicted who would drop out (Dynarski & Gleason, 2002).

Dropout statistics are particularly alarming because jobs that pay living wages and benefits have virtually disappeared for youth without a high school diploma. For society, the costs of dropout are staggering, estimated in the billions of dollars in lost revenues, welfare programs, unemployment programs, under-employment, and crime prevention and prosecution (Christenson, Sinclair, Lehr, & Hurley, 2000). Given these individual and societal consequences, facilitating school completion for all students must be a critical concern for researchers, pol-icymakers, and educators across the country.

Promoting successful school completion for students who are at risk of dropping out is recognized as especially challenging in light of current national reform efforts to achieve high academic standards, end social promotion, and ratchet up educational accountability. The need for schools and the broader edu-cational community to create opportunities for success and to provide necessary supports for all youth to meet educational standards is complicated by require-ments in many states that students must pass state high school exit exams to earn a standard diploma. Although these exams may ensure that students have attained specific competencies prior to receiving a diploma, a potential unin-tended consequence is increases in the number of students who drop out.

CRITICAL CONSIDERATIONS IN DROPOUT PREVENTION

Educators designing dropout-prevention programs will want to attend to five crit-ical considerations: dropout as a process, the role of context, alterable variables, an orientation toward completion and engagement, and the importance of empir-ical evidence.

Dropout as a Process

Early and sustained intervention is integral to the success of students because the decision to leave school without graduating is not an instantaneous one, but rather a process that occurs over many years. Teaching students to read is vital for them to become engaged learners. Research shows that leaving school early is the outcome of a long process of disengagement from school (Christenson, Sin-clair, Lehr, & Godber, 2001); dropout is preceded by indicators of withdrawal (e.g., poor attendance) or unsuccessful school experiences (e.g., academic or behavioral difficulties) that often begin in elementary school. Overt indicators of disengagement are generally accompanied by feelings of alienation, a poor sense of belonging, and a general dislike for school.

The Role of Context

The problem of school dropout cannot be understood in isolation from contex-tual factors. Early school withdrawal reflects a complex interplay among student, family, school, and community variables, as well as risk and protective factors. School and family policies and practices are critical (Christenson et al., 2000). For example, schools with the greatest holding power tend to have relatively small enrollment, fair discipline policies, caring teachers, high expectations, and opportunities for meaningful participation. Policies that support suspension and grade retention for students who are deemed not ready to advance have been linked to higher dropout rates. Family factors associated with reduced dropout rates include parental support, monitoring and supervision, high regard for education, and positive expectations regarding school performance.

Alterable Variables

The dichotomy between predictors that are more versus less easy to influence provides a suggested course of action for educators. Finn (1989) made an important distinction when he contrasted *status* predictor variables such as socioeconomic status, which educators have little ability to change, and *behavioral* or alterable predictor variables such as out-of-school suspensions and course failures, which are more readily influenced by educators. Recently, there has been a shift toward investigating alterable variables—behaviors and attitudes that reflect students' connection to school as well as family and school practices that support children's learning—because they have greater utility for interventions.

Completion and Engagement

School dropout and school completion are considered two sides of the same coin; however, school completion is the preferred term given its positive orientation and emphasis on the development of student competencies. School-completion programs require a primary focus on student engagement, particularly on finding ways to enhance students' interest in and enthusiasm for school, sense of belonging at school, motivation to learn, and progress in school, as well as the value they place on school and learning (Christenson et al., 2001). Engagement is multidimensional (Sinclair, Christenson, Lehr, & Anderson, in press). *Academic and behavioral engagement* refers to observable indicators; sustained attention to and completion of academic work and accrual of credits exemplify academic engagement, and attendance, number of suspensions, and classroom participation are measures of behavioral engagement. *Cognitive and psychological engagement* refers to internal indicators; processing academic information, thinking about how to learn, and self-monitoring progress toward task completion exemplify cognitive engagement, and identification with school, a sense of belonging and connection, and positive relationships with peers and teachers characterize psychological engagement.

Conceptually, promoting school completion encompasses more than preventing dropout. For example, it is characterized by school personnel emphasizing development of students' competencies rather than dwelling on their deficits. Successful programs are comprehensive, interfacing family, school, and community efforts rather than offering a single, narrow intervention in one environment; are implemented over time rather than at a single period in time; and make an effort to tailor interventions to fit individual students rather than adopting a programmatic "one size fits all" orientation. School-completion programs have a longitudinal focus, aiming to promote a "good" outcome, not simply prevent a "bad" outcome for students and society (Christenson et al., 2001).

Empirical Evidence

Schools across the nation have implemented dropout-prevention programs. The National Dropout Prevention Center at Clemson University has studied the issue of dropout for nearly two decades and has developed a database cataloguing such programs (Schargel & Smink, 2001). Although these programs provide general guidelines and appear promising, continued empirical study is required to determine those variables that influence the effectiveness of interventions. However, despite the importance of school completion for individuals and society as a whole, and despite the complexity of the problem, few such studies have been published. A comprehensive review of dropout interventions (Lehr, Hanson, Sinclair, & Christenson, 2003) indicated that dropout research has been overwhelmingly predictive or descriptive (i.e., there have been few controlled studies), and the methodology used to evaluate the effectiveness of the majority of dropout interventions has been judged to be of low quality or poor scientific merit. For example, many studies have not reported the statistical significance of results, and even fewer have reported effect sizes to help determine practical significance. Aptly, the need for more rigorous studies was highlighted in a recent report from the U.S. General Accounting Office (2002), which stated that "although there have been many federal, state, and local dropout prevention programs over the last 2 decades, few have been rigorously evaluated" (p. 31).

Currently, we know considerably more about who drops out than we do about efficacious intervention programs. Most interventions have been designed to remediate specific predictors of dropout, such as poor attendance and poor academic performance. Although research supports the idea that these variables should be targeted, there is little evidence to suggest that these programs change dropout rates (Dynarski & Gleason, 2002). On a more optimistic note, there are promising signs that comprehensive, personalized, long-term interventions yield positive results for students (e.g., Fashola & Slavin, 1998; Sinclair et al., in press).

INTERVENTIONS

What are the characteristics of school-based dropout-prevention interventions? An integrative review of 45 prevention and intervention studies addressing dropout or school completion, described in professional journals from 1983 through 2000 (Lehr et al., 2003), identified many similarities among the interventions, including their focus on changing the student, beginning with a *personal-affective focus* (e.g., individual counseling, participation in an interpersonal-relations class) and then shifting to an *academic focus* (e.g., specialized courses or tutoring), and their efforts to address alterable variables (e.g., poor grades, attendance, and attitude toward school). Most interventions were implemented with secondary students with a history of poor academic performance and dropping out, poor attendance, and teacher referral for supplemental support; students with disabilities were targeted in only two programs and specifically excluded from two. Interventions that yielded moderate to large effects on at least one dependent variable provided early reading programs, tutoring, counseling, and mentoring; they emphasized creating caring environments and relationships, used block scheduling, and offered community-service opportunities.

There is consensus that successful interventions do more than increase student attendance—they help students and families who feel marginalized in their relations with teachers and peers to be connected at school and with learning. Student engagement across the school years depends on the degree to which there is a match between the student's characteristics and the school environment so that the student is able to handle the academic and behavioral demands of school. For more than a decade, we and our colleagues have field-tested the Check & Connect model of student engagement among students with and without disabilities. Our field tests have been conducted in kindergarten through grade 12 and in both urban and suburban schools (Sinclair et al., in press). Applications of this evidence-based intervention approach have underscored the critical need to keep education and learning the salient issue for many students and their families. We have used the concept of "persistence-plus" to show students that there is someone who is not going to give up on them or allow them to be distracted from school; that there is someone who knows them and is available to them throughout the school year, the summer, and into the next school year; and that caring adults want them to learn, do the work, attend class regularly, be on time, express frustration constructively, stay in school, and succeed. Furthermore, McPartland (1994) cogently addressed the need for school-completion programs to be adapted to fit local circumstances when he argued, "It is unlikely that a program developed elsewhere can be duplicated exactly in another site, because local talents and priorities for school reform, the particular interests and needs of the students to be served, and the conditions of the school to be changed will differ" (p. 256).

Consensus is emerging with respect to essential intervention components. In particular, the "personalization" of education—striving to understand the nature of academic, social, and personal problems affecting students and tailoring services to address individualized concerns—is an essential component. Effective programs aimed at promoting school completion focus on building students' relationships with teachers, parents, and peers and include systematic monitoring of the students' performance; they work to develop students' problem-solving skills, provide opportunities for success in schoolwork, create a caring and supportive environment, communicate the relevance of education to future endeavors, and help with students' personal problems (McPartland, 1994; Sinclair et al., in press). In a comprehensive review of federal dropout-prevention evaluations, Dynarski and Gleason (2002) identified smaller class sizes, more personalized settings, and individualized learning plans as characteristics that lowered dropout rates in both General Educational Development (GED) programs for older students and alternative middle school programs. Of particular importance is the need for a more intensive intervention approach. Although low-intensity supplemental services such as tutoring or occasional counseling were relatively easy to implement, they had little to no impact on student outcomes, such as grades, test scores, attendance, or the dropout rate.

CHALLENGES

New federal initiatives have made it clear that decisions about educational programs should be based on empirical evidence. Research is only beginning to address the critical need for programs that promote student engagement and school completion, and thereby reduce dropout rates. Educators and policymakers are in need of sound research to guide best practice.

As programs are developed and evaluated, we must address the challenge of *student mobility,* which is significantly associated with school failure (Rumberger & Larson, 1998). High rates of mobility seriously undermine the potential for youth to value school or develop a sense of belonging. Even if a school offers services well suited to meet the needs of disenfranchised students, the potential benefit can be lost if youth do not remain in the school long enough or trust someone enough to participate. If we are to reduce significantly the dropout rate and promote the successful completion of school, we must grapple with the question of how to ensure that the protective factors of sustained intervention and continuity of relationships with teachers and peers exist when students move frequently. There may be a need for interventions that coordinate the efforts of multiple schools and multiple school districts and perhaps a mechanism for educators and mentors to track student performance and partner with families within and across states.

Another challenge that must be addressed is the acceptability of the current array of exit documents, ranging from honors diplomas to certificates of completion, attendance diplomas, and special education diplomas. The options recognize different ways in which students complete school, and which option students are encouraged to pursue has often been based on educators' expectations for their success. Yet current federal law (NCLB) indicates that for purposes of school accountability, only those students who have earned a standard diploma in 4 years will be counted in the percentage of students graduating. We must examine the consequences of this definition. Is the value of earning a diploma within 5 years or completing school via other options discounted? It will be important for the nation to consider its definition of successful school completion to ensure that the requirement for a standard diploma does not provide an incentive for students to drop out.

CONCLUDING REMARKS

The dropout problem in the United States is solvable, provided student performance is systematically monitored to ensure students are provided with realistic opportunities for academic and reading success, supported as learners by educators and families, encouraged to see the relevance of school and learning in their personal lives and future goals, and helped with personal problems across the school years. Increasing students' engagement and enthusiasm for school requires much more than simply having them stay in school—it involves supporting students to help them meet the defined academic standards of their schools, as well as the underlying social and behavioral standards. If students are engaged at school and with learning, they should not only graduate but also demonstrate academic and social competence at school completion.

NCLB demands and provides unique opportunities for educators and parents to partner in order to foster the learning of all students across school years and settings. To improve outcomes for youth at high risk for school failure, further research and evaluation must systematically document strategies that actively engage youth in the learning process and help youth to stay in school and on track to graduate while developing academic and behavioral skills. The educational success of all students will require explicit attention to social and emotional learning as well as academics, through a focus on cognitive, psychological, and behavioral engagement, along with academic engagement.

Recommended Reading

Doll, B., Hess, R., & Ochoa, S.H. (Eds.). (2001). Contemporary psychological perspectives on school completion [Special issue]. *School Psychology Quarterly, 16*(4).

Gleason, P., & Dynarski, M. (1998). *Do we know whom to serve? Issues in using risk factors to identify dropouts.* Princeton, NJ: Mathematica Policy Research.

Prevatt, F., & Kelly, F.D. (2003). Dropping out of school: A review of intervention programs. *Journal of School Psychology, 41,* 377–395.

Rosenthal, B.S. (1998). Non-school correlates of dropout: An integrative review of the literature. *Children & Youth Services Review, 20,* 413–433.

University of Minnesota, College of Education and Human Development, Institute on Community Integration. (2002). *Check & Connect.* http://www.ici.umn.edu/checkandconnect/

Note

1. Address correspondence to Sandra Christenson, University of Minnesota, School Psychology Program, 350 Elliott Hall, 75 East River Rd., Minneapolis, MN 55455; e-mail: chris002@umn.edu.

References

Children's Defense Fund. (2002). *Twenty-five facts about American children from the State of America's Children Yearbook 2001.* Retrieved October 17, 2002, from http://www.childrensdefense.org/keyfacts.htm

Christenson, S.L., Sinclair, M.F., Lehr, C.A., & Godber, Y. (2001). Promoting successful school completion: Critical conceptual and methodological guidelines. *School Psychology Quarterly, 16,* 468–484.

Christenson, S.L., Sinclair, M.F., Lehr, C.A., & Hurley, C.M. (2000). Promoting successful school completion. In K. Minke & G. Bear (Eds.), *Preventing school problems—promoting school success: Strategies and programs that work* (pp. 377–420). Bethesda, MD: National Association of School Psychologists.

Dynarski, M., & Gleason, P. (2002). How can we help? What we have learned from recent federal dropout prevention evaluations. *Journal of Education for Students Placed at Risk, 7*(1), 43–69.

Fashola, O.S., & Slavin, R.E. (1998). Effective dropout prevention and college attendance programs for students placed at risk. *Journal of Education for Students Placed at Risk, 3*(2), 159–183.

Finn, J.D. (1989). Withdrawing from school. *Review of Educational Research, 59,* 117–124.

Lehr, C.A., Hanson, A., Sinclair, M.F., & Christenson, S.L. (2003). Moving beyond dropout prevention towards school completion: An integrative review of data-based interventions. *School Psychology Review, 32,* 342–364.

McPartland, J.M. (1994). Dropout prevention in theory and practice. In R.J. Rossi (Ed.), *Schools and students at risk: Context and framework for positive change* (pp. 255–276). New York: Teachers College.

National Center for Education Statistics. (2002). *The condition of education 2002* (NCES 2002-025). Washington, DC: U.S. Department of Education, Office of Educational Research and Improvement.

National Educational Goals Panel. (2002). *Find out how the nation is doing.* Retrieved May 23, 2003, from http://www.negp.gov

Rumberger, R.W., & Larson, K.A. (1998). Student mobility and the increased risk of high school dropout. *American Journal of Education, 107,* 1–35.

Schargel, F.P., & Smink, J. (2001). *Strategies to help solve our school dropout problem.* Larchmont, NY: Eye on Education.

Sinclair, M.F., Christenson, S.L., Lehr, C.A., & Anderson, A.R. (in press). Facilitating student engagement: Lessons learned from Check & Connect longitudinal studies. *Journal of California Association of School Psychologists.*

U.S. Department of Education. (2001). *Twenty-third annual report to Congress on the implementation of the Individuals With Disabilities Education Act.* Washington, DC: Author.

U.S. General Accounting Office. (2002). *School dropouts: Education could play a stronger role in identifying and disseminating promising prevention strategies.* Washington, DC: Author.

This article has been reprinted as it originally appeared in *Current Directions in Psychological Science*. Citation information for this article as originally published appears above.

Mentoring Relationships and Programs for Youth

Jean E. Rhodes[1]
University of Massachusetts, Boston
David L. DuBois
University of Illinois at Chicago

Abstract

Mentoring is one of the most popular social interventions in American society, with an estimated three million youth in formal one-to-one relationships. Studies have revealed significant associations between youth involvement in mentoring relationships and positive developmental outcomes. These associations are modest, however, and depend on several intervening processes. Centrally important is the formation of close, enduring connections between mentors and youth that foster positive developmental change. Effects of mentoring programs likewise typically have been small in magnitude, but they increase systematically with the use of program practices likely to support relationship development. Gaps between research and practice are evident both in the indiscriminate use of the term mentoring in the prevention field and in a focus on the growth and efficiency of mentoring programs at the expense of quality. Continued expansion of effective mentoring will require a better alignment of research and practice.

Keywords

mentoring; preventive intervention; nonparent adults; youth

Organized approaches to mentoring youth in the United States date back to reform-oriented initiatives in the juvenile court system more than a century ago. These efforts gave rise to Big Brothers Big Sisters of America (BBBSA), the largest and most well-known program of its kind. The past decade has witnessed a remarkable proliferation of similarly focused programs that pair caring, adult volunteers with youth from at-risk backgrounds. An estimated three million youth are in formal one-to-one mentoring relationships in the United States, and funding and growth imperatives continue to fuel program expansion (MENTOR, 2006). Even larger numbers of youth report experiencing mentoring relationships outside of these types of programs with adults such as teachers, coaches, neighbors, and extended family.

Anecdotal accounts of the protective qualities of mentoring relationships and their life-transforming effects on young people abound in the media. Youth mentoring has entered the American lexicon, appearing on a U.S. postage stamp and in countless public service announcements. Federal funding for mentoring programs has increased substantially as well, with annual congressional appropriations of $100 million since 2004. It is only relatively recently, however, that social and behavioral scientists have focused their attention on a more rigorous examination of mentoring for children and adolescents. In this article, we review the highlights of this research. We then critically examine recent trends in practice and policy in view of current directions in research.

MENTORING RELATIONSHIPS AND YOUTH OUTCOMES

Numerous studies have examined mentoring relationships and their consequences for youth development. Illustratively, in a longitudinal study of a nationally representative sample of young adults, DuBois and Silverthorn (2005) found that those who reported having had a mentoring relationship during adolescence exhibited significantly better outcomes within the domains of education and work (high-school completion, college attendance, employment), mental health (self-esteem, life satisfaction), problem behavior (gang membership, fighting, risk taking), and health (exercise, birth control use). (They controlled where possible for the same or related measures at the start of the study as well as indices of individual and environmental risk.) The magnitude of these associations, however, was fairly small, with the reduction in risk for negative outcomes attributable to having a mentor typically less than 10%. Similar findings have emerged in evaluations of programs in which mentoring relationships are arranged and supported by program staff. A meta-analysis of 55 mentoring program evaluations (DuBois, Holloway, Valentine, & Cooper, 2002) found benefits of participation in the areas of emotional/psychological well-being, involvement in problem or high-risk behavior, and academic outcomes. Yet, in comparison to other prevention programs for children and adolescents (Durlak & Wells, 1997), the effectiveness of mentoring programs was found to be relatively small. The few studies that collected follow-up assessments of mentoring programs revealed even weaker effects, suggesting an eroding of benefits after youth left programs and relationships with mentors ended.

More recently, Jolliffe and Farington (2007) explored the effects of youth mentoring on recidivism among juvenile offenders. Their analyses, which were based on 18 evaluations, revealed a somewhat smaller overall effect of mentoring than was reported in the meta-analysis conducted by DuBois and colleagues. Still another recent meta-analysis looked at a broader range of outcomes associated with mentoring relationships for youth across 40 investigations (Eby, Allen, Evans, Ng, & DuBois, 2008). Results indicated that youth experiencing mentoring fared significantly better than those who did not, but the size of these differences again was relatively small and below those associated with mentoring for college students and adults.

Findings in evaluations of individual mentoring programs have also been mixed. This includes the BBBSA mentoring program. This program has been widely touted as effective based on the findings of a large, random-assignment evaluation of the program (Grossman & Tierney, 1998). Yet the magnitude of these effects was small and generally reflected a relative slowing of negative trajectories rather than outright improvements among those receiving mentoring (Rhodes, 2002). A recent large random-assignment evaluation of BBBSA's newer, school-based mentoring program (Herrera, Grossman, Kauh, Feldman, & McMaken, 2007) revealed similar findings. At the end of the school year, there were significant improvements in participants' academic performance, perceived scholastic efficacy, school misconduct, and attendance relative to nonmentored youth.

These effects were again generally small in magnitude and, when youth were reassessed a few months into the following school year, they had for the most part eroded to nonsignificance.

Taken together, available research indicates that, although mentoring relationships can indeed promote positive development among young people, these benefits are modest in size. Nevertheless, when all relationships are combined, as in most of the analyses described above, notably more positive outcomes for some youth may be masked by neutral and even negative outcomes for youth involved in less effective mentoring relationships. For mentoring to fully realize its promise as a safe and effective intervention for young persons, programs will need to be informed by a deeper understanding of the processes that are the root of these differences.

WHEN AND HOW DO MENTORING RELATIONSHIPS WORK?

To this end, it is critically important to understand *how* mentoring relationships affect youth. Based on empirical and theoretical literature, Rhodes (2005) has proposed a model that delineates several processes and conditions presumed to be important for understanding the effects of mentoring relationships on youth (see Fig. 1). First and foremost, beneficial effects are expected only to the extent that the mentor and youth forge a strong connection that is characterized by

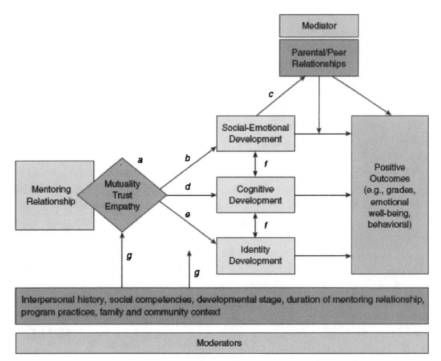

Fig. 1. Model of youth mentoring (Rhodes, 2005). Close, enduring mentoring relationships influence youth outcomes through social/emotional, cognitive, and identity development.

mutuality, trust, and empathy (component *a* in Fig. 1). For this type of bond to arise, mentors and youth are likely to need to spend time together on a consistent basis over some significant period of time (Spencer, 2007). Only then may youth derive significant benefits. In a reanalysis of data from the previously noted evaluation of the BBBSA program, for example, positive effects on youth outcomes became progressively stronger as relationships persisted for longer periods of time and were greatest when relationships lasted at least 1 year (Grossman & Rhodes, 2002). For youth in relationships that terminated prematurely within the first 6 months (i.e., less than half the 1-year commitment that volunteers were asked to make), there were no clear benefits and, in at least one instance (alcohol use), a significant increase in problems relative to a randomly assigned control group. Beyond issues of time, research indicates that the extent to which mentors and youth establish a strong connection is influenced by the dynamics of their interactions with each other. Langhout, Rhodes, and Osborne (2004), for example, found that outcomes were most favorable when youth reported experiencing not only support but also some degree of structure in their relationships with their mentors. In general, close and enduring ties appear to be fostered when mentors adopt a flexible, youth-centered style in which the young person's interests and preferences are emphasized, rather than when they focus predominantly on their own agendas or expectations for the relationship (Morrow & Styles, 1995).

As shown in Figure 1, well-established mentoring relationships may contribute to positive youth outcomes through three interacting developmental processes: social-emotional, cognitive, and identity-related. There are several ways in which the social-emotional development of children and adolescents may be furthered through mentoring (path *b* in Fig. 1). By serving as a sounding board and providing a model of effective adult communication, for example, mentors may help youth to better understand, express, and regulate their emotions (Rhodes, Grossman, & Resch, 2000).

The model further assumes that positive socio-emotional experiences with mentors can generalize, enabling youth to interact with others more effectively (path *c*). In support of this prediction, benefits of mentoring relationships have been indicated to accrue in part through improvements in youths' perceptions of their parental relationships as well as their relationships with peers and other adults in their social networks (Rhodes, Reddy, & Grossman, 2005; Rhodes et al., 2000). Mentoring relationships similarly may affect a range of cognitive developmental processes (path *d*). This aspect of the model is derived from theory and research that highlights the role of social support from adults in fostering cognitive gains during development. In particular, through interactions with mentors, children and adolescents may acquire and refine new thinking skills, becoming more receptive to adult values, advice, and perspectives. In support of these possibilities, close, enduring ties with mentors have been found to predict improvements in academic and vocational outcomes (e.g., Herrera et al., 2007; Klaw, Fitzgerald, & Rhodes, 2003). Finally, as noted, mentoring relationships also may facilitate identity development (path *e*). Illustratively, mentors may help shift youths' conceptions of both their current and future identities. Markus and Nurius (1986) have referred in this regard to "possible selves," or individuals' ideas of what they might become, what they would like to become, and what they fear becoming. More generally, relationships with mentors may open doors to activities, resources, and educational or occupational opportunities on which youth can draw to construct their sense of identity (Darling, Hamilton, Toyokawa, & Matsuda, 2002). Findings regarding mentors' protective influence on risk behavior (Beier, Rosenfeld, Spitalny, Zanksy, & Bontempo, 2000) and academic outcomes (Rhodes et al., 2000) are suggestive of a more positive future orientation in their identities. For this type of guidance and support to be realized, however, mentors may need to model appropriate behaviors and values. When youth perceive potential adult mentors to be involved in problem behavior, they are more likely to engage in the same types of behavior themselves (Beam, Gil-Rivas, Greenberger, & Chen, 2002).

In the theoretical model, both mentoring relationships and the pathways linking them to youth outcomes may be conditioned by a range of individual, family, and contextual influences (see Fig. 1, g arrows). Several findings are consistent with this assumption. Youth who are overwhelmed by social and behavioral problems, for example, appear to be less likely to experience strong, enduring ties with their mentors and, perhaps consequently, also receive fewer benefits (Rhodes, 2005). Environmental adversities such as family instability and socioeconomic disadvantage also frequently can pose challenges to the formation of mentoring relationships (Spencer, 2007). Yet, youth from backgrounds of environmental risk have been found to be especially likely to benefit from mentoring (DuBois et al., 2002), thus suggesting that the challenges presented by such circumstances need not form barriers to effective relationships.

Returning to the issue of mentoring program effectiveness, it is noteworthy that significantly stronger positive effects on youth have been found when programs have incorporated a range of different practices that would be expected to promote the types of close, enduring, and developmentally enriching relationships that are highlighted as desirable by the preceding theory and research. These practices include training and ongoing supervision of mentors, expectations of relatively frequent meetings and long-lasting relationships between mentors and youth, program-sponsored activities to enhance the development of mentoring relationships, parent support and involvement, and the addition of other programs and services to supplement mentoring (DuBois et al., 2002; Herrera et al., 2007; Jolliffe & Farington, 2007). In their analysis, DuBois et al. (2002) found that expected effects for programs utilizing the full complement of evidence-based practices that they identified were nearly three times as large as the benefits found for youth in the typical program.

CONCLUSIONS

Recent research indicates that mentoring programs are likely to be effective to the extent that they are successful in establishing close, enduring connections that promote positive developmental change. Policies that demand greater adherence to evidence-based practice and the use of rigorous evaluations are needed to ensure that quality receives as much attention as does quantity. Models of successful program replication can help guide such growth (see Box 1).

Box 1. *The across ages mentoring program*

One mentoring program, Across Ages, has achieved the status of "model program" on the Substance Abuse and Mental Health Services Administration's National Registry of Evidence-based Programs and Practices. Even as Across Ages has expanded to over 75 sites nationwide, it has continued to demonstrate adherence to its core set of practices, relatively low volunteer attrition, match durations that greatly exceed national averages, and evidence of encouraging behavioral, academic, and psychosocial outcomes (Taylor, LoSciuto, & Porcellini, 2005). In this program, 10- to 13-year-olds are matched with volunteers aged 50 or older. Volunteers undergo a rigorous screening followed by 10 hours of preservice training. Additional features of Across Ages include:

- Pre-match training of youth
- 1-year commitment (mentors and youth)
- Weekly face-to-face contact for a minimum of 2 hours
- Monthly in-service meetings for mentors for supervision, training and support
- Weekly phone calls to mentors/weekly meetings with youth
- Community service projects
- Structured activities and goal setting

Practices and policies to cultivate greater availability of mentoring relationships for youth are based on the assumption that these ties can offer measurable benefits to young people. Findings from recent research offer support for this viewpoint. Yet there are equally important ways in which the available evidence fails to support current trends in practice and policy. One area of concern is the increasingly broad range of activities—such as tutoring, after-school, and service learning programs—that are argued to constitute mentoring. Underlying this trend seems to be the perspective that any program in which adults are brought into contact with young people may count as providing mentoring regardless of the nature or time frame of the relationships that are involved. Yet, because the processes involved appear to be complex and, in some cases, entail fundamental changes in the ways that children and adolescents think about themselves and their relationships, it should not be assumed that all programs connecting youth with adults would tap into relationship processes in a meaningful or beneficial way.

A second area of concern is that mentoring programs and policies too often have been implemented with insufficient attention to available research. Mentoring strikes deep emotional chords and has attracted powerful constituents who, at some level, have looked to research only to confirm what they intuitively hold to be true. Many organizations and funding sources have adopted aggressive growth goals to increase the numbers of youth mentored. Consequently, largely untested approaches to mentoring (e.g., group, peer, online) have been championed, while existing models have relaxed minimum requirements for volunteer screening, commitment, and training. These approaches have been successful in reducing the burden that is placed on agencies and volunteers yet seem to be directly at odds with the types of practices that research indicates are needed to establish and sustain high-quality mentoring relationships (Rhodes & DuBois, 2006). In effect, mentoring programs have moved in a direction that is in danger of trivializing what research indicates is at the very heart of their intervention: a caring adult–youth relationship. If youth mentoring relationships are to offer optimal and sustained benefit to young people, theory and research will need to assume a more central role in the development and growth of interventions to cultivate and support such caring relationships between adults and youth.

Recommended Reading

DuBois, D.L., & Karcher, M.J. (Eds.). (2005). *Handbook of youth mentoring*. Thousand Oaks, CA: Sage. A well-organized collection of rigorous, scholarly reviews of theory, research, and practice for a wide range of topics pertaining to youth mentoring.

Hirsch, B.J. (2005). *A place to call home: After-school programs for urban youth*. Washington, DC: American Psychological Association and New York: Teachers College Press. An in-depth and informative account of mentoring relationships between staff and youth in after-school programs.

Rhodes, J.E. (2002). (See References). A comprehensive, highly accessible overview of what is known about youth mentoring.

Acknowledgments—Both authors are grateful for the support they have received for their research on mentoring and its relation to practice as Distinguished Fellows of the William T. Grant Foundation.

Note

1. Address correspondence to Jean Rhodes, Department of Psychology, University of Massachusetts, 100 Morrissey Blvd, Boston, MA 02125; e-mail: jean.rhodes@umb.edu.

References

Beam, M.R., Gil-Rivas, V., Greenberger, E., & Chen, C. (2002). Adolescent problem behavior and depressed mood: Risk and protection within and across social contexts. *Journal of Youth & Adolescence, 31,* 343–357.

Beier, S.R., Rosenfeld, W.D., Spitalny, K.C., Zansky, S.M., & Bontempo, A.N. (2000). The potential role of an adult mentor in influencing high risk behaviors in adolescents. *Archives of Pediatrics and Adolescent Medicine, 154,* 327–331.

Darling, N., Hamilton, S., Toyokawa, T., & Matsuda, S. (2002). Naturally occurring mentoring in Japan and the United States: Roles and correlates. *American Journal of Community Psychology, 30,* 245–270.

DuBois, D.L., Holloway, B.E., Valentine, J.C., & Cooper, H. (2002). Effectiveness of mentoring programs for youth: A meta-analytic review. *American Journal of Community Psychology, 30,* 157–197.

DuBois, D.L., & Silverthorn, N. (2005). Natural mentoring relationships and adolescent health: Evidence from a national study. *American Journal of Public Health, 95,* 518–524.

Durlak, J.A., & Wells, A.M. (1997). Primary prevention mental health programs for children and adolescents: A meta-analytic review. *American Journal of Community Psychology, 25,* 115–152.

Eby, L.T., Allen, T.D., Evans, S.C., Ng, T.W.H., & DuBois, D.L. (2008). Does mentoring matter? A multidisciplinary meta-analysis comparing mentored and non-mentored individuals. *Journal of Vocational Behavior, 72,* 254–267.

Grossman, J.B., & Rhodes, J.E. (2002). The test of time: Predictors and effects of duration in youth mentoring relationships. *American Journal of Community Psychology, 30,* 199–219.

Grossman, J.B., & Tierney, J.P. (1998). Does mentoring work? An impact study of the Big Brothers Big Sisters program. *Evaluation Review, 22,* 403–426.

Herrera, C., Grossman, J.B., Kauh, T.J., Feldman, A.F., & McMaken, J. (2007). *Making a difference in schools: The Big Brothers Big Sisters school-based mentoring impact study*. Philadelphia, PA: Public/Private Ventures.

Jolliffe, D., & Farington, D.P. (2007). A rapid evidence assessment of the impact of mentoring on re-offending: A summary. Cambridge University: Home Office Online Report 11/07. http://www.crimereduction.gov.uk/workingoffenders/workingoffenders069.htm

Klaw, E.L., Fitzgerald, L.F., & Rhodes, J.E. (2003). Natural mentors in the lives of African American adolescent mothers: Tracking relationships over time. *Journal of Youth and Adolescence, 32*, 322–332.

Langhout, R.D., Rhodes, J.E., & Osborne, L.N. (2004). An exploratory study of youth mentoring in an urban context: Adolescents' perceptions of relationship styles. *Journal of Youth and Adolescence, 33*, 293–306.

Markus, H., & Nurius, P. (1986). Possible selves. *American Psychologist, 41*, 954–969.

MENTOR. (2006). *Mentoring in America 2005: A snapshot of the current state of mentoring.* Retrieved August 3, 2007, from http://www.mentoring.org/downloads/mentoring_333.pdf

Morrow, K.V., & Styles, M.B. (1995). *Building relationships with youth in program settings: A study of Big Brothers/Big Sisters.* Philadelphia, PA: Public/Private Ventures.

Rhodes, J.E. (2002). *Stand by me: The risks and rewards of mentoring today's youth.* Cambridge, MA: Harvard University Press.

Rhodes, J.E. (2005). A model of youth mentoring. In D.L. DuBois & M.J. Karcher (Eds.), *Handbook of youth mentoring* (pp. 30–43). Thousand Oaks, CA: Sage.

Rhodes, J.E., & DuBois, D.L. (2006). Understanding and facilitating the youth mentoring movement. *Social Policy Report, 20*(3), 3–20.

Rhodes, J.E., Grossman, J.B., & Resch, N.R. (2000). Agents of change: Pathways through which mentoring relationships influence adolescents' academic adjustment. *Child Development, 71*, 1662–1671.

Rhodes, J.E., Reddy, R., & Grossman, J.B. (2005). The protective influence of mentoring on adolescents' substance use: Direct and indirect pathways. *Applied Developmental Science, 9*, 31–47.

Spencer, R. (2007). "It's not what I expected": A qualitative study of youth mentoring relationship failures. *Journal of Adolescent Research, 22*, 331–354.

This article has been reprinted as it originally appeared in *Current Directions in Psychological Science*. Citation information for this article as originally published appears above.

Coaching the Coaches: Youth Sports as a Scientific and Applied Behavioral Setting

Ronald E. Smith and Frank L. Smoll[1]
Department of Psychology, University of Washington, Seattle, Washington

In U.S. culture, sport touches the lives of a great many people, whether as participants or as spectators. It is also touching the lives of a growing number of psychologists who have come to appreciate the world of athletics as a fertile setting for the study of psychological phenomena, for the development and testing of psychological theories, and for the application of psychological principles. Very few psychological processes that are of interest within "mainstream" psychology do not occur within the context of sport, meaning that they can often be studied within a naturalistic setting in which participants are heavily involved and committed.

The most heavily publicized area of sport psychology tends to be interventions for enhancing performance of elite athletes, as the recent Olympic games have shown. However, another sport setting that is worthy of attention is youth sports, which involve some 26 million children and some 3 million adult supervisors in the United States alone. Proponents of youth sports emphasize ways in which the experience can contribute to personal development. Within sport, youngsters can learn adaptive ways of competing and cooperating with other people; they can learn risk taking, personal commitment, and self-control; and they can learn to deal with success and failure. Important attitudes about achievement, authority, and persistence in the face of adversity are formed. In addition, advocates point out, lifelong patterns of physical activity that promote health and fitness can be initiated through involvement in youth sports. Yet a realistic appraisal of youth sports indicates that participation does not automatically result in these outcomes. The most important factor determining outcomes is the manner in which this important social learning situation is structured and supervised by the adults who play an increasingly active role in the highly organized youth sport programs of today.

In a research program that has spanned nearly two decades, we have focused on interactions between coaches and young athletes. Most athletes have their first sport experiences in programs staffed by volunteer coaches. Although many of these coaches are fairly well versed in the technical aspects of the sport, they rarely have had any formal training in creating a healthy psychological environment for youngsters. We have been concerned with identifying the coaching practices that foster positive psychosocial outcomes and with developing an empirically based intervention program that trains coaches in how to create an athletic environment that fosters positive coach–athlete and peer interactions, increases the pleasure of participating, enhances self-esteem, and reduces attrition from sport programs. In this article, we demonstrate linkages between basic and applied research, theory testing, and program evaluation in this important area of sports.

BASIC RESEARCH: MEASURING COACHING
BEHAVIORS AND THEIR EFFECTS ON CHILDREN

In its initial phase, the project was guided by a simple mediational model having the following components: coach's behaviors → athletes' perceptions and recall → athletes' evaluative reactions. This model stipulates that the ultimate effects of coaching behaviors are mediated by the children's recall and the meaning they attribute to the coach's actions. We therefore developed methods for measuring all of these elements of the model. First, in collaboration with Earl Hunt, we developed the 12-category Coaching Behavior Assessment System to directly assess coaching behaviors during practices and games (Smith, Smoll, & Hunt, 1977). This observational coding system allowed us to measure individual differences in the use of positive reinforcement, various types of technical instruction, punitive responses to mistakes, encouragement, organizational and order-maintaining behaviors, attention paid to athletes' positive behaviors and mistakes, and other coaching practices. Second, we developed corresponding rating scales to assess children's and coaches' independent recall of how frequently the 12 classes of behaviors had occurred. Finally, we developed a battery of attitudinal and personality measures to assess the children's reactions to the coach and their teammates, enjoyment of their athletic experience, and self-esteem.

We found that the typical baseball or basketball coach engages in more than 200 codable actions during an average game. We were thus able to generate behavioral profiles of up to several thousand responses over the course of a season. In large-scale observational studies, we coded more than 80,000 behaviors of some 70 male coaches, then interviewed and administered questionnaires to nearly 1,000 children in their homes after the season to measure their recall of their coaches' behaviors and their evaluative reactions to the coach, their sport experience, and themselves (e.g., Curtis, Smith, & Smoll, 1979; Smith, Zane, Smoll, & Coppel, 1983). We also obtained coaches' postseason ratings of how frequently they engaged in each of the observed behaviors.

These data provided clear evidence for the crucial role of the coach. We found that won-lost records bore little relation to our psychosocial outcome measures (i.e., reaction to coach, enjoyment, and self-esteem); virtually all the systematic variance in outcome was accounted for by differences in coaching behaviors. Not surprisingly, we found that the most positive outcomes occurred when children played for coaches who engaged in high levels of positive reinforcement for both desirable performance and effort, who responded to mistakes with encouragement and technical instruction, and who emphasized the importance of fun and personal improvement over winning. Not only did the children who had such coaches like their coaches more and have more fun, but they also liked their teammates more.

There were also some surprises in the data. First, we found that punitive and hostile actions occurred less frequently but had more devastating effects than we had anticipated. Although only 1.5% of the behaviors we coded were punitive and critical, they correlated more strongly (and negatively) than any other behavior with children's attitudes. Second, we found that general encouragement bore a curvilinear relation to children's attitudes; both very low and very high levels were linked to negative attitudes toward the coach. Finally, we found that coaches were, for the most part, blissfully unaware of how they behaved. The only actions on their self-report measure that correlated significantly (around .50) with the observational measures were the punitive behaviors. In all other behavioral categories, the children were more accurate in their perceptions than were the coaches. This finding clearly indicated the need to increase coaches' self-awareness when developing an intervention program.

APPLIED RESEARCH: DEVELOPING AN INTERVENTION PROGRAM

Data from the basic research provided a strong empirical foundation for developing a behavioral intervention program for youth coaches. They serve two other functions as well: They allow us to structure the intervention as an information-sharing rather than speculative enterprise, and their scientific origin increases the credibility of the behavioral guidelines that we communicate to the coaches.

Core Principles

Five core principles underlie the behavioral coaching guidelines communicated in our program, which is called Coach Effectiveness Training (CET; Smith, Smoll, & Curtis, 1979). First, we emphasize the important differences between the professional sports model, in which winning and financial gain are the bottom line, and a developmental model, in which the focus is on providing a positive developmental context for the child. In the latter model, "winning" is defined not in terms of won-lost records, but in terms of giving maximum effort and making improvement. The explicit and primary focus of a youth sport program is on having fun, deriving satisfaction from being on the team, learning sport skills, and increasing self-esteem and reducing fear of failure.

Our second principle emphasizes what we term a "positive approach" to coaching. In such an approach, coach–athlete interactions are characterized by the liberal use of positive reinforcement, encouragement, and sound technical instruction that help create high levels of interpersonal attraction between coaches and athletes. Punitive and hostile responses are strongly discouraged, as they have been shown to create a negative team climate and to promote fear of failure in athletes. We emphasize that reinforcement should not be restricted to the learning and performance of sport skills. Rather, it should be liberally applied to strengthen other desirable responses as well (e.g., teamwork, leadership, sportsmanship). Coaches are urged to reinforce effort as much as they do results. This guideline has direct relevance to developing a healthy philosophy of winning and reducing performance anxiety. CET also includes several guidelines for a positive approach to technical instruction. For example, we encourage coaches to emphasize in their instruction the good things that will happen if athletes execute correctly rather than focusing on the negative things that will occur if they do not. We believe that this approach motivates athletes to make desirable things happen (i.e., helps develop a positive achievement orientation) rather than building fear of making mistakes.

The third coaching principle is to establish norms that emphasize athletes' mutual obligations to help and support one another. Such norms increase social support and attraction among teammates and thereby enhance cohesion and commitment to the team, and they are most likely to develop when coaches are themselves supportive models and reinforce athletes' behaviors that promote team unity. We also instruct coaches in how to develop a "we're in this together" group norm. This norm can play an important role in building team cohesion, particularly if the coach frequently reinforces athletes' demonstrations of mutual supportiveness.

A fourth principle is that compliance with team roles and responsibilities is most effectively achieved by involving athletes in decisions regarding team rules and by reinforcing compliance with them rather than punishing non-compliance. We believe that coaches should recognize that youngsters want clearly defined limits and structure. By setting explicit guidelines and using positive reinforcement to strengthen desirable responses, coaches can often prevent athletes from misbehaving.

Finally, CET coaches are urged to obtain behavioral feedback and to engage in self-monitoring to increase awareness of their own actions and to encourage compliance with the guidelines.

CET Procedures

In a CET workshop, which lasts approximately 3 hours, behavioral guidelines are presented both verbally and in written materials (a printed outline and a 24-page manual) given to the coaches. The manual (Smoll & Smith, 1997) supplements the guidelines with concrete suggestions for communicating effectively with young athletes, for gaining their respect, and for relating effectively to athletes' parents. The importance of sensitivity and responsiveness to individual differences among athletes is also stressed. The written materials keep the workshop organized, facilitate the coaches' understanding of the information, eliminate the need for coaches to take notes, and give coaches a tangible resource to refer to in the future. During the workshop, we also use modeling and role-playing procedures to demonstrate how the guidelines can be applied in specific situations.

One of the striking findings from our initial research was that coaches have very limited awareness of their own actions while coaching. Thus, an important goal of CET is to increase awareness, for no change is likely to occur without it. To this end, coaches are given a brief self-monitoring form that they complete after each practice and game. On this form, they indicate how frequently they complied with each of the behavioral guidelines. Coaches report that they find this form very useful in fostering self-awareness and in helping them identify areas for potential improvement.

PROGRAM EVALUATION: ASSESSING THE EFFICACY OF CET

We have focused on five important outcome questions in our program evaluation studies. First, does the CET program affect the actions of the trained coaches in a manner consistent with the behavioral guidelines? Second, given that the program is designed to help coaches create an environment that increases children's positive reactions to coach, teammates, and their sport experience, are athletes who play for trained coaches actually affected in these ways? Third, does the positive interpersonal environment created by trained coaches result in an increase in general self-esteem, particularly among children with low self-esteem? Fourth, does CET training help coaches to reduce performance anxiety among young athletes? And, finally, do positive changes in the first four outcomes increase the likelihood that the young athletes will remain in sports, rather than dropping out?

All five of these desirable outcomes have been demonstrated in a series of outcome studies in which experimental groups of youth coaches exposed to the CET program were compared with untrained coaches or with an attention-placebo control group that attended a technical skills teaching clinic conducted by the Seattle Mariners professional team. The behavior of coaches exposed to CET differed from the behavior of coaches in the control groups in a manner consistent with CET's behavioral guidelines. Both observation and athletes' perceptions indicated that trained coaches were more reinforcing, were more encouraging, gave more technical instruction, and were less punitive and controlling than were control group coaches. In turn, the athletes who played for the trained coaches indicated that they enjoyed their experience more and liked their coach and teammates more (Smith et al., 1979). Such children also demonstrated significant increases in general self-esteem and significant decreases in performance anxiety over the course of the season (Smith, Smoll, & Barnett, 1995; Smoll, Smith, Barnett, & Everett, 1993). We also found that athletes who are low in self-esteem are the ones who react most positively to trained coaches, indicating that the program has a salutary impact on the children who are most in need of a positive sport experience. Finally, a study of attrition showed a dropout rate of 26% among children who played for control group coaches, a figure that is quite consistent with previous reports of 30% to 40% annual attrition rates in youth sport programs. In contrast, only 5% of the children who had played for CET-trained coaches failed to return to the sport program the next season (Barnett, Smoll, & Smith, 1992). These positive psychosocial outcomes are all the more noteworthy in light of the fact that experimental and control groups have not differed in average won-lost percentages in any of the studies. We attribute the consistently positive outcomes derived from our relatively brief intervention to the fact that our basic research helped us to identify a set of core principles that are relatively easy for coaches to learn and that have a strong impact on young athletes.

Heartened by the positive outcomes of CET demonstrated in our program evaluation studies, we have now applied the program widely in the United States and Canada. More than 13,000 youth sport coaches have taken part in CET workshops. The principles of CET have also been applied at the high school, college, and professional levels within staff development projects (e.g., Smith & Johnson, 1990). Moreover, we believe that these principles apply to a wide range of nonathletic leadership situations as well.

THEORY TESTING

Whenever possible, theory testing should involve an interplay between the controlled laboratory setting, where internal validity can be more readily attained, and the less controllable but externally valid naturalistic setting. Because of our interest in self-esteem as a moderator variable that might influence responses to coaches' behaviors, we tested the self-enhancement model of Tesser (1988) against a consistency model (e.g., Rogers, 1951). The self-enhancement model states that most people have a strong need to enhance their self-evaluations and to feel positively about themselves. People who are low in self-esteem are thought to have particularly strong self-enhancement needs. Therefore, they should value positive feedback and respond very positively to people with whom they have self-enhancing interactions. A different prediction is derived from the consistency model, which suggests that people with low self-esteem may actually be more comfortable with someone who provides negative feedback that is congruent with their negative self-image, thereby satisfying needs for cognitive consistency.

To test the models, we examined the reactions of children with low, moderate, and high scores on a measure of general self-esteem to coaches who were either quite high or quite low on a behavioral dimension that we term supportiveness (the tendency to reinforce desirable performance and effort and to respond to mistakes with encouragement rather than punitiveness). Responses revealed a significant interaction between the coach's supportiveness and the athlete's level of self-esteem. As shown in Figure 1, children with low self-esteem were more responsive than other children to variations in supportiveness, and the pattern of their responses favors the self-enhancement model. Rather than liking the

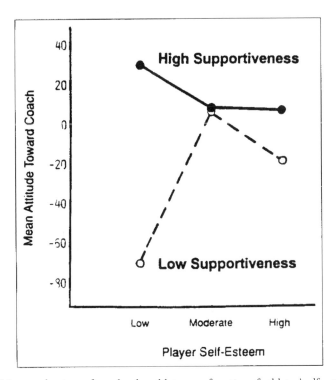

Fig. 1. Mean evaluations of coaches by athletes as a function of athletes' self-esteem and supportiveness of the coach (data from Smith & Smoll, 1990).

nonsupportive coaches, these children reacted especially negatively to them, presumably because the coaches frustrated their self-enhancement needs by being nonsupportive (Smith & Smoll, 1990). This finding extends to a naturalistic setting a body of results derived from laboratory studies which, collectively, suggest that self-enhancement motivation causes people who are low in self-esteem to be especially responsive to variations in supportiveness. Indeed, the pattern of results in Figure 1 almost directly parallels the pattern obtained in a laboratory study by Dittes (1959) involving college students' responses to accepting or nonaccepting group members. The striking similarity of the two sets of results indicates a rather notable consistency of findings across differing populations and situations.

FUTURE DIRECTIONS

Youth sports is one of several sport settings that invite the increased attention of behavioral researchers. Our work is one example of research that needs to be extended in several directions. At the basic-research level, we have focused primarily on boys' programs and male coaches to this point. Girls' programs clearly deserve empirical attention, and comparative studies of boys' and girls' reactions to specific relationships with coaches could reveal important sex differences. One of our studies suggests that girls may be more responsive to variations in supportiveness than are boys, whereas the latter may be more responsive to differences in adequacy of technical instruction. The study of attachment relationships could likewise add an important element to research in this area. For example, how are parental attachments related to the kinds of attachments that children form with coaches?

From an intervention perspective, the results from evaluations of the CET program have been encouraging. Again, however, these evaluations have been done with a limited range of samples, mainly white, middle-class participants. Extensions of the program to other populations could have notable benefits. For example, the low dropout rates among children who play for trained coaches could have important implications for preventing delinquency. Reducing attrition by applying CET within inner-city settings, where dropout rates often exceed 50%, could yield significant payoffs by keeping youngsters who are at risk for delinquency involved in sports and out of gangs and other unfavorable activities.

The range of psychological phenomena and developmental issues that can be studied within sports is extensive. Given the many significant issues yet to be explored, it is our hope that more psychological scientists will come to appreciate the youth sport setting as an inviting naturalistic laboratory for basic and applied research.

Recommended Reading

Smith, R.E., & Smoll, F.L. (1996). *Way to go, Coach!: A scientifically validated approach to coaching effectiveness*. Portola Valley, CA: Warde Publishers.

Smoll, F.L., & Smith, R.E. (1989). Leadership behaviors in sport: A conceptual model and research paradigm. *Journal of Applied Social Psychology, 19*, 1522–1551.

Smoll, F.L., & Smith, R.E. (Eds.). (1996). *Children and youth in sport: A biopsychosocial perspective*. Dubuque, IA: McGraw-Hill.

Note

1. Address correspondence to Ronald E. Smith, Department of Psychology, Box 351525, University of Washington, Seattle, WA 98195-1525; e-mail: resmith@u.washington. edu. Inquiries concerning Coach Effectiveness Training can also be addressed to smoll@ u.washington.edu.

References

Barnett, N.P., Smoll, F.L., & Smith, R.E. (1992). Effects of enhancing coach-athlete relationships on youth sport attrition. *The Sport Psychologist, 6,* 111–127.

Curtis, B., Smith, R.E., & Smoll, F.L. (1979). Scrutinizing the skipper: A study of leadership behaviors in the dugout. *Journal of Applied Psychology, 64,* 391–400.

Dittes, J. (1959). Attractiveness of a group as a function of self-esteem and acceptance by group. *Journal of Abnormal and Social Psychology, 59,* 77–82.

Rogers, C.R. (1951). *Client-centered therapy.* Boston: Houghton Mifflin.

Smith, R.E., & Johnson, J. (1990). An organizational empowerment approach to consultation in professional baseball. *The Sport Psychologist, 4,* 347–357.

Smith, R.E., & Smoll, F.L. (1990). Self-esteem and children's reactions to youth sport coaching behaviors: A field study of self-enhancement processes. *Developmental Psychology, 26,* 987–993.

Smith, R.E., Smoll, F.L., & Barnett, N.P. (1995). Reduction of children's sport performance anxiety through social support and stress-reduction training for coaches. *Journal of Applied Developmental Psychology, 16,* 125–142.

Smith, R.E., Smoll, F.L., & Curtis, B. (1979). Coach Effectiveness Training: A cognitive-behavioral approach to enhancing relationship skills in youth sport coaches. *Journal of Sport Psychology, 1,* 59–75.

Smith, R.E., Smoll, F.L., & Hunt, E.B. (1977). A system for the behavioral assessment of athletic coaches. *Research Quarterly, 48,* 401–407.

Smith, R.E., Zane, N.W.S., Smoll, F.L., & Coppel, D.B. (1983). Behavioral assessment in youth sports: Coaching behaviors and children's attitudes. *Medicine and Science in Sports and Exercise, 15,* 208–214.

Smoll, F.L., & Smith, R.E. (1997). *Coaches who never lose: A 30-minute primer for coaching effectiveness.* Portola Valley, CA: Warde Publishers.

Smoll, F.L., Smith, R.E., Barnett, N.P., & Everett, J.J. (1993). Enhancement of children's self-esteem through social support training for youth sport coaches. *Journal of Applied Psychology, 78,* 602–610.

Tesser, A. (1988) Toward a self-evaluative maintenance model of social behavior. In L. Berkowitz (Ed.), *Advances in experimental social psychology* (Vol. 21, pp. 69–92). Orlando, FL: Academic Press.

This article has been reprinted as it originally appeared in *Current Directions in Psychological Science.* Citation information for this article as originally published appears above.

Empirical and Theoretical Conclusions of an Analysis of Outcomes of HIV-Prevention Interventions

Dolores Albarracín[1], Marta R. Durantini, and Allison Earl
University of Florida

Abstract

Over two decades of HIV-prevention attempts have generated a most impressive ecological data set for the test of behavioral-change and persuasion theories in the domain of condom use. An analysis of this evidence has yielded five important empirical and theoretical conclusions. First, interventions are more successful at achieving immediate knowledge and motivational change than they are at achieving immediate behavioral change. Second, the immediate motivational change decays over time, whereas behavior change increases over the same period. Third, interventions that engage audiences in particular activities, such as role-playing condom use, are more effective than presentations of materials to passive audiences. Fourth, interventions consistent with the theories of reasoned action and planned behavior, with self-efficacy models, and with information-motivation and behavioral-skills models prove effective, whereas interventions designed to induce fear do not. Fifth, expert intervention facilitators are more effective than lay community members in almost all cases. When populations are unempowered, expert facilitators are particularly effective, and they are most effective if they also share the gender and ethnicity of the target audience.

Keywords

HIV; health promotion; persuasion; behavior change; attitude change; source effects

The HIV epidemic has resulted in a mushrooming of prevention programs and research on these programs. As a result, the literature on HIV prevention is possibly the most extensive, up-to-date, and diverse laboratory to study change in health behavior and behavioral change in general. In this article, we discuss the conclusions from two comprehensive statistical analyses of this literature. These conclusions pertain to how much change different interventions elicit, how such change evolves over time, and how the data support or contradict theories of behavior change.

SOURCES OF THIS REVIEW

Over the course of 8 years, we (Albarracín et al., in press) conducted a comprehensive meta-analysis (i.e., statistical analysis of a pool of studies on an issue) of the outcomes of interventions to increase condom use to prevent HIV. As part of this project, over 350 interventions and around 100 control groups were selected, comprising a large number of countries, U.S. states, and years. For each of these groups or conditions, we calculated amount of change in behavior (e.g., increases in condom-use frequency) and various psychological variables including HIV-related knowledge (how much one knows about HIV and how to protect oneself), attitudes and intentions about condom use (whether one thinks that condom use is good and desirable and is willing to use condoms), perceived norms about the use of condoms (thoughts that others support one's use of condoms), perceived HIV threat (feelings of fear and being personally at risk for HIV), perceptions of control over using condoms (perceiving that one can do it if one wants to), and behavioral skills (knowing how to obtain and apply condoms and negotiate condom use with a partner). In addition, characteristics of the intervention content (what is said and done), source (who says it), and target population (the actual audience) were coded and used to analyze the effects of these factors on change, in light of theoretical predictions about the mechanisms and interpersonal sources of behavior change. Many potential methodological aspects were explored. The results we present were not affected by the type of design used, the presence or absence of control groups, or whether or not participants were randomly assigned to study groups.

CONCLUSIONS ABOUT THE AMOUNT AND DURABILITY OF CHANGE

Amount of Change

A first empirical conclusion from our meta-analysis is that, immediately after the intervention, knowledge and motivational change (change in attitudes, intentions, perceived norms, control perceptions) are much more pronounced than is actual behavioral change. The estimates of standardized change (amount of change when all measures of a variable are comparable) plotted in Figure 1 (panel A shows change from the intervention at the immediate follow-up) lead to the conclusion that recipients of HIV interventions initially experience moderate changes in knowledge and motivation and small changes in behavior.[2] In other words, as measured in the studies, interventions were least effective at increasing immediate behavioral change.

Durability of Change

The durability of change is also important and can be examined by analyzing reports that had two follow-ups (in our meta-analysis, at an average of 2 and 4 months). Although knowledge and motivational change outweigh behavioral change immediately following an HIV-prevention intervention, not all these changes persist over time in the same way (panels B and C of Fig. 1). The motivational impact of intervention programs decays; and although behavioral change is small immediately following an intervention, it increases at the time of the delayed follow-up (see last bar of panel C in Fig. 1).[3] Therefore, although knowledge change continues to be greater than behavior change at the delayed follow-up, any initial advantage for the motivational change has faded at the delayed follow-up. Intriguing possibilities are that condom use may become relatively automatic or that the motivation to use condoms may be shared and implemented by both sexual partners; both may cause condom use to increase even when motivation decreases.

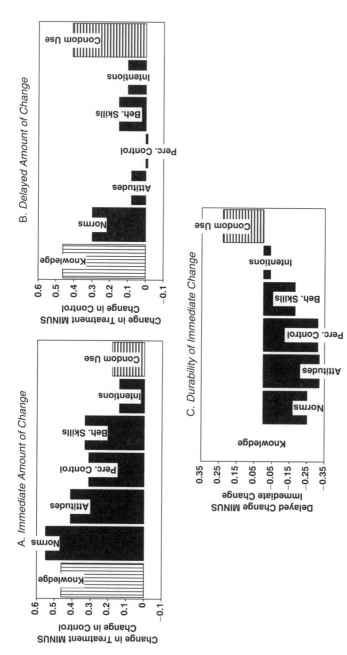

Fig. 1. Immediate and delayed change in HIV knowledge, condom-related motivations, and condom use after HIV-prevention intervention (panels A and B) and durability of these changes (panel C). Vertical shading indicates knowledge change; solid shading indicates motivational change (including condom-related perceived norms, attitudes, and perceptions of control, as well as behavioral skills and intentions regarding condom use), and horizontal shading indicates behavioral change. The results in panel B minus the results in panel A produce the results in panel C. (A score of 0.2 is considered small, a score of 0.5 moderate, and a score of 0.8 large.)

CONCLUSIONS ABOUT VIABILITY
OF THEORIES OF BEHAVIOR CHANGE

Theories on Which Behavioral-Change
Interventions Are Currently Based

One key objective of analyzing the outcomes of HIV-prevention interventions was to test theories of behavior change. Several theoretical models that specify the motivational and knowledge antecedents of health behaviors have guided intervention design in the area of HIV prevention. For example, the theory of reasoned action and the theory of planned behavior (Ajzen & Fishbein, 2005; for a meta-analysis, see Albarracín, Johnson, Fishbein, & Muellerleile, 2001) state that protection behaviors are contingent on positive attitudes about a behavior and on social norms favoring it. The theory of planned behavior also takes into account perceptions that the behavior is easy and up to the individual (i.e., perceived behavioral control). According to social-cognitive theory (Bandura, 1994), people will engage in protective behaviors when they perceive that they are capable of doing so, because self-efficacy is central to implementing behavior. Furthermore, social-cognitive theory (Bandura, 1994) and the information–motivation–behavioral-skills model (Fisher & Fisher, 1992) both assume that people are more likely to perform a behavior once they acquire relevant knowledge and behavioral skills.

Other models have concentrated on the role of the perceived threat posed by a health problem. The health-belief model (Rosenstock, Strecher, & Becker, 1994) and the protection-motivation theory (Floyd, Prentice-Dunn, & Rogers, 2000) hypothesize that people are motivated to initiate healthy behaviors when they (a) fear the severity of the disease and (b) believe that they are personally susceptible to it.

Linking specific theories to specific intervention contents is useful for examining the degree to which the various theories are plausible. Interventions that attempt to modify attitudes (i.e., attitudinal arguments) usually consist of assertions that the behavior being advocated will benefit one's physical health or psychological comfort. Arguments to increase favorable norms with respect to condom use (i.e., normative arguments) are often designed to convince an audience that its social network supports the practice. An informational communication typically conveys data on the nature of HIV, modes of transmission, mechanisms of the disease, and methods of prevention.

According to the information–motivation–behavioral-skills model, however, HIV-prevention programs are generally not successful unless they manage to increase behavioral skills as well. Thus, interventions based on this model—which incorporates the theories of reasoned action, planned behavior, and social-cognitive theory—also contain behavioral scripts about strategies that yield successful performance of the behavior. For example, an intervention may attempt to motivate recipients by increasing favorable attitudes and norms. Further, a persuasive message may not only tout the benefits of condom use (i.e., attitudinal arguments) or mention groups that support it (i.e., normative arguments), but also describe how success in condom use depends on preparatory actions (i.e., behavioral skills arguments), such as carrying condoms around all the time or discussing condom use with potential partners. As another example, a widely accepted strategy is to have individuals role-play condom application or negotiation (i.e., behavioral skills training), with the idea that the behavioral practice and the instructional feedback will facilitate the acquisition of the key behavioral skills. In addition to teaching behavioral skills, interventions of this type presumably increase perceptions of control (i.e., perceived behavioral control and self-efficacy), which are a critical element in the theory of planned behavior and social-cognitive theory.

As indicated before, the health-belief model and the protection-motivation theory both suggest that inducing perceptions of threat concerning HIV should increase condom use, particularly when interventions also increase response efficacy (Rogers, 1975). Therefore, communications designed on this basis typically use highly emotional scare tactics (i.e., fear-inducing arguments) in the hope that negative affect will stimulate condom use. For example, a campaign evaluated by Rigby, Brown, Anagnostou, Ross, and Rosser (1989) presented an image of the Grim Reaper as the source of an HIV-prevention message. Other less extreme communications based on the same assumptions describe the consequences of the disease, provide data on infection rates, or conduct a detailed interview about HIV risk behaviors to sensitize participants to risk.

Viability of the Theories of Behavior Change

The universe of interventions and control groups we meta-analyzed was used to test the effects of components of different theories (e.g., normative arguments or threat-inducing contents) on actual changes in condom use (as well as the mediators of this change). The findings of these analyses revealed that, overall, active interventions—that is, ones that required activities by the recipients (either behavioral-skills training or undergoing HIV counseling and testing)—were more effective than passive interventions that only presented material without the recipients engaging in specific activities. Within passive interventions, the most effective strategies were attitudinal arguments discussing the beneficial outcomes of using condoms and behavioral-skills-inducing arguments explaining how to best implement condom use, along with the distribution of condoms to participants. Within active interventions, the most effective strategies were presenting information, presenting behavioral-skills arguments, and training people in the management of their mood and situations in which drugs and alcohol are involved. Further, fear-inducing arguments were not effective when introduced in either passive or active interventions, either immediately or later in time, for any population or in combination with any other strategy (e.g., behavioral skills training). Thus, these findings provided support for the theories of reasoned action and planned behavior, for self-efficacy models, and for the information–motivation–behavioral-skills model, but did not support the main premise of the health-belief model and the protection-motivation theory.

Another important conclusion of our review is that the theories that were viable were viable across many gender, age, ethnic, and risk-behavior groups. For example, strategies targeting attitudes, perceived control, or behavioral skills were effective in all cases (see Fig. 2). To the extent that the theories of reasoned action and planned

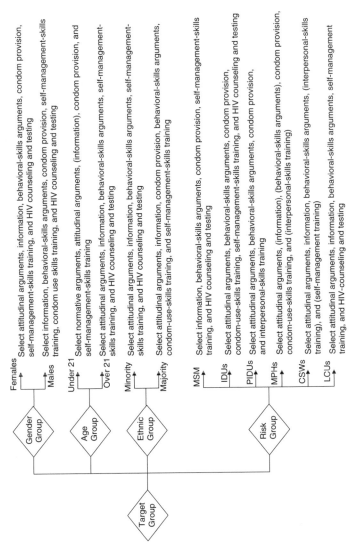

Fig. 2. The most effective active interventions for specific groups. (Interventions in parentheses were partially verified but appear to be reasonable assumptions given the data; MSM = men who have sex with men, IDUs = intravenous-drug users, PIDUs = partners of intravenous drug users, MPHs = multiple-partner heterosexuals, CSWs = commercial sex workers, and LCUs = low condom users.) Adapted from Albarracín, Gillette, et al. (in press).

behavior, self-efficacy models, and the information–motivation–behavioral-skills model propose that information, motivation, and/or behavioral skills must be present to induce behavioral change, these models received support for all populations.

At the same time, disenfranchised groups differed from more powerful groups (see Fig. 2). For instance, normative arguments were reportedly effective only for teenage populations. Likewise, training in interpersonal skills (e.g., proposing and negotiating condom use) was effective only for female partners of injection-drug users. In general, the less a group had access to social resources, the more that group benefited from provision of condoms and behavioral-skills training.

Viability of Different Sources in Charge of Delivering HIV-Prevention Interventions

Another recent advance in knowledge was to identify who can best present or facilitate HIV-prevention programs (see Durantini, Albarracín, Earl, & Mitchell, in press). Specifically, this work investigated the links of source characteristics and similarity between the source and the recipient to actual behavioral changes after the interventions. With regard to who should be the source of the intervention, this review compared two hypotheses. On the one hand, some researchers have argued that persuasive communications (and therefore behavioral interventions) should use experts as sources (Hovland, Janis, & Kelley, 1953). On the other hand, there is extensive work and policy favoring the use of laypersons selected from the target community (Freire, 1972; Putnam, 1911; in the domain of HIV prevention, see Kelly et al., 1997). Although there are some deeply-held beliefs about these issues, there have been no direct comparisons. That is, researchers have compared peer- or expert-led interventions with control groups, but no one has directly compared peer-led interventions with expert-led interventions.

By dividing interventions into those presented by experts (e.g., public health educators, physicians, nurses, research staff) and those presented by lay community members (e.g., community leaders, artists, religious ministers), our meta-analysis (Durantini et al., in press) permitted determining what type of source is more effective and for whom. Findings indicated that expert sources were more effective than lay-community members for most populations. The exceptions were men and teens (for a meta-analysis of HIV prevention among teens, see Johnson, Carey, Marsh, Levin, & Scott-Sheldon, 2003), for whom both types of sources were equally effective.

In addition, the results from this review revealed that even when experts were generally effective, they were most effective for populations that typically have restricted power in society. That is, the beneficial impact of having an expert source was much stronger for ethnic minorities and women than it was for ethnic majorities and men. Importantly, however, women and ethnic minorities were also sensitive to sources who shared whatever characteristic makes that audience different from the mainstream. For one thing, women changed more in response to other women, and ethnic minorities changed more in response to other ethnic minorities. Also, most populations whose behaviors place them at risk for HIV (injection drug users, multiple-partner heterosexuals, low condom users) benefited from having both an expert and somebody from their group as intervention facilitators. Presumably, lacking power made individuals more sensitive to intervention sources as potential points of access to resources.

FUTURE DIRECTIONS

Since the HIV epidemic first struck, there has been a remarkable increase in our understanding about how to change behaviors that prevent infection with HIV. However, this understanding raises important, currently unanswered issues. First, although some skills interventions are effective, how to exactly match them to the gender and needs of particular audiences is not clear. Social psychologists are ideally positioned to conceptualize the problem and contribute to the design of a more varied, population-tailored arsenal. Second, with the exception of teenage audiences, presenting normative arguments often works less well than not doing so. It is surprising that years of work on social influence have still not generated any model about how to effectively create norms in the real world. Third, it appears that the source of the intervention is the most direct and beneficial normative influence on behavior change. Our meta-analytic results are particularly provocative because community psychologists and other scholars have touted peer education as the gold standard. However, the results described here say nothing about the processes at stake. Future research must investigate the effects of actual and apparent expertise and community membership and the verbal and nonverbal interactions that transpire when behavioral interventions are implemented.

Recommended Reading

Albarracín, D., Gillette, J., Earl, A., Glasman, L.R., Durantini, M.R., & Ho., M.H. (in press). (See References)
Durantini, M.R., Albarracín, D., Earl, A., & Mitchell, A.L. (in press). (See References)
Fishbein, M. (2000). The role of theory in HIV prevention. *AIDS Care, 12,* 273–278.
Fisher, J.D. & Fisher, W.A. (1992). (See References)
Kalichman, S.C., Carey, M.P., & Johnson, B.T. (1996). Prevention of sexually transmitted HIV infection: A meta-analytic review of the behavioral outcome literature. *Annals of Behavioral Medicine, 18,* 6–15.

Acknowledgments—The research was supported by Grant K01-MH01861 from the National Institute of Mental Health and facilitated by grants from the National Institutes of Health (R03-MH58073 and R01-NR08325). We thank Jeffrey Gillette, Laura R. Glasman, Ringo Ho, Cynthia Klein, Penny S. McNatt, Amy L. Mitchell, G. Tarcan Kumkale, and Ece Kumkale for their invaluable contributions and assistance. We thank Joel B. Cohen for comments on an earlier version of this manuscript.

Notes

1. Address correspondence to Dolores Albarracín, Psychology Department, University of Florida, Gainesville, FL 32611; e-mail: dalbarra@ufl.edu.

2. Increases in fear or threat perceptions only occurred when the interventions included fear-inducing arguments. The overall effects of all interventions on this variable were nil.

3. Forty-six of the conditions in the meta-analysis had positive behavioral change.

References

Ajzen, I., & Fishbein, M. (2005). The influence of attitudes on behavior. In D. Albarracín, B.T. Johnson, & M.P. Zanna (Eds.), *The handbook of attitudes* (pp. 173–222). Mahwah, NJ: Erlbaum.

Albarracín, D., Gillette, J., Earl, A., Glasman, L.R., Durantini, M.R., & Ho., M.H. (in press). A test of major assumptions about behavior change: A comprehensive look at HIV prevention interventions since the beginning of the epidemic. *Psychological Bulletin.*

Albarracín, D., Johnson, B.T., Fishbein, M., & Muellerleile, P. (2001). Reasoned action and planned behavior as models of condom use: A meta-analysis. *Psychological Bulletin, 127,* 142–161.

Bandura, A. (1994). Social cognitive theory and control over HIV infection. In R. DiClemente & J. Peterson (Eds.), *Preventing AIDS: Theories and methods of behavioral interventions* (pp. 25–59). New York: Plenum.

Durantini, M.R., Albarracín, D., Earl, A., & Mitchell, A.L. (in press). Conceptualizing the influence of social agents of change: A meta-analysis of HIV prevention interventions for different groups. *Psychological Bulletin.*

Fisher, J.D. & Fisher, W.A. (1992). Changing AIDS-risk behavior. *Psychological Bulletin, 111,* 455–474.

Floyd, D.L., Prentice-Dunn, S., & Rogers, R.W. (2000). A meta-analysis of research on protection motivation theory. *Journal of Applied Social Psychology, 30,* 407–429.

Freire, P. (1972). *Pedagogy of the oppressed.* Harmondsworth: Penguin.

Hovland, C.I., Janis, I.L., & Kelley, H.H. (1953). *Communication and persuasion: Psychological studies of opinion change.* New Haven, CT: Yale University Press.

Johnson, B.T., Carey, M.P., Marsh, K.L., Levin, K.D., & Scott-Sheldon, L.A. (2003). Interventions to reduce sexual risk for the human immunodeficiency virus in adolescents, 1985–2000: A research synthesis. *Archives of Pediatrics and Adolescent Medicine, 157,* 381–388.

Kelly, J.A., Murphy, D.A., Sikkema, K.J., McAuliffe, T.L., Roffman, R.A., Solomon, L.J., Winett, R.A., Kalichman, S.C., & the Community HIV Prevention Research Collaborative (1997). Randomised, controlled, community-level HIV-prevention intervention for sexual-risk behavior among homosexual men in US cities. *The Lancet, 350,* 1500–1505.

Putnam, R.D. (1911). *Making democracy work.* Princeton, NJ: Princeton University Press.

Rigby, K., Brown, M., Anagnostou, P., Ross, M.W., & Rosser, B.R.S. (1989). Shock tactics to counter AIDS: The Australian experience. *Psychology and Health, 3,* 145–159.

Rogers, R.W. (1975). A protection motivation theory of fear appeals and attitude change. *Journal of Psychology, 91,* 93–114.

Rosenstock, I.M., Strecher, V.J., & Becker, M.H. (1994). The health belief model and HIV risk behavior change. In R.J. DiClemente, & J.L. Peterson (Eds.), *Preventing AIDS: Theories and methods of behavioral interventions* (pp. 5–24). New York: Plenum Press.

This article has been reprinted as it originally appeared in *Current Directions in Psychological Science*. Citation information for this article as originally published appears above.

Psychosocial Impact of Job Loss on Individuals and Families

Richard H. Price[1]
University of Michigan

A large number of studies have been undertaken to evaluate the psychosocial impact of involuntary job loss on unemployed workers and their families,[2] but until recently the findings have been mixed and inconclusive. The primary reason is that it has been difficult to firmly establish that job loss causes psychosocial difficulties. The rival hypothesis, that persons with mental health problems are more likely than others to lose their jobs, is difficult to rule out unless representative samples of both employed and unemployed persons can be followed over time.

In addition, most studies on the impact of unemployment have focused on individuals rather than on families. It is only recently that we have begun to gather evidence that the impact of unemployment can radiate throughout the personal-social network of the unemployed individual to his or her spouse, signficant other, or children. Furthermore, most studies have gathered only a limited amount of information about the nature of the difficulties confronted by the unemployed and their families, thus limiting the opportunity to understand the processes by which job loss has its effects on individuals and their families.

MENTAL HEALTH IMPACT

A recent study by Kessler, Turner, and House[3] documented the mental health impact of involuntary job loss in a probability sample of currently unemployed, previously unemployed, and steadily employed persons drawn from high-unemployment census tracts in southeastern Michigan. These investigators were able to show that unemployed groups showed more symptoms of anxiety and depression than did steadily employed individuals. Furthermore, unemployed persons in the sample were three times as likely as steadily employed persons to show extreme scores on mental health symptoms.

To strengthen the evidence that unemployment was causing mental health problems rather than the reverse, Kessler and his colleagues identified a subsample of unemployed persons who had lost their jobs as a result of mass layoffs and plant closings. These people were unlikely to have become unemployed because of mental health problems. The results for this sub-sample were identical to those of the larger study, suggesting that involuntary job loss does indeed create mental health problems.

Considerably less research has been done to determine the causal mechanisms responsible for the mental health impact of job loss. Among the possible mechanisms for this impact are the effects of financial strain, marital difficulty and conflict, reduced affiliation in personal and social networks, and financial loss events such as loss of a house or of personal property.

Kessler and his colleagues[4] have reported a series of path analyses indicating that financial strain accounts for the largest proportion of the effects of unemployment on mental health and that all other factors play a relatively minor role. These results help us gain insight into how unemployment can be translated into mental health symptoms and help explain why reemployment frequently produces a nearly complete reversal of the psychological distress associated with job loss.

FAMILY IMPACT

Although there is a substantial body of anecdotal evidence that job loss can have an impact on family relationships, much of the research evidence on this question is mixed and subject to some of the same difficulties described above.[5,6] In addition to problems of sample representativeness, few studies have been able to examine the impact of job loss on family life and other family members, and fewer still have obtained measures of processes by which unemployment may have its effect on family relationships. However, recently, Broman, Hamilton, and Hoffman[7] studied a large, representative sample of families of auto workers who had recently lost their jobs or were anticipating unemployment. In particular, these investigators were able to obtain measures of conflict between the unemployed person and (a) his or her spouse and (b) children. In addition, respondents were asked about problems their children exhibited, including problems in school, behavioral and emotional problems, and sleep problems or nightmares. The results indicated that the unemployment experience has powerful negative effects on the families of workers, increasing the level of conflict, tension, and stress reported in their households. Compared with currently employed control groups, unemployed workers reported more conflict with their spouses and with their children, and reported that they were more likely to have hit, slapped, or spanked their children.

While other studies have also documented elevated family conflict and child abuse among the unemployed, few studies have obtained information on the likely reasons for this increase. However, Broman, Hamilton, and Hoffman were able to establish that financial hardship was the mechanism through which unemployment increased family conflict. Furthermore, they found that financial hardship produced more conflict for men than for women. This finding may reflect traditional beliefs that males are failing in a major social role when they become unemployed.

FAMILY SUPPORT

Although job loss appears to increase family conflict, primarily as a consequence of financial strain, does the family play a role in ameliorating the impact of unemployment? House and his colleagues[8] examined this question, focusing on a variety of forms of social support, including integration into affiliative networks and the availability of crisis support from friends, relatives, and co-workers. Overall, House and his colleagues found that social support works very differently for married and unmarried unemployed persons. The marital relationship provides a strong support system that has protective effects on mental health. Being married, particularly for men, increases social integration and the availability of informal social support. For the unmarried, however, social integration is a critical protective factor. Unemployed persons who are unmarried and lack strong supportive social networks are particularly at risk for mental health problems.

THE DOUBLE BURDEN OF UNEMPLOYMENT

Unemployed persons and their families face a double burden. Not only must they cope with the circumstances of unemployment itself, including financial hardship and the possibility of increased family conflict, but the unemployed person must also engage in a job search that places high demands on his or her coping resources. Any intervention that attempts to aid individuals in coping with the transition back into the world of work must recognize this double burden.

Interventions that aid the unemployed in returning to the work force may reduce the risks associated with prolonged unemployment. Such interventions may also help the unemployed person to cope with the difficult task of job seeking, which frequently involves numerous rejections and setbacks and requires the use of social networks and effective self-presentation. One such intervention, the Jobs Project,[9] which was evaluated in the context of the randomized field experiment, involved four major overlapping components: (1) training in job search skills, (2) an active learning process with considerable time spent rehearsing new skills, (3) inoculation against setbacks (i.e., learning groups anticipated setbacks or barriers and developed problem-solving strategies for coping with them), and (4) social support from both other group members and trainers, including the expression of empathy and validation of the participant's concerns and feelings.

Results of the randomized field experiment indicated that the Jobs intervention produced higher quality reemployment in terms of earnings and job satisfaction, as well as higher motivation among participants who continued to be unemployed. A $2\frac{1}{2}$-year follow-up[10] demonstrated continued higher monthly earnings, higher levels of employment, and fewer episodes of employer and job changes. In addition, benefit-cost analyses indicated that the higher earnings and tax revenues produced would pay for the intervention in less than 1 year.

WHO BENEFITS MOST?

One critical question about preventive interventions of the kind described is whether they benefit the people who need them most. To answer this question, with van Ryn and Vinokur,[11] I conducted analyses to identify the persons at highest risk for depression among the unemployed. In a $2\frac{1}{2}$-year longitudinal study, we found that those most at risk were those who experienced high levels of financial hardship and were low in social assertiveness. These individuals also benefited most from the intervention. In fact, among high-risk individuals, the intervention cut the risk of severe depressive episodes from 50% to about 30%.

It remains to be seen if such interventions can be made even more effective by actively involving family members in the provision of social support during the job search process. This is a promising new line of inquiry and may well yield new insights about family dynamics and support among the unemployed, as well as provide intervention prototypes that have the possibility of broad policy impact. In addition, such interventions, if made available in downsizing organizations, can have beneficial effects both for the individuals who must seek reemployment and for the work organizations, which can reduce their liability in a variety of ways.[12]

Notes

1. Address correspondence to Richard H. Price, Institute for Social Research, University of Michigan, Ann Arbor, M1 48106.

2. J. Barling, *Employment, Stress and Family Functioning* (John Wiley & Sons, West Sussex, England, 1990).

3. R.C. Kessler, J.B. Turner, and J.S. House, Unemployment and health in a community sample, *Journal of Health and Social Behavior, 28,* 51–59 (1987).

4. R.C. Kessler, J.B. Turner, and J.S. House, Intervening processes in the relationship between unemployment and health, *Psychological Medicine, 17,* 949–961 (1987).

5. R. Liem and J.H. Liem, Psychological effects of unemployment on workers and their families, *Journal of Social Issues, 44*(4), 87–105 (1988)

6. P. Moen, E. Kain, and G.H. Elder, Jr., Economic conditions and family life: Contemporary and historical perspectives, in *American Families and the Economy,* R. Nelson and F. Skidmore, Eds. (National Academic Press, Washington, DC, 1983), pp. 213–259.

7. C.L. Broman, V.L. Hamilton, and W.S. Hoffman, Unemployment and its effects on families: Evidence from a plant closing study, *American Journal of Community Psychology, 18,* 643–659 (1990).

8. J.S. House, D.R. Williams, and R.C. Kessler, Unemployment, social support, and health, in *Social Support—Health and Disease,* S.O. Isacsson and L. Janzon, Eds. (Almqvist & Wik-sell, Stockholm, Sweden, 1986), pp. 93–111.

9. R.D. Caplan, A.D. Vinokur, R.H. Price, and M. van Ryn, Job seeking, reemployment and mental health: A randomized field experiment in coping with job loss, *Journal of Applied Psychology, 74,* 759–769 (1989).

10. A.D. Vinokur, M. van Ryn, E.M. Gramlich, and R.H. Price, Long-term follow-up and benefit/cost analysis of the Jobs Project: A preventive intervention for the unemployed, *Journal of Applied Psychology, 76*(2), 1–7 (1991).

11. R.H. Price, M. van Ryn, and A.D. Vinokur, *Impact of a Preventive Job Search Intervention on High and Low Risk Unemployed Persons,* working paper, Michigan Prevention Research Center, Institute for Social Research, University of Michigan, Ann Arbor, MI (1991).

12. R.H. Price, Strategies for managing plant closings and downsizing, in *The Human Side of Corporate Competitiveness,* D. Fishman and C. Cherniss, Eds. (Sage Publications, Beverly Hills, CA, 1990), pp. 127–151.

Section 4: Critical Thinking Questions

1. Christenson and Thurlow argue that a focus on promotion of school completion differs from a focus on preventing school dropout. Is this more than a change in nomenclature? How would you classify the other papers in this section with respect to their prevention or promotion orientation?

2. The Olweus bullying prevention program focuses on multiple levels of intervention (schools, classrooms, etc.). How do these different levels of intervention reinforce one another?

3. What is internal validity? How did the theory-testing study of self-esteem and self-enhancement described by Smith and Smoll contribute to the internal validity of the self-enhancement model? What is external validity? How was it supported?

4. What features do successful mentoring programs as described by Rhodes and DuBois, and positive coaching relationships as described by Smith and Smoll have in common? How can these features be promoted?

5. What ingredients do the successful interventions to prevent HIV and to prevent depression following job loss have in common? Why might these features be generally important in prevention efforts?

6. Why are considerations of cost-benefit analysis, as described by Price, important for psychologists creating prevention programs?

This article has been reprinted as it originally appeared in *Current Directions in Psychological Science*. Citation information for this article as originally published appears above.

Section 5: From Specific Programs to Widespread Impact of Intervention

Prevention and promotion programs of the sort described in the previous section are quite successful in reducing problems and fostering well-being for participants. For example, a meta-analysis (quantitative review and synthesis of research) by Durlak and Wells in a community psychology journal showed that prevention programs for youth are overall as successful as medical treatments, based upon the percentage of individuals in the experimental groups (the prevention programs) that have better outcomes than those in the control groups (the medical treatment programs). However, community psychologists and their colleagues have been better at creating effective programs than at getting them into widespread practice; conversely, some popular prevention programs lack any scientific basis. The National Institutes of Health are responding to this problem by funding "translational research," which helps to bridge the gap between what researchers know and what most people actually experience so that the population as a whole can benefit from advances in prevention and treatment.

The three papers in this section describe prerequisites for broad-based impact of intervention programs. Spoth suggests that impact depends on effectiveness of interventions (i.e. the sort of evidence provided in the last section), the extensiveness of coverage for all segments of the population, the efficiency of the intervention, and the engagement of populations and organizations that deliver the intervention. Although researchers understand most about effectiveness, even here he suggests more information is needed about replications of interventions, long-term outcomes, effects on different subgroups, and the ways that interventions work (mediating mechanisms).

With respect to extensiveness, Spoth suggests that we need research about different developmental stages, different demographic and cultural groups, and different levels of risk. Prochaska suggests that another crucial dimension is stage of readiness to engage in behavior change. He argues that different interventions are suitable for people who are not yet prepared to change, who are prepared, and who have already changed but need help to maintain their success.

With respect to efficiency, Spoth argues for inexpensive formats that reach broader segments of the population. Prochaska demonstrates that in-home and computer-based programs can reach more people than clinic programs and reports data showing that less is sometimes more: adding help from counselors did not increase the success of computer-based "expert systems" in sustained behavior change. However, both researchers advocate targeting multiple behaviors concurrently to increase program impact.

Engagement, according to Spoth, is important both for target populations and for organizations that deliver prevention programs. Prochaska addresses the first of these issues, showing that efforts targeted at all stages of change can involve more people with lower drop-out rates. Klein and Knight focus on organizational engagement. They propose that implementation of innovative programs is a problem that transcends all subdisciplines of psychology and describe both common barriers to the implementation of new practices in organizations and factors that support putting innovations into practice. Their guidelines are as relevant to prevention programs in schools and community-based organizations as to business innovations in profit-making firms.

Translating Family-Focused Prevention Science Into Effective Practice: Toward a Translational Impact Paradigm

Richard Spoth[1]

Partnerships in Prevention Science Institute, Iowa State University

Abstract

Family-focused preventive intervention research could serve as an exemplar for the translation of science into practice on a scale that achieves public health impact. This article outlines advances in the field and translational research that still is needed, presenting these within a heuristic framework. The framework is designed to guide a broad translational research agenda fostering a shift toward a paradigm of public health impact—called a translational impact paradigm. Current advances and needed research in the subfield are mapped onto a set of four translational impact factors: effectiveness of interventions; extensiveness of their population coverage; efficiency of interventions; and engagement of eligible populations or organizations, including widespread adoption and sustained, quality implementation (the "4 Es" of intervention impact). The article then highlights key tasks required to progress in this area: improving practitioner–scientist partnership networks embedded in systems for delivery of evidence-based interventions; application of research guidelines and standards that facilitate translational impact; and policy change that supports needed research.

Keywords

family-focused preventive interventions; translational science; public health impact

The subfield of family-focused preventive intervention science addresses a broad range of public health objectives, many of which are included in the Department of Health and Human Services' strategic plan, *Healthy People 2010* (U.S. Department of Health and Human Services, 2000), articulating goals for a healthier U.S. population. Advances in the translation of family-focused preventive intervention science into widespread community-based practices with children, youth, and families would contribute substantially to accomplishing those public health objectives.

This article lays out a heuristic framework intended to guide definition of a research agenda that would foster the translation of family-focused intervention science into real-world public health practices. In this framework, key translational factors are linked to the primary means for addressing them—networks of partnerships between practitioners and scientists, the infrastructure supporting those partnerships, standards guiding their research, and necessary policy change.

ORIENTATION TOWARD THE TRANSLATION FUNCTION

Sussman, Valente, Rohrbach, Skara, & Pentz (2006) compare multiple models guiding prevention intervention research and frame them in terms of their "translational function," defined as the translation of prevention research, across multiple phases, into real-world applications. Although this function includes both (a) translation of research on the etiology of public health problems into the design of interventions (e.g., using research on childrearing factors predicting youth substance abuse to guide intervention design) and (b) translation of effective interventions into widespread practice. My focus in this article is on the latter type, frequently called Type 2 (see http://obssr.od.nih.gov/). Leaders in the field argue that Type 2 translation is the most difficult challenge in achieving public health impact, but that it has received much less funding and attention (Glasgow, Lichtenstein, & Marcus, 2003; Woolf, 2008). These leaders also suggest that Type 2 translation include consideration of factors at the intervention-development stage (e.g., consumer preferences) that might influence the extent of translation after the intervention is fully developed and tested.

Better serving translation for "real world applications" requires that family-focused intervention scientists value maximizing impact on all populations that ultimately could benefit and that they carefully consider the necessary research, and standards guiding it, across all phases of intervention development and testing. This type of orientation is a first step in a shift from a more narrow focus on intervention design and efficacy testing toward a translational impact paradigm. Figure 1 outlines this and three other important steps that serve as an organizational frame for the paper.

THE IMPORTANCE OF A TRANSLATIONAL SCIENCE ORIENTATION

The problems addressed by family-focused intervention, such as youth substance use and conduct problems—particularly among youth and families where multiple problems co-occur—have tremendous social, health, and economic consequences for U.S. populations (Biglan & Metzler, 1998). Presently, little of the potential impact of family-focused intervention science is being realized. If a pie chart represented the sum total of family-focused preventive intervention that is actually being implemented in the United States, it would show that, by far, the largest slice consists of interventions that have not been rigorously tested. Only a relatively small slice of the remaining pie would consist of interventions with demonstrated positive, long-term effects, and an even smaller slice would represent such evidence-based interventions that are being well implemented and sustained over the long term. Research addressing the translational function is aimed at expanding the high-quality, real-world implementation of evidence-based interventions over the long term so that they will have greater public health impact.

MAPPING ADVANCES ONTO A COMPREHENSIVE SET OF TRANSLATION-RELEVANT FACTORS

A second step in plotting the translational-related research course (see Fig. 1) is further attending to (a) effectiveness of interventions, that is, rigorously testing well-designed interventions for a range of outcomes; (b) extensiveness of their population coverage, that is, addressing all population segments that might benefit;

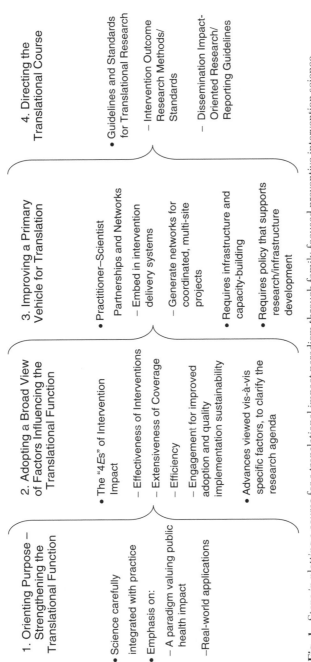

Fig. 1. Steps in plotting a course for a translational impact paradigm through family-focused preventive intervention science.

1. Orienting Purpose – Strengthening the Translational Function

- Science carefully integrated with practice
- Emphasis on:
  - A paradigm valuing public health impact
  - Real-world applications

2. Adopting a Broad View of Factors Influencing the Translational Function

- The "4Es" of Intervention Impact
  - Effectiveness of Interventions
  - Extensiveness of Coverage
  - Efficiency
  - Engagement for improved adoption and quality implementation sustainability
- Advances viewed vis-à-vis specific factors, to clarify the research agenda

3. Improving a Primary Vehicle for Translation

- Practitioner–Scientist Partnerships and Networks
  - Embed in intervention delivery systems
  - Generate networks for coordinated, multi-site projects
- Requires infrastructure and capacity-building
- Requires policy that supports research/infrastructure development

4. Directing the Translational Course

- Guidelines and Standards for Translational Research
  - Intervention Outcome Research Methods/Standards
  - Dissemination Impact-Oriented Research/Reporting Guidelines

(c) efficiency of intervention; and (d) engagement of diverse populations and organizations, including study of how to get interventions adopted and implemented with high quality, on a large scale, in a sustained way. Briefly, these are the "4 Es" for intervention impact; they are summarized in Table 1 (p. 184), along with areas of research related to each factor and illustrative advances that have been made.

Effectiveness of Interventions for Translation

The literature reveals a wide range of positive outcomes produced by evidence-based interventions, or EBIs (i.e., those tested in well-designed, methodologically sound studies demonstrating practically significant outcomes); a number of these EBIs have proven effective across multiple settings. Notably, studies of interventions implemented with families during the preschool years have shown significant positive effects on measures of caregiver–child bonding and child management, along with reduction of child aggressive behavior and enhancement of social, emotional, and cognitive competencies in children as they prepare to enter school (e.g., Webster-Stratton & Taylor, 2001). Positive outcomes from family-focused interventions for school-aged children (K–12) include improved life skills, grades, and health behaviors, as well as reduced substance use, delinquency, conduct problems, and depression or other mental health problems, along with improved caregiver–child bonding and more effective child management (Lochman & van den Steenhoven, 2002; Spoth & Redmond, 2002). Positive intervention effects on caregiver–child relationships are especially noteworthy because they serve as "scaffolds" for building adaptive self-regulation, emotion, and behavior in children. The number of family-focused interventions meeting criteria for evidence-based interventions (see www.preventionresearch.org) has been increasing (see http://modelprograms.samhsa.gov/).

Needed Intervention Outcome-Related Research

Independent replication studies of specific interventions, currently rare, are needed to show that positive outcomes are reliably achieved. Also, few studies so far reviewed have included long-term follow-up evaluations showing positive outcomes. Such studies are needed because of the possible dissipation of effects over time or the possibility that some positive effects may have delayed emergence. Further, despite advances in the conduct of core-component analyses— to identify which intervention components are those that most contribute to positive outcomes—more mediational analyses are needed—particularly, study of variation in mediating factors by population or setting. For example, these analyses identify which among a range of parenting skills mediate intervention effects on specific youth outcomes (see www.bocyf.org/prevention_of_mental_health_disorders.html). Key mediating variables could be used to tailor interventions to the needs of participating individuals (e.g., see the adaptive intervention approach described by Collins, Murphy, & Bierman, 2004). In addition, in order to have an impact at the population level, interventions demonstrating effects across risk-related subgroups (Offord, Kraemer, Kazdin, Jensen, & Harrington, 1998) are required. Notably, existing evidence suggests that general-population interventions for young adolescents can either benefit risk-related subgroups equally or benefit higher-risk youth more than lower-risk youth, thus achieving "universality of effects" (see www.ppsi.iastate.edu/abstracts.htm#96).

Extensiveness of Coverage for All Population Segments

Across Developmental Stages   For broad population impact, EBIs will be required for families with children in all developmental stages—from the prenatal period to late adolescence—for a range of developmentally specific outcomes. There has been considerable progress in the development of family-focused EBIs that address the full range of developmental stages. The "tween" stage, or the transition period between elementary and middle school, is one for which more interventions need to be developed and tested, given that research highlights the early emergence during this stage of substantial problem behaviors that could be addressed with timely intervention. Also, despite evidence of the high prevalence of certain problem behaviors (e.g., binge drinking) among high-school juniors and seniors in the general population, there has been limited research directed toward family-focused interventions for them (Spoth, Greenberg, & Turrisi, in press).

Across Sociodemographically Diverse Populations, With Necessary Cultural Adaptations   Also critically important for wider population impact is the application of EBIs to diverse populations in various settings. Research on interventions for families of adolescents with existing behavior problems or disorders has advanced to the point where interventions with multiple populations of youth and their families—ranging from school referrals to incarcerated youth—have been tested and found effective (Alexander, Robbins, & Sexton, 2000). It also is clear, however, that more research is needed concerning the development of culturally competent or appropriate interventions—or adaptation of existing interventions—to address diverse ethnic or sociodemographic characteristics of populations in the United States, ranging from inner-city to rural settings (e.g., Castro, Barrera, & Martinez, 2004).

Across Levels of Population Risk   To maximize population impact, researchers have suggested using a mix of types of interventions focusing on different levels of participant risk. This approach is increasingly feasible because several family-focused interventions with positive efficacy data in general populations have become available in the last decade, along with interventions for higher-risk subpopulations. There also is evidence for the benefit of combining all levels through an intervention process that starts with brief interventions for general populations and facilitates movement from them into more intensive interventions for higher-risk families (a "stepped" intervention process—see Table 1, Engagement of populations/organizations–Illustrative advances).

Efficiency of Implemented Interventions

Efficient General-Population Formats   Brief, lower-cost interventions, such as self-administered programs, have high potential for achieving broad impact by being disseminated in community practice (see Taylor & Biglan, 1998). One example is Family Matters (www.nrepp.samhsa.gov/programfulldetails.asp?PROGRAM_ID=89), an intervention for young adolescents and their parents that utilizes

Table 1. *Translation-relevant impact factors, areas of relevant research, and illustrative advances*

Translational function-related factor	Areas of relevant research	Illustrative advances
Effectiveness of interventions (outcomes evidence base)	—Establishing what works for a range of positive outcomes —Replication of effects —Long-term effects —Core components/key mechanisms of effects —Effects across risk-related subgroups	An illustration of an intervention with replicated, long-term effects and quality implementation is the *Nurse–Family Partnership*; it aims to improve the health and self-sufficiency of low-income, first-time parents and the positive development of their children. Multiple randomized, controlled trials have been conducted and show positive longitudinal mother and child outcomes, including reductions in child abuse or neglect and fewer arrests for both mothers and their children (at age 15)—associated with these outcomes, economic benefits also have been demonstrated. Importantly, the program has developed a dissemination system to support sustained, quality implementation through a network that currently serves families in 280 counties in 22 states (see www.nursefamilypartnership.org).
Extensiveness of intervention coverage across all population segments	—Coverage across all developmental stages —Coverage of sociodemographically-diverse populations/cultural adaptations —Coverage of levels of population risk	Addressing the need for broader population coverage and cultural adaptations, the design of the universal *Strong African American Families Program* was guided by an empirically based model for the key processes associated with psychological adjustment, substance use, and high-risk behavior of African American youth. The intervention focuses on enhancing youth competencies through (a) parent–child relationship quality and parenting skills, including "no-nonsense discipline" and family activities; (b) youth self- and emotional regulation; and (c) reduction of youth willingness to drink or to engage in risky, destructive behavior. Positive results include more regular, communicative parenting and reduced initiation of alcohol use among youth (see http://www.cfr.uga.edu/html/saaf.html).

Efficiency of interventions	–Formats that can enhance intervention efficiency
	  • Brief interventions
	  • Self-administered
	  • CD- or DVD-based/ computer-assisted
	–Crossover/non-targeted effects
	  • Generalization to nontargeted outcomes
	  • Generalization to nontargeted participants
	–Economic analyses
	  • Cost effectiveness
	  • Benefit cost
		An excellent example of advances in *economic analyses* is provided by the Washington State Institute for Public Policy (WSIPP). WSIPP followed a directive from the Washington State Legislature to conduct a comprehensive cost-benefit analysis of preventive interventions, in order to provide guidance to decision makers in identification of interventions that would be a good investment of funds. The WSIPP conducted a thorough review of the scientific literature on preventive intervention outcomes, estimated the costs and benefits of those that met their positive outcome criteria, developed recommendations for quality implementation of the selected interventions, and also suggested funding mechanisms. Their economic analysis showed that a number of family-focused preventive interventions clearly have economic benefits (see http://www.wsipp.wa.gov/).

Engagement of populations/ organizations	–Recruitment of eligible populations –Retention and family involvement –Engagement of organizations adopting interventions for sustained, quality implementation	Illustrating effective strategies for engaging families in evidence-based interventions, the *Family Check Up* (FCU) and *Motivation-Enhancing Intervening* (MEI) are integrated components of the *Adolescent Transitions Program*. The FCU involves parent-centered services, including brief consultations with parents, feedback to parents about their child's behavior at school and a range of videotapes and books. MEI entails a three-session program for higher-risk youth and families designed to educate parents in proven family management practices and to encourage them to avail themselves of related services. Analyses have shown that youth whose parents engaged in the FCU showed less growth in substance use during ages 11–17 and decreased risk for substance use diagnosis and police records of arrest (see http://www.strengtheningfamilies.org/html/programs_1999/08_ATP.html).

material mailed to their homes and follow-up phone calls from health educators. CD- or DVD-based and computer-assisted interventions, particularly those teaching parenting skills, are promising in this regard.

Crossover Effects—Additional Outcomes at No Additional Cost   Youth who engage in one type of problem behavior also frequently are at risk for engaging in other problem behaviors, and multi-problem youth and their families are disproportionately responsible for prevalent public health problems. Interventions are more efficient when they effectively address risk and protective factors common to multiple problems. Those aimed at the reduction of a specific problem behavior like substance use have the potential to also reduce youth conduct problems or, in addition, symptoms of anxiety and depression (see Summary Sheets, www.ppsi.iastate.edu). Efficiency is further enhanced when, for example, an intervention not only reduces substance use by a youth family member but, in doing so, also reduces sibling problem behavior and parental stress (see Alexander et al., 2000).

Economic Analyses   It is important to assess economic benefits of family-focused interventions (both cost effectiveness and benefit–cost analyses) because of the degree to which such information influences administrators when they select interventions (Karoly et al., 1998). Although rigorous economic analyses have been conducted with a number of family-focused interventions and have shown positive results (e.g., www.colorado.edu/cspv/blueprints/; www.wsipp.wa.gov/rptfiles/costbenefit.pdf; Spoth, Guyll, & Day, 2002), most interventions with positive outcomes have not been evaluated for economic benefits.

Engagement of Populations/Organizations

Even the most effective interventions cannot have widespread impact without adequately engaging possible eligible populations, so strategies to improve engagement in family-focused EBIs are critically important. Effective engagement includes recruitment (e.g., well-designed marketing, multipronged strategies for increasing awareness of appealing intervention features, flexible scheduling) and retention (e.g., relationship building and use of participation incentives like door prizes). Research clearly is needed on the effectiveness of recruitment strategies (Haggerty et al., 2002), and more study of community-based (vs. researcher-driven) recruitment is necessary (e.g., Spoth, Clair, Greenberg, Redmond, & Shin, 2007).

Because widespread implementation depends on the engagement of key decision-makers and stakeholders who influence adoption of evidence-based interventions at the organizational level, it is also necessary to study factors influencing the decision to implement an EBI (e.g., an organization's readiness for change) in a range of practice settings, along with effectiveness of education of policy and decision makers about the benefits of adopting EBIs (Glasgow et al., 2003). Following adoption, EBIs also must be implemented with quality (e.g., with adherence to manuals and protocols specifying core components and allowable adaptation), so that positive effects can be realized in real-world settings. Research on implementation quality has increased greatly over the last decade (see http://nirn.fmhi.usf.edu/resources/publications/Monograph). A number of family-focused EBIs have demonstrated high-quality implementation, and the link between implementation quality and positive outcomes has been demonstrated (Forgatch, Patterson, & DeGarmo, 2005). There has been, however, very limited demonstration of engagement in the long-term sustainability of such interventions; much work remains to be done on key characteristics of interventions and implementers that influence both quality and sustainability.

The Society for Prevention Research has developed a framework for translational research requiring a broad perspective encompassing the 4 Es of intervention impact—that is, effectiveness, extensiveness, efficiency, and engagement, as well as intervention adoption, implementation, and sustainability, key areas of translational study in their own right (see www.preventionresearch.org, MAPS II).

PLOTTING THE FUTURE COURSE: KEY TASKS AND NEEDED POLICY CHANGE

Practitioner–Scientist Partnerships and Networks

One of the single most important means of future advances in accomplishing greater population impact through translational science—and a third step in a course toward an enhanced translational function (see Fig. 1)—would be the development of partnerships between practitioners and scientists. Especially important are networks of partnerships embedded in population-based delivery systems for EBIs. These partnerships would address specific public health outcome objectives for family-focused interventions, such as the reduction of substance use, conduct problems, mental health problems, or obesity, and achieving positive youth-development milestones.

Descriptions of practitioner–scientist partnerships and their potential for benefitting public health have been summarized elsewhere (e.g., Spoth & Greenberg, 2005). For present purposes, it is noteworthy that there are many existing infrastructures for the delivery of family-focused interventions that could serve as the basis for translational research. Examples include population-based networks of public health and human service agencies used by the Blueprints programs (e.g., Nurse Family Partnerships; also see Multisystemic Therapy and Functional Family Therapy—www.colorado.edu/cspv/blueprints/). Another illustration is a network of practitioner–scientist partnerships that link the Cooperative Extension System with the Public School Systems (PROSPER—see www.prosper.ppsi.iastate.edu), which has the potential to reach every community in the country.

Guidelines and Standards for Impact-Oriented Intervention Research

A fourth step toward an enhanced translational impact paradigm concerns research guidelines and standards (Fig. 1, p. 181).

Standards for Outcome Research   It is critically important to foster the current trend toward more rigorous standards for assessing intervention efficacy, including paying closer attention to possible threats to all types of validity (internal, external, construct, and statistical conclusion) in intervention research. Research could be improved through actions such as (a) increasing use of statistical techniques such as Hierarchical Linear Modeling, to address the common practice of "cluster sampling" (e.g., families recruited through schools or community organizations who are randomly assigned to study conditions); (b) application of methods for addressing missing data, especially in longitudinal designs where sample attrition is an issue; and (c) validation of constructs and use of multiple methods of measurement (e.g., observational and self-reported interview data) with multiple informants (e.g., parents and youth).

Guidelines for Assessing and Reporting Impact   It also is important to encourage broader application of comprehensive guidelines for impact-oriented intervention research (see standards summarized at www.preventionresearch.org) and to increase the number of intervention literature reviews that report impact measures for the populations eligible for the intervention (e.g., the product of the efficacy of the intervention and the proportion of the eligible population engaged—see Abrams, 1999). Most importantly, further adoption of study-reporting standards indicating the level and quality of the real-world validity of an intervention, across development and testing phases, would foster a translational impact paradigm. A specific system to measure and evaluate validity has been devised and is applicable to family-focused interventions (Glasgow et al., 2003).

In closing, there have been many calls for strategies to address the challenges faced by youth and families in this country and to strengthen translational science currently receiving limited funding (Woolf, 2008). Greater attention to the translational function of intervention research will be necessary. Further, bold new policymaking will be required to realize the potential of the emerging advances in family-focused preventive interventions. An example would be "braided" funding for intervention-outcome research conducted by practitioner–researcher partnerships, integrating both research and public health service funding streams (see www.preventionresearch.org). Networks of practitioner–scientist partnerships, operating under existing infrastructures and following standards for impact-oriented research, could accelerate population-level effects—propelled by broader community-based implementation of family-focused EBIs. Greater investment in this effort would be akin to the investment in the research and public health-oriented infrastructure for vaccines that had such profound public health impact earlier in this century.

Recommended Reading

Ashery, R.S., Robertson, E.B., & Kumpfer, K.L. (Eds.). (1998). *Drug abuse prevention through family interventions* [Electronic version] (NIDA Research Monograph 177, NIH Publication No. 97–4135). Rockville, MD: National Institute on Drug Abuse. A thorough treatment of topical areas in family-focused intervention science, with chapters addressing the rationale for family-centered interventions targeting substance abuse, family-related etiological factors, varied types of interventions, advances in research methodology, and dissemination approaches, along with summary recommendations that remain timely today.

Bausell, R.B., & Sussman, S. (Eds.). (2006). *Evaluation and the Health Professions* (Special issues on translational research), 29(1–3). A series of three special issues addressing the full range of translational research topics, including the history of translational research, an overview of conceptual frameworks, exemplary studies across diverse substantive areas, methodological and research-reporting issues, as well as future directions in the field.

Evans, D.L., Foa, E.B., Guy, R.E., Hendin, H., O'Brien, C.P., Seligman, M.E.P., & Walsh, B.T. (Eds.). (2005). *Treating and preventing adolescent mental health disorders: What we know and what we don't know.* NY: Oxford University Press. A comprehensive review of the evidence base for both prevention and treatment of adolescent mental health disorders, along with advances in research on positive youth development and specification of the most important areas of future research.

Spoth, R., Dishion, T., & Kavanagh, K. (Eds.). (2002). *Prevention Science* (Special issue on family-focused preventive intervention research), 3(3). A special issue that reviews salient developments in family-focused prevention intervention research and identifies key tasks in meeting the challenges of scaling up interventions for greater public health impact, with illustrative findings from family-centered studies involving infants, children and adolescents.

Acknowledgments—Work on this paper was supported by research grants DA010815 and DA013709 from the National Institute on Drug Abuse and by grant AA014702-13 from the National Institute on Alcohol Abuse and Alcoholism. A special note of appreciation to Lisa Schainker, Linda Trudeau, Mark Greenberg and Alex Mason for invaluable editing and feedback on earlier versions of this manuscript.

Note

1. Address correspondence to Richard Spoth, Partnerships in Prevention Science Institute, ISU Research Park, Building 2, Suite 500, 2625 North Loop Drive, Iowa State University, Ames, Iowa 50010; e-mail: rlspoth@iastate.edu.

References

Abrams, D.B., (1999). Nicotine addictions: Paradigms for research in the 21st century. *Nicotine & Tobacco Research, 1,* S211–S215.

Alexander, J.F., Robbins, M.S., & Sexton, T.L. (2000). Family-based interventions with older, at-risk youth: From promise to proof to practice. *The Journal of Primary Prevention, 21,* 185–205.

Biglan, A., & Metzler, C.W. (1998). A public health perspective for research on family-focused interventions. In R.S. Ashery, E.B. Robertson, & K.L. Kumpfer (Eds.), *Drug abuse prevention through family interventions* (NIDA Research Monograph 177, NIH Publication No. 97–4135, pp. 430–458). Rockville, MD: National Institute on Drug Abuse.

Castro, F.G., Barrera, M., Jr., & Martinez, R., Jr. (2004). The cultural adaptation of prevention interventions: Resolving tensions between fidelity and fit. *Prevention Science, 5,* 41–45.

Collins, L.M., Murphy, S.A., & Bierman, K.A. (2004). A Conceptual framework for adaptive preventive interventions. *Prevention Science, 5,* 185–196.

Forgatch, M.S., Patterson, G.R., & DeGarmo, D.S. (2005). Evaluating fidelity: Predictive validity for a measure of competent adherence to the Oregon Model of Parent Management Training (PMTO). *Behavior Therapy, 36,* 3–13.

Glasgow, R.E., Lichtenstein, E., & Marcus, A. (2003). Why don't we see more translation of health promotion research to practice? Rethinking the efficacy to effectiveness transition. *American Journal of Public Health, 93,* 1261–1267.

Haggerty, K.P., Fleming, C.B., Lonczak, H.S., Oxford, M., Harachi, T.W., & Catalano, R.F. (2002). Predictors of participation in parenting workshops. *Journal of Primary Prevention, 22,* 375–387.

Karoly, L.A., Greenwood, P.W., Everingham, S.S., Hoube, J., Kilburn, M.R., Rydell, C.P., et al. (1998). *Investing in our children: What we know and don't know about the costs and benefits of early childhood interventions.* Santa Monica, CA: RAND.

Lochman, J.E., & van den Steenhoven, A. (2002). Family-based approaches to substance abuse prevention. *Journal of Primary Prevention, 23,* 49–114.

Offord, D.R., Kraemer, H.C., Kazdin, A.E., Jensen, P.S., & Harrington, R. (1998). Lowering the burden of suffering from child psychiatric disorder: Trade-offs among clinical, targeted, and universal interventions. *Journal of the American Academy of Child and Adolescent Psychiatry, 37,* 686–694.

Spoth, R., Clair, S., Greenberg, M., Redmond, C., & Shin, C. (2007). Toward dissemination of evidence-based family interventions: Maintenance of community-based partnership recruitment results and associated factors. *Journal of Family Psychology, 21,* 137–146.

Spoth, R., & Greenberg, M.T. (2005). Toward a comprehensive strategy for effective practitioner–scientist partnerships and larger-scale community benefits. *American Journal of Community Psychology, 35,* 107–126.

Spoth, R., Greenberg, M., & Turrisi, R. (2008). Preventive interventions addressing underage drinking: State of the evidence and steps toward public health impact. *Pediatrics, 121* (Suppl. 4), 311–336.

Spoth, R., Guyll, M., & Day, S.X. (2002). Universal family-focused interventions in alcohol-use disorder prevention: Cost-effectiveness and cost-benefit analyses of two interventions. *Journal of Studies on Alcohol, 63,* 219–228.

Spoth, R., & Redmond, C. (2002). Project Family prevention trials based in community-university partnerships: Toward scaled–up preventive interventions. *Prevention Science, 3,* 203–221.

Sussman, S., Valente, T.W., Rohrbach, L.A., Skara, S., & Pentz, M.A. (2006). Translation in the health professions: Converting science into action. *Evaluation & the Health Professions, 29,* 7–32.

Taylor, T.K., & Biglan, A. (1998). Behavioral family interventions for improving child-rearing: A review of the literature for clinicians and policy makers. *Clinical Child and Family Psychology Review, 1,* 41–60.

U.S. Department of Health and Human Services. (2000). *Healthy people 2010: Understanding and improving health* (2nd ed.). Washington, DC: U.S. Government Printing Office.

Webster-Stratton, C., & Taylor, T. (2001). Nipping early risk factors in the bud: Preventing substance abuse, delinquency, and violence in adolescence: Interventions targeted at young children (ages 0–8 years). *Prevention Science, 2,* 165–192.

Woolf, S.H. (2008). The meaning of translational research and why it matters. *JAMA: The Journal of the American Medical Association, 222,* 211–213.

This article has been reprinted as it originally appeared in *Current Directions in Psychological Science.* Citation information for this article as originally published appears above.

Population Treatment for Addictions

James O. Prochaska[1]

University of Rhode Island

Abstract

Addictive behaviors are major causes of chronic disease, premature death, and high health care costs. Such behaviors have not been treated seriously by health care systems, and this is a major reason why such systems face an unhealthy future. Treating addictions seriously requires complementing a traditional individual-patient paradigm with a population paradigm, an action paradigm with a stage paradigm, clinic practices with home-based practices, a clinician paradigm with a computer paradigm, and programs that focus on changing single behaviors with programs that focus on changing multiple behaviors.

Keywords

addictions; population treatment; stages of change

Addictive behaviors are major causes of chronic disease, disability, and death. They are also major causes of high costs for health care systems, legal systems, employers, and educational systems. A promising approach for more effective treatment of addictions involves complementing traditional treatment and research paradigms with more comprehensive and innovative paradigms.

PATIENT AND POPULATION PARADIGMS

Historically, as a profession and as a science, psychology took responsibility only for those persons in treatments or clinical trials. Psychotherapy research was preoccupied with efficacy for the individual patient. A therapy yielding 30% abstinence from the targeted undesired behavior would have 50% greater efficacy than a treatment yielding 20% abstinence. However, most addictions go undiagnosed and untreated. When health care systems offer smoking-cessation clinics for free, for example, 1% of eligible smokers participate. About 4% of primary-care patients with mental health problems receive appropriate treatments (Cummings, 2003).

In contrast to the traditional patient paradigm, a population paradigm focuses on impact, which is calculated as efficacy times participation. A therapy with 30% efficacy and 5% participation has an impact of 1.5%. A therapy with 20% efficacy and 75% participation has an impact of 15%. In this example, the therapy with 33% less efficacy has 10 times greater impact. In short, higher efficacy does not necessarily translate into greater impact, a fact that is easily overlooked if treatment efforts are framed within the patient paradigm. Complementing the patient paradigm with the population paradigm has the potential to produce unprecedented impact.

PASSIVE-REACTIVE AND PROACTIVE PARADIGMS

High percentages of addicted persons can be reached only if a passive-reactive approach to treatment is complemented by proactive practices. Most health professionals are socialized to passively wait for patients and then react. This is appropriate for patients who are acutely sick, in pain, or distressed. However, in the case of chronic behaviors that are causes of chronic disease, most patients are not sick, in pain, or distressed. Professionals need to think of these behaviors as silent killers, the way they think of hypertension, and take a proactive approach, assessing relevant populations for their readiness to change these behaviors. Treatments matched to individuals' stages of change could then be prescribed.

ACTION AND STAGE PARADIGMS

The traditional outcome paradigm construed behavior change as equaling action. Behavior change occurs, for example, when individuals quit smoking, drinking, or abusing drugs. In the stage paradigm, in contrast, behavior change is understood as a process that unfolds over time and involves progress through a series of stages: precontemplation, contemplation, preparation, action, and maintenance. In the United States, about 40% of smokers are in the precontemplation stage— that is, they do not intend to quit in the next 6 months. About 40% are in contemplation, meaning that they intend to quit in the next 6 months but not in the next month. Only about 20% are in preparation, prepared to quit in the next month. Of daily smokers, less than 10% are prepared to quit.

The vast majority of research and services for smoking cessation are based on the action paradigm and are designed for smokers who are prepared to quit. For example, the U.S. Public Health Service's clinical guidelines for the treatment of tobacco (Fiore et al., 2000) had access to more than 6,000 studies on tobacco covering a broad range of evidence-based treatments for smokers motivated to quit, defined as those in the preparation stage. But the authors concluded that there was not an adequate evidence base for treatments for the 80% or more of smokers in the precontemplation and contemplation stages. It is troubling that so much research excluded the vast majority of people with the most deadly of addictions. No wonder free action-oriented cessation clinics reach only 1% of smokers!

Action-oriented cessation treatments would serve even fewer smokers in countries that have not had extensive public-health campaigns. In countries like China, Germany, and Turkey, about 70% of all smokers are in precontemplation, and only about 5% are prepared to quit. If treatment programs are going to be designed to serve addicted populations, then action-oriented treatments need to be complemented by treatments that match patients' needs at each stage of change.

In one study, my colleagues and I reached out by telephone to a representative sample of 5,000 smokers and offered home-based treatments tailored to whether they were ready to quit, getting ready, or not ready. We recruited 80% of the people we contacted (Prochaska, Velicer, Fava, Rossi, & Tsoh, 2001), which is much better than typical with a standard action approach. In another stage-matched study, we recruited 85% of 4,500 smokers in a health maintenance organization (Prochaska, Velicer, Fava, Ruggiero, et al., 2001). We recruited over 70% of alcohol abusers on a college campus (Laforge, 2004), even though 70% were in precontemplation and only 10% were prepared to take action.

Once a program reaches a high percentage of the target population, will they complete treatment? A meta-analysis (i.e., a statistical analysis combining the results of multiple studies) that analyzed the rates and causes of dropout from psychotherapy for a broad range of problems found that about 50% of participants discontinued treatment quickly (Wierzbicki & Pekarik, 1993). These dropout rates for "behavior medicines" are very similar to discontinuation rates across most biological medicines. In the meta-analysis, education, minority status, and having an addiction were the best predictors of dropout but still accounted for only a small percentage of dropouts. In studies of therapies for mental health, heroin addiction, obesity, smoking, and exercise, the best predictors of dropout were stage of change and the individual's ratings of the pros and cons of changing (e.g., Brogan, Prochaska, & Prochaska, 1999). In the Brogan et al. study on mental health problems, we predicted over 90% of dropouts using stage of change and related variables. The entire 40% of premature dropouts were in the precontemplation stage. The 15% of participants who finished therapy quickly but appropriately were in the action stage. The treatment focus for patients who are in the action stage and have quit an addiction within the past 6 months should be relapse prevention. (Relapse prevention can help people progress to the maintenance stage, that is, to quit for more than 6 months; at this point, risks of relapse can continue to decrease.) But relapse prevention would not fit clients in the precontemplation stage, who would benefit instead from a clinical strategy focusing on dropout prevention. If treatment is matched to stage, people in precontemplation, who are most likely to drop out, can complete treatment at much higher rates.

In a review of the addiction literature, Connors, Walitzer, and Dermen (2002) found dropout rates ranged from 50% to 75%. They compared standard care with motivational interviewing (MI) based on a stage paradigm. Patients who received a single MI session completed treatment 25% to 50% more often than those who received standard care only.

These studies indicate that using a stage-based approach in treatment programs increases the enrollment rate and also reduces the dropout rate.

FROM CLINIC- TO HOME-BASED PARADIGMS

Individualized and interactive interventions have the greatest efficacy. Historically, such interventions were available mainly from clinic-based counselors. But clinic-based treatments are not reaching enough people. For example, obesity has increased at epidemic proportions in the past 16 years, yet participation in weight-management clinics has not increased appreciably. Obesity is the number-two cause of preventable death in the United States, but the nation's largest clinic-based delivery systems reach less than 5% of the overweight and obese populations. The problem appears to be not only that such programs are action oriented rather than stage based, but also that the settings in which the programs are delivered are themselves barriers. Marketing research revealed that 5% of

Americans want clinic-based weight-management programs, but 50% want home-based programs.

Home-based programs can increase not only participation, but also efficacy. Even when people attend clinics, they spend 99% of their waking week outside of therapy, and what they do during that time is more important in determining their outcomes than is what happens within therapy sessions. Imagine medicine trying to improve efficacy by focusing only on the interactions in physicians' offices. Most primary-care treatment is provided by the pharmaceutical industry, which specializes in therapeutics delivered at home. Treatment for addictions needs to be home based as well as clinic based.

CLINICIAN AND COMPUTER PARADIGMS

Delivering treatments at home requires using computers to complement a traditional clinician paradigm. Computers can provide individualized and interactive interventions that model the efforts of expert clinicians. A growing consensus holds that computer-generated communications that are tailored to the individual are the most promising approach for population-based interventions (Kreuter, Strecher, & Glassman, 1999). Interactive technologies are likely to be to behavior treatments what pharmaceuticals are to biological treatments: the most cost-effective means of bringing optimal amounts of science to bear on major health problems in entire populations in relatively user-friendly ways. Unlike pharmaceuticals, however, interactive technologies have no known side effects.

By providing guidance on principles and processes of change, an expert computer system can facilitate progress through the stages. For example, one such system asks a smoker 40 questions and on the basis of the answers provides feedback about the person's stage of change and whether he or she underestimates the benefits of quitting and overestimates the cons. The system also includes feedback on a total of 10 change processes (e.g., commitment, reinforcement, and social support), and participants receive feedback on a maximum of 6 processes relevant to their stage. The feedback indicates which processes the smoker is underutilizing, overutilizing, or utilizing appropriately compared with a group of peers in the same stage who made the most progress toward quitting. In follow-up interactions, participants receive feedback comparing them with their peers and feedback indicating how they have changed since their previous assessments. Participants learn what they are doing right, what mistakes they are making, and what they can concentrate on to progress the most. The system can also tell clinicians about their clients' progress and indicates how they can most help particular clients. In one study, such feedback reduced the percentage of clients who got worse by 50% and doubled positive outcomes (Lambert et al., 2001).

In our first clinical trial with smoking cessation, my colleagues and I compared four treatments: the American Lung Association's action and maintenance self-help manuals; stage-matched self-help manuals that targeted the precontemplation, contemplation, and preparation stages as well; stage-matched manuals plus three expert computer-system guides; and a combination of the manuals, the guides, and four proactive telephone calls from counselors over a 6-month period (Prochaska, DiClemente, Velicer, & Rossi, 1993). The self-help manuals and expert computer-system guides were mailed to smokers, who then followed the manuals and guides as best they could. The counselor calls added professional counseling to help the smokers progress from one stage to the next.

From a total sample of 753, smokers within each stage were randomly assigned to the four conditions. Eighteen months after the manuals and guides were distributed, the data showed that the combination of expert computer systems with manuals was more than twice as effective as the American Lung Association's treatments (24% vs. 11% abstinence). Computers plus manuals and the combination of computers, manuals, and counselors were tied for efficacy at 12 months, but at 18 months the latter condition produced 18% abstinence, whereas the former produced 24% abstinence.

The counselors were distressed over their failure to outperform the expert computer systems. The computers told them to seek social support. But the counselors did not give up. Unlike computers, clinicians learn from clinical experience. They changed protocols for future applications.

In another study that involved 4,500 smokers proactively recruited from a health maintenance organization, results after 12 months were better among clients who were helped by expert systems plus counselors for 6 months than among those who worked with the expert systems only (25.6% vs. 20.6%). At 18 months, results for the expert systems plus counselors declined, and those for the expert computer systems alone increased, so that the two conditions were tied at 23.2% abstinence (Prochaska, Velicer, Fava, Ruggiero, et al., 2001).

Why did the counselors plus computers not outperform the expert systems alone? One hypothesis is that some clients became dependent on counselors, much as they were dependent on nicotine. Historically, studies of therapies for addictions have shown a pattern of rapid relapse when therapy terminates. Such relapse has been attributed to addictions being resistant to change, but it is partly due to the loss of social support and social monitoring treatment provides.

With computer guides, rates of abstinence keep increasing for at least the 18- and 24-month follow-ups that have been used, rather than showing the rapid declines that often occur following counseling. Perhaps this is because computers enhance self-efficacy (i.e., increasing confidence in one's ability to continue making changes on one's own). When intervention ends, people can keep progressing through their own efforts based on self-efficacy or self-reliance. If people become dependent on clinicians, then one strategy for improving treatment would be to fade out therapists, much as nicotine is faded out in smoking-cessation programs.

In a review of 150 studies applying the transtheoretical model (TTM) of behavior change[2] to smoking, Spencer, Pagell, Hallien, and Adams (2002) identified 22 that tested stage-matched interventions. In my own analysis of the studies reviewed by Spencer et al., I identified 12 that used only stage for treatment matching: Four showed significant positive effects, 4 showed no significant effects, and 4 had results that were unclear. Five studies tested treatments that were tailored on a larger but partial set of TTM variables, such as stage, pros and cons of quitting, and self-efficacy. Three demonstrated significant positive results, and 2 did not. Five studies tested treatments that matched feedback to the participant using all TTM variables, including 10 processes of change, and 4 of these produced significant positive results. These results indicate that the greater the number of theoretical variables used for tailoring treatment to the client, the greater the chances that the treatment will be successful.

The studies varied on other key variables. The five using partial TTM tailoring had follow-ups of 10 weeks to 6 months and used reactive recruitment (i.e., the participants were smokers who had reached out to programs for help). The studies using treatments that were tailored on all the TTM variables had 18- to 24-month follow-ups, and four of the five were proactive population-based trials (i.e., they reached out to smokers to offer help). The more demanding the study (full TTM tailoring, long-term follow-ups, and high percentage of eligible smokers participating), the greater the likelihood of significant positive effects.

In population trials of treatment for alcohol abuse on college campuses, Laforge (2004) proactively recruited 70% of eligible students. Three expert computer systems that were fully TTM tailored produced significant reductions in alcohol problems in females but not males. To defend against pressures to change, males relied more than females on processes of resistance, such as reactance (getting angry and defensive when feeling pressure to change) and rationalization (excusing the problem behavior). These processes of resistance were an important reason why the treatment was ineffective for males. Future treatments should attempt to reduce processes of resistance in order to help male alcohol abusers progress to less risky drinking. Resistance to change is a challenge clinicians also face when treating individuals with other addictive behaviors.

FROM SINGLE TO MULTIPLE BEHAVIORS

Attempts to enhance the impacts of our expert computer-system guides by increasing efficacy or participation have failed. Because our proactive methods already recruit 80+%, they have limited potential to increase their recruitment rates. Efforts to increase efficacy for smoking cessation by doubling the number of contacts with participants, adding counseling calls, or providing nicotine replacement patches have been unsuccessful. However, the impact of treatments can be increased if they broaden their focus and treat multiple rather than single behaviors.

Clinical trials have the luxury of treating one problem. In studies of nicotine-replacement therapy, for example, smokers with mental health problems are typically excluded. Yet 45% of cigarettes in the United States are bought by smokers with mental health problems. In practice, the majority of clients have multiple problems. The people with the highest risk and highest potential cost to the health care system are those with multiple behavior problems. Individuals who become free from two behavior risks reduce their health care costs on average by $2,000 per year (Eddington, 2001).

In our first multiple-behavior trial, my colleagues and I recruited at home 2,360 parents (83.6% of the target population) of teenagers who were in a prevention program at school. Using three fully TTM-tailored expert-system guides for each relevant behavior, we produced significant impacts on smoking, diet, and sun exposure at a 24-month follow-up (Prochaska et al., 2004). From primary care, we recruited 5,500 patients to the same treatments, and assessments

24 months later showed significant effects on the same three behaviors and on compliance with recommended schedules for mammograms (Prochaska et al., in press). Treatments for smoking only and for multiple behaviors including smoking yielded the same long-term rates of abstinence from smoking (22 to 25%). Thus, it is possible to increase impacts by treating multiple behaviors without decreasing efficacy for the individual behaviors that are targeted.

FUTURE BREAKTHROUGHS AND CONCLUSION

Traditional paradigms were based on the assumption that relapse-prevention programs would produce breakthroughs in the efficacy of addiction treatments. To better understand relapse, my colleagues and I recently compared smokers who quit in our population-based study and remained abstinent (maintainers), smokers who quit and relapsed, and smokers who had not stopped smoking (stable smokers) for their use of 14 principles and processes of change (e.g., decision making, social support, and self-reinforcement). The study also included a control group, and all three categories of smokers were found in this group, too. Over 2 years, the maintainers demonstrated expert applications of the processes. The stable smokers showed little use of these processes. The smokers who quit and then relapsed initially paralleled the maintainers, but as they relapsed they began to behave like the stable smokers. Patterns of process use across the three groups were almost identical for treatment and control groups, but the treatment condition produced more maintainers.

Among maintainers and relapsers, the pathways of change do not differ between treatment and control groups. The common pathways for treatment and control groups could explain the mystery of how diverse treatments produce common outcomes. For example, Project Match, one of the largest therapy studies on alcohol problems, found no significant differences in outcomes for groups who were randomly assigned to cognitive-behavior therapy, MI, or 12-step treatment.

Traditional clinical paradigms have assumed that improved relapse-prevention strategies are likely to produce a breakthrough in treatment outcomes. But for relapse prevention to produce a breakthrough, from 25% to 30% abstinence, in our best practice for smoking cessation, it would have to succeed with 70% of smokers who quit but then relapse with the current treatment, because relapsers constitute only 7% of the participants in our programs. This is not possible. However, a breakthrough of 5% could be produced by helping 7% of stable smokers quit, because stable smokers are 70% of our treatment population. This is possible. This example shows how traditional clinical paradigms and emerging population approaches provide different perspectives on what research and treatment strategies are likely to produce breakthroughs in efficacy.

A popular hypothesis is that multiple-level interventions are most likely to produce breakthroughs. According to this hypothesis, addictions are best treated by combining social controls (e.g., social policies), biological controls (e.g., pharmaceuticals), and self-controls (e.g., therapy). Experts advocating this position provide little evidence beyond a few well-known case studies, however. In our population trials, adding 2 years of multiple behavior interventions at the worksite (e.g., self-help groups and environmental policies) or 2 years of primary-care interventions (e.g., physician counseling) has failed to produce better results than our individual-level expert computer systems alone. These results are consistent with our previous research showing that more is not necessarily better. More treatment contacts, more treatment modalities (e.g., computer system plus counselor), and more treatment levels (e.g., interventions at both the worksite and individual levels) do not necessarily produce more successful outcomes.

What has produced breakthroughs in the impact of treatments for addictions are new paradigms. These new paradigms include proactive recruitment that targets entire populations and stage-matched interventions for multiple behaviors, delivered at home by individualized expert-system computers. Future breakthroughs are likely to emerge from innovative integrations of these new paradigms with best practices from traditional paradigms that have reached individual patients with action-oriented interventions for single behaviors, delivered in clinics by expert clinicians. Complementing established paradigms with new paradigms can produce more comprehensive approaches to the study and treatment of addictions.

Recommended Reading

Prochaska, J.O. (2003). Enhancing motivation to change. In B.B. Wilford, A.W. Graham, & T.K. Schultz (Eds.), *Principles of addiction medicine* (3rd ed., pp. 825–838). Chevy Chase, MD: American Society of Addiction Medicine.

Prochaska, J.O., Norcross, J.C., & DiClemente, C.C. (1994). *Changing for good*. New York: Morrow.

Spencer, L., Pagell, F., Hallien, M.E., & Adams, T.B. (2002). (See References)

Notes

1. Address correspondence to James O. Prochaska, Cancer Prevention Research Center, University of Rhode Island, 2 Chafee Rd., Kingston, RI 02881; e-mail: jop@uri.edu.

2. TTM is intended to be a comprehensive and integrative model of behavior change and therapy. In this model, behavior change is understood as a process that unfolds over time and involves progress through stages of change. Variables such as 10 processes of change, self-efficacy, and decision making (the balance of the pros and cons of changing) are applied to produce progress at each stage of change.

References

Brogan, M.M., Prochaska, J.O., & Prochaska, J.M. (1999). Predicting termination and continuation status in psychotherapy using the Transtheoretical Model. *Psychotherapy, 36,* 105–113.

Connors, G.J., Walitzer, K.S., & Dermen, K.H. (2002). Preparing clients for alcoholism treatment: Effects on treatment participation and outcomes. *Journal of Consulting and Clinical Psychology, 70,* 1161–1169.

Cummings, W.A. (2003, February). *The implosion of managed care*. Keynote address presented at the 14th Annual Art and Science Health Promotion Conference, Washington, DC.

Eddington, D.W. (2001). Emerging research. *American Journal of Health Promotion, 15,* 341–369.

Fiore, M.C., Bailey, W.C., Cohen, S.J., et al. (2000). *Treating tobacco use and dependence: Clinical practice guideline*. Rockville, MD: U.S. Department of Health and Human Services, Public Health Service.

Kreuter, M.K., Strecher, V.J., & Glassman, B. (1999). One size does not fit all: The case for tailoring cancer prevention materials. *Annals of Behavioral Medicine, 21,* 276–283.

Laforge, R.G. (2004). *A population based individualized alcohol harm reduction program feedback intervention*. Manuscript submitted for publication.

Lambert, M.J., Whipple, J.L., Smart, D.W., Vermeersch, D.A., Nielsen, S.L., & Hawkins, E.J. (2001). The effects of providing therapists with feedback on patient progress during psychotherapy. *Psychotherapy Research, 11*, 49–68.

Prochaska, J.O., DiClemente, C.C., Velicer, W.F., & Rossi, J.S. (1993). Standardized, individualized, interactive and personalized self-help programs for smoking cessation. *Health Psychology, 12*, 399–405.

Prochaska, J.O., Redding, C.A., Goldstein, M., Velicer, W.F., Rossi, J.S., Sun, X., Rakowski, W., Rossi, S.R., Greene, G.W., DePue, J., Fava, J., Laforge, R., Ehrlich, B., Willey, C., & Niaura, R. (in press). Stage-based expert systems to guide a population of primary care patients to quit smoking, eat healthier, prevent skin cancer, and receive regular mammograms. *Preventive Medicine.*

Prochaska, J.O., Velicer, W.F., Fava, J., Ruggiero, L., Laforge, R., & Rossi, J.R. (2001). Counselor and stimulus control enhancements of a stage matched expert system for smokers in a managed care setting. *Preventive Medicine, 32*, 23–32.

Prochaska, J.O., Velicer, W.F., Fava, J.L., Rossi, J.S., & Tsoh, J.Y. (2001). Evaluating a population-based recruitment approach and a stage-based expert system intervention for smoking cessation. *Addictive Behaviors, 26*, 583–602.

Prochaska, J.O., Velicer, W.F., Rossi, J.S., Redding, C.A., Greene, G.W., Rossi, S.R., Sun, X., Fava, J.L., Laforge, R., & Plummer, B. (2004). Multiple risk expert systems interventions: Impact of simultaneous stage-matched expert system interventions for smoking, high-fat diet and sun exposure in a population of parents. *Health Psychology, 23*, 503–516.

Spencer, L., Pagell, F., Hallien, M.E., & Adams, T.B. (2002). Applying the Transtheoretical model to tobacco cessation and prevention: A review of the literature. *American Journal of Health Promotion, 17*, 7–71.

Wierzbicki, M., & Pekarik, G. (1993). A meta-analysis of psychotherapy dropout. *Professional Psychology, 29*, 190–195.

This article has been reprinted as it originally appeared in *Current Directions in Psychological Science*. Citation information for this article as originally published appears above.

Innovation Implementation:
Overcoming the Challenge

Katherine J. Klein[1] and Andrew P. Knight
The Wharton School, University of Pennsylvania

Abstract

In changing work environments, innovation is imperative. Yet, many teams and organizations fail to realize the expected benefits of innovations that they adopt. A key reason is not innovation failure but implementation failure—the failure to gain targeted employees' skilled, consistent, and committed use of the innovation in question. We review research on the implementation process, outlining the reasons why implementation is so challenging for many teams and organizations. We then describe the organizational characteristics that together enhance the likelihood of successful implementation, including a strong, positive climate for implementation; management support for innovation implementation; financial resource availability; and a learning orientation.

Keywords

innovation; implementation; learning

In the life of an individual, a family, a team, an organization, or a community, innovation is critical. Individuals, families, teams, organizations, and communities must grow and change—adopting and implementing innovations—if they are to survive and thrive in a changing environment.

In the language of innovation researchers, an *innovation* is a product or practice that is new to its developers and/or to its potential users. Innovation *adoption* is the decision to use an innovation. Innovation *implementation,* in contrast, is "the transition period during which [individuals] ideally become increasingly skillful, consistent, and committed in their use of an innovation. Implementation is the critical gateway between the decision to adopt the innovation and the routine use of the innovation" (Klein & Sorra, 1996, p. 1057). The difference between adoption and implementation is fundamental: Individuals, teams, organizations, and communities often adopt innovations but fail to implement them successfully.

Consider an example that is as mundane as it is close to home: Do you own an exercise machine of some kind? If so, that's innovation adoption. When you bought the machine, you adopted it. If you own a machine, did you in fact use it in the past week? That's innovation implementation. If you use the exercise machine regularly, in a skilled, consistent, and committed manner, you've excelled at implementation.

As a general rule, adoption is much easier—although sometimes more expensive—than implementation. Many innovations, like exercise machines, are implemented ineffectively. Thus, innovation failure—the failure of an innovation to achieve the gains expected by the adopting individual or individuals—often reflects not the ineffectiveness of the innovation per se but the ineffectiveness of the implementation process (Klein & Sorra, 1996). In short, the innovation fails because it is not used with the consistency, skill, and care required to achieve its expected benefits.

In this article, we focus on the implementation of innovations that require the active and coordinated use of multiple organizational members. Examples include computerized manufacturing automation and organizational quality-improvement programs such as total-quality management. Although research on the implementation of such innovations is limited, the topic is of great interest to organizational psychologists, to other organizational scholars, and to managers. But, innovation implementation is an issue that transcends psychological sub-disciplines. Psychologists who hope that their research will inform the design of, say, school-based prevention programs, drug-treatment programs, or training systems must grapple, ultimately, with implementation: If adopted, will the interventions they recommend be implemented? Even the family therapist who suggests to a family that they regularly eat dinner together faces the challenge of implementation: A family may "adopt" the idea, but will they implement it?

We begin with a brief overview of the state of innovation-implementation research. We then draw on research findings to describe (a) the obstacles that organizations face during innovation implementation and (b) organizational factors that may allow organizations to overcome these obstacles. We conclude with a brief discussion of the practical implications of the research and of new directions for implementation research.

STUDYING INNOVATION IMPLEMENTATION

Research on the implementation of organizational innovations is both labor intensive and rare. The ideal study of team or organizational innovation implementation, we believe, is one that examines the implementation of a single innovation, or a common set of innovations, across a sample of adopting organizations or teams over time. For example, Edmondson, Bohmer, and Pisano (2001) combined qualitative and quantitative data collection in a longitudinal study of 16 surgical teams' efforts to implement a new technique—minimally invasive cardiac surgery—in the operating room. Klein, Conn, and Sorra (2001) conducted a multilevel, longitudinal study of the implementation of a single type of computerized manufacturing technology (manufacturing resource planning or MRP II) across 39 manufacturing plants. And Holahan, Aronson, Jurkat, and Schoorman (2004) examined the implementation of computer technology in science education in 69 schools. The findings of these studies, and of in-depth qualitative case studies of organizational innovation implementation (e.g., Nutt, 1986; Nord & Tucker, 1987; Repenning & Sterman, 2002), illuminate stumbling blocks and best practices in innovation implementation.

STUMBLING BLOCKS ON THE ROAD
TO INNOVATION IMPLEMENTATION

The implementation of team and organizational innovations is difficult for numerous reasons. Six interrelated reasons figure prominently in the implementation literature.

First, many innovations—particularly technological innovations—are unreliable and imperfectly designed. The newer the technology, the more likely it is to have bugs, break down, and be awkward to use. This "hassle factor" can render even the most enthusiastic technophile frustrated and annoyed. In their review of the literature on computerized-technology implementation, Klein and Ralls (1995) reported that 61% of the qualitative studies they reviewed documented the negative consequences of low technology quality and availability on employee satisfaction and innovation use.

Second, many innovations require would-be users to acquire new technical knowledge and skills. For many people, this may be tedious or stressful. In an individual-level study of project engineers' implementation of information-technology innovations, Aiman-Smith and Green (2002) found that innovation complexity—the extent to which the new technology was more complicated than the technology it replaced—was significantly negatively related to user satisfaction and the speed required to become competent in using the innovation.

Third, the decision to adopt and implement an innovation is typically made by those higher in the hierarchy than the innovation's targeted users. Targeted users, however, often have great comfort in the status quo and great skepticism regarding the merits of the innovation. Nevertheless, they may be instructed by upper management to use the innovation against their wishes. Indeed, based on interviews in 91 organizations, Nutt (1986) concluded that managers' most common strategies in guiding innovation implementation are "persuasion" and "edict"—both of which involve little or no user input in decisions regarding adoption and implementation.

Fourth, many team and organizational innovations require individuals to change their roles, routines, and norms. Innovation implementation may require individuals who have previously worked quite independently to coordinate their activities and share information (Klein & Sorra, 1996). It may also disrupt the status hierarchy, requiring individuals who have previously worked as boss and subordinates to now work as peers. In a qualitative study of the implementation of an empowerment-education intervention for diabetes patients, Adolfsson, Smide, Gregeby, Fernström, and Wikblad (2004) found that doctors and nurses struggled with the role changes that the intervention required. Although the doctors and nurses believed that the empowerment approach was beneficial for their patients, they found it difficult to step out of their expert roles to interact with their patients as facilitators.

Fifth, implementation is time consuming, expensive, and, at least initially, a drag on performance. Effective innovation implementation often requires hefty investments of time and money in technology start-up, training, user support, monitoring, meetings, and evaluation. Thus, even the most beneficial innovation is likely to result in poorer team and/or organizational performance in the short run, as Repenning and Sterman (2002) documented in their study of the implementation of two process-improvement innovations—one designed to reduce expensive stores of work-in-progress inventory and one designed to speed new product development—in a division of a major U.S. automaker. Good things— implementation benefits—may come to those who wait, but targeted users and their managers may feel greater pressure to maintain pre-existing levels of performance than to invest in the uncertain and long-term potential of innovation implementation.

And, sixth, organizations are a stabilizing force. Organizational norms and routines foster maintenance of the status quo. Even when organizational members recognize that a specific change would be beneficial, they often fall prey to the "knowing–doing gap" (Pfeffer & Sutton, 2000). That is, they often fail, for a variety of reasons, to actually do the things that they know would enhance performance or morale. Organizational members may adhere rigidly to the past, fear reprisal for suggesting bold changes, or substitute talk for action, for example (Pfeffer & Sutton, 2000). The result, unfortunately, is a failure to adopt, and certainly to implement, potentially beneficial innovations.

Given these challenges to implementation success, it is perhaps no wonder that observers estimate that nearly 50% or more of attempts to implement major technological and administrative changes end in failure (e.g., Aiman-Smith & Green, 2002; Baer & Frese, 2003; Repenning & Sterman, 2002). Indeed, a 2002 report by financial giant Morgan Stanley estimated that, of the $2.7 trillion that companies pour into technology each year, more than $500 billion is wasted—in large part due to implementation failure.

ANTECEDENTS OF INNOVATION-IMPLEMENTATION EFFECTIVENESS

Our review of the literature on innovation implementation suggests that six key factors shape the process and outcomes of innovation implementation.

One key factor is the package of implementation policies and practices that an organization establishes (Klein & Ralls, 1995). Implementation policies and practices include, for example, the quality and quantity of training available to teach employees to use the innovation; the provision of technical assistance to innovation users on an as-needed basis; the availability of rewards (e.g., praise, promotions) for innovation use; and the quality, accessibility, and user-friendliness of the technology itself. The influence of such policies and practices is cumulative and compensatory. No single implementation policy or practice seems to be absolutely critical for an organization's innovation-implementation effectiveness. But, the overall quality of an organization's implementation policies and practices is predictive. Klein et al. (2001) found that manufacturing plants that established numerous high-quality implementation policies and practices were more successful in implementing manufacturing-resource planning, a major technological innovation, than were manufacturing plants whose implementation policies and practices were meager and of lesser quality.

The second critical factor is the team's or organization's climate for innovation implementation—that is, employees' shared perceptions of the importance of innovation implementation within the team or organization. When a unit's climate for innovation implementation is strong and positive, employees regard innovation use as a top priority, not as a distraction from or obstacle to the performance of their "real work." Both Klein et al. (2001) and Holahan et al. (2004) found that implementation climate was a significant predictor of innovation use.

Managers play a critical role in the implementation process, so their support of the innovation is the third critical factor. In the absence of strong, convincing, informed, and demonstrable management support for implementation, employees are likely to conclude that the innovation is a passing managerial fancy: Ignore it and it will go away. As Repenning (2002) admonished, "Managers may be understandably suspicious of the recommendation that, once they choose to adopt an innovation, they support it wholeheartedly irrespective of any reservations concerning lack of appropriateness. To do otherwise, however, insures that the implementation effort will fail" (pp. 124–125). Sharma and Yetton (2003) found that the more an innovation requires employees to work together—as the innovations on which we focus in this article do—the stronger the positive relationship between management support and implementation success.

The fourth factor is the availability of financial resources. Implementation is, of course, not cheap. It takes money to offer extensive training, to provide ongoing user support, to launch a communications campaign explaining the merits of the innovation, and to relax performance standards while employees learn to use the innovation. Like Nord and Tucker (1987), Klein et al. (2001) found that financial-resource availability was a significant predictor of the overall quality of an organization's implementation policies and practices and thus, indirectly, a predictor of the organization's implementation effectiveness.

The fifth necessary factor is a learning orientation: a set of interrelated practices and beliefs that support and enable employee and organizational skill development, learning, and growth. In organizations and teams that have a strong learning orientation, employees eagerly engage in experimentation and risk taking; they are not constrained by a fear of failure. A learning orientation is critical during innovation implementation because implementation is rarely an easy, smooth process or an instant success. Bugs, errors, and missteps are likely. A strong learning orientation allows organizational members to overcome such obstacles, experimenting, adapting, and persevering in innovation use. The research of Edmondson et al. (2001) suggests that leaders create a shared team learning orientation by (a) articulating a compelling and inspiring reason for innovation use; (b) expressing their own fallibility and need for team members' assistance and input; and (c) communicating to team members that they are essential, valued, and knowledgeable partners in the change process. As a result, team members—targeted innovation users—come to see innovation implementation as an exciting learning opportunity, not as a burden to be endured. Further, team members must feel sufficient psychological safety (Edmondson, 1999; Baer & Frese, 2003) to express their ideas and opinions, as well as to admit their errors. A psychologically safe social environment is one in which group members collectively feel secure taking interpersonal risks (Edmondson, 1999). Indeed, Baer and Frese (2003) found that psychological safety moderates the effects of process innovation on organizational performance: The greater an organization's climate for psychological safety, the stronger the positive relationship between the organization's adoption and implementation of process innovations and its financial performance.

Lastly, the sixth critical factor is managerial patience—that is, a long-term time orientation. Managers who are committed to achieving the long-term benefits of innovation implementation understand that the implementation process may diminish unit productivity and efficiency in the short term. The more managers push employees to maintain or improve immediate task performance, the less time and energy employees can devote to the implementation of innovations that offer long-term, and potentially more enduring, performance gains (Repenning & Sterman, 2002).

CONCLUSION: PRACTICAL IMPLICATIONS AND NEW DIRECTIONS FOR RESEARCH

Researchers have begun to identify the practices and characteristics that allow organizations to overcome the challenges of innovation implementation. Clearly, top management cannot close the book on an innovation after they have decided to adopt it. To ensure targeted users' sustained and skillful use of innovative technologies and practices, managers must devote great attention, conviction, and resources to the implementation process.

While important strides have been made in understanding the process of innovation implementation, more research is needed and important questions remain. How does the implementation of technological innovations like new computer systems differ from the implementation of nontechnological innovations such as new managerial, educational, training, or patient-treatment interventions? How does success or failure at implementing an innovation in one team or location spread through an organization or community? Do units that succeed in implementing one innovation succeed in implementing others as well? Though questions remain, the growing innovation-implementation literature draws needed attention to the challenge and the importance of effective innovation implementation. In the absence of effective implementation, the benefits of innovation adoption are likely to be nil. After all, how physically fit can you get if you buy a top-of-the-line exercise bike or treadmill but never use it?

Recommended Reading

Edmondson, A.C. (2003). (See References)
Klein, K.J., Conn, A.B., & Sorra, J.S. (2001). (See References)
Klein, K.J., & Sorra, J.S. (1996). (See References)
Pfeffer, J., & Sutton, R.I. (2000). (See References)
Repenning, N.P., & Sterman, J.D. (2002). (See References)

Note

1. Address correspondence to Katherine J. Klein, Management Department, The Wharton School, University of Pennsylvania, 2000 Steinberg Hall – Dietrich Hall, Philadelphia, PA 19104-6370; e-mail: kleink@wharton.upenn.edu.

References

Adolfsson, E.T., Smide, B., Gregeby, E., Fernström, L., & Wikblad, K. (2004). Implementing empowerment group education in diabetes. *Patient Education and Counseling, 53*, 319–324.

Aiman-Smith, L., & Green, S.G. (2002). Implementing new manufacturing technology: The related effects of technology characteristics and user learning activities. *Academy of Management Journal, 45,* 421–430.

Baer, M., & Frese, M. (2003). Innovation is not enough: Climates for initiative and psychological safety, process innovations, and firm performance. *Journal of Organizational Behavior, 24,* 45–68.

Edmondson, A.C. (1999). Psychological safety and learning behavior in work teams. *Administrative Science Quarterly, 44,* 350–383.

Edmondson, A.C., Bohmer, R., & Pisano, G.P. (2001). Disrupted routines: Team learning and new technology adaptation. *Administrative Science Quarterly, 46,* 685–716.

Holahan, P.J., Aronson, Z.H., Jurkat, M.P., & Schoorman, F.D. (2004). Implementing computer technology: A multiorganizational test of Klein and Sorra's model. *Journal of Engineering and Technology Management, 21,* 31–50.

Klein, K.J., Conn, A.B., & Sorra, J.S. (2001). Implementing computerized technology: An organizational analysis. *Journal of Applied Psychology, 86,* 811–824.

Klein, K.J., & Ralls, R.S. (1995). The organizational dynamics of computerized technology implementation: A review of the empirical literature. In L.R. Gomez-Mejia & M.W. Lawless (Eds.), *Implementation management of high technology* (pp. 31–79). Greenwich, CT: JAI Press.

Klein, K.J., & Sorra, J.S. (1996). The challenge of innovation implementation. *Academy of Management Review, 21,* 1055–1080.

Nord, W.R., & Tucker, S. (1987). *Implementing routine and radical innovations.* San Francisco: New Lexington Press.

Nutt, P.C. (1986). Tactics of implementation. *Academy of Management Journal, 29,* 230–261.

Pfeffer, J., & Sutton, R.I. (2000). *The knowing–doing gap: How smart companies turn knowledge into action.* Boston: Harvard Business School Press.

Repenning, N.P. (2002). A simulation-based approach to understanding the dynamics of innovation implementation. *Organization Science, 13,* 109–127.

Repenning, N.P., & Sterman, J.D. (2002). Capability traps and self-confirming attribution errors in the dynamics of process improvement. *Administrative Science Quarterly, 47,* 265–295.

Sharma, R., & Yetton, P. (2003). The contingent effects of management support and task interdependence on successful information systems implementation. *MIS Quarterly, 27,* 533–555.

Section 5: Critical Thinking Questions

1. Prochaska shows that expert computer systems are helpful in creating behavior change and that the addition of help from counselors does not add much over the long run. What has to go into an expert computer system to make it work, and why might counselors not add much to the mix?

2. Klein and Knight argue that the challenges of implementing innovations in organizations are similar, whether the organization is a school implementing a prevention program or a manufacturing firm implementing a new technology. Do you agree? Can you think of any ways that the type of organization or the type of innovation might influence the relative importance of their six stumbling blocks or six antecedents?

3. Spoth says that the impact of an intervention is a product of its efficacy and the proportion of the eligible population it engages. How do the "4 Es" (effectiveness, extensiveness, efficiency, and engagement) translate into efficacy and proportion of the population that is engaged?

4. Spoth focuses on family-focused prevention, and Prochaska focuses on addictions. Are their conclusions applicable in each other's domain?

5. What are the implications of considering population impact for traditional clinical practice? What are the implications for the kind of training that future psychologists should receive?

This article has been reprinted as it originally appeared in *Current Directions in Psychological Science*. Citation information for this article as originally published appears above.